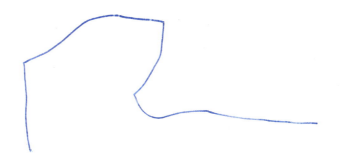

WORLD WAR II

WORLD WAR II

Loyd E. Lee

Greenwood Press Guides to
Historic Events of the Twentieth Century
Randall M. Miller, Series Editor

Greenwood Press
Westport, Connecticut • London

Library of Congress Cataloging-in-Publication Data

Lee, Loyd E., 1939–
    World War II / Loyd E. Lee.
      p.   cm.—(Greenwood Press guides to historic events of the
  twentieth century, ISSN 1092–177X)
    Includes bibliographical references and index.
    ISBN 0–313-29998–6 (alk. paper)
    1. World War, 1939–1945—Influence.   2. History, Modern—1945–
  I. Title. II. Series.
  D744.L44 1999
  940.53—dc21   98–22903

British Library Cataloguing in Publication Data is available.

Library of Congress Catalog Card Number: 98–22903
ISBN: 0–313–29998–6
ISSN: 1092–177X

First published in 1999

Greenwood Press, 88 Post Road West, Westport, CT 06881
An imprint of Greenwood Publishing Group, Inc.

Printed in the United States of America

The paper used in this book complies with the
Permanent Paper Standard issued by the National
Information Standards Organization (Z39.48–1984).

10 9 8 7 6 5 4 3 2 1

Front cover photo: American soldiers debark from Coast Guard landing barges on D-Day.
CORBIS-BETTMANN.

Black cover photo: Soviet T-34 tanks in action against the German Army. Franklin D. Roosevelt Library.

For William, Alexander, and Nicholas

Contents

A photo essay follows page 104

Series Foreword

As the twenty-first century approaches, it is time to take stock of the political, social, economic, intellectual, and cultural forces and factors that have made the twentieth century the most dramatic period of change in history. To that end, the Greenwood Press Guides to Historic Events of the Twentieth Century presents interpretive histories of the most significant events of the century. Each book in the series combines narrative history and analysis with primary documents and biographical sketches, with an eye to providing both a reference guide to the principal persons, ideas, and experiences defining each historic event, and a reliable, readable overview of that event. Each book further provides analyses and discussions, grounded in both primary and secondary sources, of the causes and consequences, in thought and action, that give meaning to the historic event under review. By assuming a historical perspective, drawing on the latest and best writing on each subject, and offering fresh insights, each book promises to explain how and why a particular event defined the twentieth century. No consensus about the meaning of the twentieth century emerges from the series, but, collectively, the books identify the most salient concerns of the century. In so doing, the series reminds us of the many ways those historic events continue to affect our lives.

Each book follows a similar format designed to encourage readers to consult it both as a reference and a history in its own right. Each volume opens with a chronology of the historic event, followed by a narrative overview, which also serves to introduce and examine briefly the main themes and issues related to that event. The next set of chapters is composed of topical essays, each analyzing closely an issue or problem of interpretation introduced in the opening chapter. A concluding chapter suggesting the long-term implications and meanings of the historic event brings the strands of the preceding chapters together while placing the event in the larger historical context. Each book also includes a section of short biographies of the principal persons related to the event, followed by a section introducing and reprinting key historical documents illustrative of and pertinent to the event. A glossary of selected terms adds to the utility of each book. An annotated bibliography—of significant books, films, and CD-ROMs—and an index conclude each volume.

The editors made no attempt to impose any theoretical model or historical perspective on the individual authors. Rather, in developing the series, an advisory board of noted historians and informed high school history teachers and public and school librarians identified the topics needful of exploration and the scholars eminently qualified to examine those events with intelligence and sensitivity. The common commitment throughout the series is to provide accurate, informative, and readable books, free of jargon and up to date in evidence and analysis.

Each book stands as a complete historical analysis and reference guide to a particular historic event. Each book also has many uses, from understanding contemporary perspectives on critical historical issues, to providing biographical treatments of key figures related to each event, to offering excerpts and complete texts of essential documents about the event, to suggesting and describing books and media materials for further study and presentation of the event, and more. The combination of historical narrative and individual topical chapters addressing significant issues and problems encourages students and teachers to approach each historic event from multiple perspectives and with a critical eye. The arrangement and content of each book thus invite students and teachers, through classroom discussions and position papers, to debate the character and significance of great historic events and to discover for themselves how and why history matters.

The series emphasizes the main currents that have shaped the modern world. Much of that focus necessarily looks at the West, especially Europe and the United States. The political, commercial, and cultural expansion of the West wrought largely, though not wholly, the most fundamental changes of the century. Taken together, however, books in the series reveal the interactions between Western and non-Western peoples and society, and also the tensions between modern and traditional cultures. They also point to the ways in which non-Western peoples have adapted Western ideas and technology and, in turn, influenced Western life and thought. Several books examine such increasingly powerful global forces as the rise of Islamic fundamentalism, the emergence of modern Japan, the Communist revolution in China, and the collapse of communism in eastern Europe and the former Soviet Union. American interests and experiences receive special attention in the series, not only in deference to the primary readership of the books but also in recognition that the United States emerged as the dominant political, economic, social, and cultural force during the twentieth century. By looking at the century through the lens of American events and experiences, it is possible to see why the age has come to be known as "The American Century."

Assessing the history of the twentieth century is a formidable prospect. It has been a period of remarkable transformation. The world broadened and narrowed at the same time. Frontiers shifted from the interiors of Africa and Latin America to the moon and beyond; communication spread from mass circulation newspapers and magazines to radio, television, and now the Internet; skyscrapers reached upward and suburbs stretched outward; energy switched from steam, to electric, to atomic power. Many changes did not lead to a complete abandonment of established patterns and practices so much as a synthesis of old and new, as, for example, the increased use of (even reliance on) the telephone in the age of the computer. The automobile and the truck, the airplane, and telecommunications closed distances, and people in unprecedented numbers migrated from rural to urban, industrial, and ever more ethnically diverse areas. Tractors and chemical fertilizers made it possible for fewer people to grow more, but the environmental and demographic costs of an exploding global population threatened to outstrip natural resources and human innovation. Disparities in wealth increased, with developed nations prospering and underdeveloped nations starving. Amid the crumbling of former European colonial empires, Western technology, goods, and culture increasingly enveloped the globe, seeping into, and undermining, non-Western cultures—a process that contributed to a surge of religious fundamentalism and ethno-nationalism in the Middle East, Asia, and Africa. As people became more alike, they also became more aware of their differences. Ethnic and religious rivalries grew in intensity everywhere as the century closed.

The political changes during the twentieth century have been no less profound than the social, economic, and cultural ones. Many of the books in the series focus on political events, broadly defined, but no books are confined to politics alone. Political ideas and events have social effects, just as they spring from a complex interplay of non-political forces in culture, society, and economy. Thus, for example, the modern civil rights and woman's rights movements were at once social and political events in cause and consequence. Likewise, the Cold War created the geopolitical framework for dealing with competing ideologies and nations abroad and served as the touchstone for political and cultural identities at home. The books treating political events do so within their social, cultural, and economic contexts.

Several books in the series examine particular wars in depth. Wars are defining moments for people and eras. During the twentieth century war became more widespread and terrible than ever before, encouraging new efforts to end war through strategies and organizations of international cooperation and disarmament while also fueling new ideologies and instruments of mass persuasion that fostered distrust and festered old national rivalries. Two world wars during the century redrew the political map, slaughtered or uprooted two generations of people, and introduced and hastened the development of new technologies and weapons of mass destruction. The First World War spelled the end of the old European order and spurred communist revolution in Russia and fascism in Italy, Germany, and elsewhere. The Second World War killed fascism and inspired the final push for freedom from European colonial rule in Asia and Africa. It also led to the Cold War that suffocated much of the world for almost half a century. Large wars begat small ones, and brutal totalitarian regimes cropped up across the globe. After (and in some ways because of) the fall of communism in eastern Europe and the former Soviet Union, wars of competing cultures, national interests, and political systems persisted in the struggle to make a new world order. Continuing, too, has been the belief that military technology can achieve political ends, whether in the superior American firepower that failed to "win" in Vietnam or in the American "smart bombs" and other military wizardry that "won" in the Persian Gulf.

Another theme evident in the series is that throughout the century nationalism has continued to drive events. Whether in the Balkans in 1914 triggering World War I or in the Balkans in the 1990s threatening the post–Cold War peace—or in many other places—nationalist ambitions and forces would not die. The persistence of nationalism is yet another reminder of the many ways that the past becomes prologue.

We thus offer the series as a modern guide to and interpretation of the historic events of the twentieth century and as an invitation to consider how and why those events have defined not only the past and present but also charted the political, social, intellectual, cultural, and economic routes into the next century.

Randall M. Miller
Saint Joseph's University, Philadelphia

Preface

Taken in its entirety, World War II is the greatest single catastrophe human-kind has inflicted upon itself. Few people alive at the time escaped its impact; its consequences still visit those unborn in 1945 and will continue to shape our future.

For the extent of mass destruction of human life, no related series of historical events comes close to matching those of this war. The killing and maiming during the course of mechanized, industrial warfare, deliberate genocide of civilian populations, aerial bombing starvation from the dislocation of agricultural production and industrial economies, diseases spread from the collapse of organized medical services, and tens of millions of refugees ("displaced persons" in the jargon of the day)—these are only some of the measures of the war, whose true cost in lives may never be known. Previous estimates of 30,000,000–40,000,000 dead are now seen as too few. The real price was at least 50,000,000 dead, with 60,000,000, or perhaps as many as 70,000,000, the final cost in human life. Of these, about 22,000,000 were soldiers and 54,000,000 were civilians. Among the civilians were 6,000,000 Jews killed in the Holocaust and another 4,000,000 who also perished in German concentration and death camps. We will never have true figures, as the very wartime upheaval prevented the keeping of accurate records.

World War II was also the most global of human conflicts. True, the Anglo-French rivalry of the 1700s and early 1800s was conducted around the globe, and its outcome portended significant future changes. But its direct impact was generally limited to Europe and maritime peoples in direct contact with Europeans. World War I had a deeper impact, and it can be compared more clearly to World War II, but the world of 1918, except for Europe, was not as dramatically different from that of 1914 as was the world of 1945 compared to 1939.

World War II marked the death knell for European imperialism, though that was not entirely clear for a while. The United States, admittedly the globe's largest industrial economy in 1914, was a military midget in the 1930s. It emerged from the Great Depression of the 1930s and mobilized during the war to become the world's premier military power, with a long-distance air force, bases scattered around the world, and an arsenal of nuclear weapons. The United States, unlike other major powers, emerged economically stronger in 1945 as the world's leading trading nation.

The eclipse of Europe at the center of the world's international system was paralleled both by the leadership of the West by the United States and by the advent of the Soviet Union as the would-be nemesis of the world's capitalist societies. With Europe a military cipher, the colonial world in disorder, and capitalism associated with a defeated fascist order, Soviet communism received a new appeal worldwide. The Chinese communists might have defeated their nationalist opponents in civil war without the larger conflict, but those events were so intertwined with the Japanese drive for empire that it is impossible to separate the communists' triumph from the war years. The same is true of nationalist revolts throughout Asia, from Vietnam and Indonesia to India and the Arab world.

World War II saw an unprecedented growth in state power as democratic, parliamentary regimes as well as totalitarian ones centralized and organized social and economic life as never before. Managed economies, whether capitalist or socialist, seemed to be one necessary outcome. Along with managed economies came state direction of educational institutions, scientific research, and collaboration between government and basic industries, in many cases the nationalization of such industries.

The following chapters examine key aspects of the war. Relations among the primary opponents of the Axis powers, the Soviet Union, Great Britain, and the United States, greatly affected the shape of the postwar world and the world in which we still live. The relationship between warfare and ever-changing technology characterizes modern armed conflict in ways that complicate strategic planning and preparation for war. World War II clearly shows this change. The impact of the war on the societies of the major belligerent powers provides insight into the relationship between war and society as well as indicates the ways war transforms societies. Finally, a chapter on resistance movements suggests that World War II was more than a conflict over national sovereignty and the survival of states. It was also a war over deeply held social and political values.

The last half of this volume includes biographical sketches of twenty-seven participants in the war, mostly leaders, but also some not so well-known who illustrate the variety of individuals and their activities during the war. There are seventeen primary wartime documents ranging from declarations and speeches by the leaders of the Allies, to key ideas on the emerging new military technologies, to resistance pronouncements. An annotated bibliography will guide the readers to some of the most important literature relating to all aspects of the war. There is also a glossary of selected terms and an essay of eight photographs illustrating themes covered in the narrative chapters. Three maps aid the reader in locating major military events by detailing German conquests between 1939 and 1941, showing Allied advances against Germany from 1944, and outlining Allied offensives after 1942 against the empire carved out by the Japanese in 1941–1942. Finally, a chronology of key events follows this introduction.

The impact of the war was not unilaterally good or bad, though the immediate uncertainty generated by its horrors suggested the latter. Whatever the reader's judgment on these matters, it is hard to resist the conclusion that the world was a very different place after six years of accelerating mayhem. War was not just something that the world suffered through. It had indelibly changed the world's psychological, social, and spiritual environment.

In the course of studying and writing about such a vast topic as World War II, one becomes indebted to thousands of writers and observers on various aspects of the war. I am especially thankful, however, for the advice and encouragement of Professor Robin Higham and the many contributors to the two handbooks on the literature and research of *World War II in Europe* and *World War II in Asia and the Pacific* published by Greenwood Press. More directly, in preparing this manuscript I owe much to Professor Randall Miller, the series editor, and Barbara Rader of Greenwood Press. And, of course, the support of the librarians of the Sojourner Truth Library at the College of New Paltz was indispensable to acquiring the material and information needed to complete this book.

Chronology of Events

1933

January 30   Hitler appointed chancellor of Germany

1936

July 18   The Spanish Civil War begins

1937

July 7   Sino-Japanese War begins

1938

March 12   German annexation (Anschluss) of Austria

July 28   Russo-Japanese conflict begins in Manchuria

September 29   Munich Agreement concedes the Sudetenland to Germany

1939

March 15   Germany occupies the remainder of Czechoslovakia

March 28   End of Spanish Civil War

April 7   Italy invades Albania

May 28   Russo-Japanese fighting breaks out again

August 20   Surprise Russian attack on Japanese at Nomonhan (Khalkhin-gol)

August 23   Soviet-German Non-Aggression Pact signed

September 1   Germany invades Poland

September 15	Russo-Japanese cease-fire begins
September 17	Russian troops invade Poland
November 2	U.S. Congress modifies the Neutrality Acts by passing "Cash and Carry"
November 20	Russia invades Finland and starts the Winter War
December 14	Russia expelled from the League of Nations

1940

March 12	Russia and Finland sign peace treaty
March 20	Wang Jiangwei forms pro-Japanese government in Nanjing
April 9	Germany invades Denmark and Norway
May 10	Germany invades the Lowlands and France; Churchill becomes prime minister of Great Britain
May 26–June 4	Evacuation at Dunkirk
June 6	German High Command issues Commissar Order
June 10	Italy declares war on Britain and France
June 16	Pétain becomes prime minister of France
June 18	de Gaulle broadcasts from London
June 22	Pétain's government signs an armistice with Germany
June 23	de Gaulle declares his intention to continue the war against Germany
June 27	Romania cedes territory to Russia, which also annexes the Baltic states
July 3	Britain attacks French fleet at Mers-el Kebir
July 26	The United States begins partial embargo of Japan
August 15	Eagle Attack begins Battle of Britain
September 2	Britain receives American destroyers in return for leasing bases for 99 years
September 16	U.S. Selective Service and Training Act passed
September 22	Japan occupies Indochina
September 27	Tripartite Pact signed
October 28	Italy invades Greece
November 5	Roosevelt reelected for third term

1941

January 22	British take Tobruk for first time
March 11	Lend-Lease signed
April 2–May 30	Rashid Ali's pro-Axis coup in Iraq
April 6	Germany invades Yugoslavia and Greece
April 13	Russia and Japan sign Neutrality Pact
May 27	German battleship *Bismarck* sunk
June 22	Operation Barbarossa begins
July 5	The United States occupies Iceland
August 14	Atlantic Charter signed
August 25	British and Russians occupy Iran
September 18	Tito takes command of partisans in Yugoslavia
October 11	Tojo replaces Konoe as prime minister of Japan
December 6	Russia opens counteroffensive against Germany before Moscow
December 7	Japan attacks Pearl Harbor, the Philippines, Hong Kong, Malaya, and other bases
December 10	Japan sinks *Prince of Wales* and *Repulse*; Germany and Italy declare war on the United States
December 25	Hong Kong surrenders

1942

January 1	United Nations Declaration signed
January 20	Wannsee Conference on the "Final Solution to the Jewish Problem"
February 2	Stillwell becomes Chiang's Chief of Staff
February 15	Singapore surrenders
April 18	Doolittle raids
May 6	Corregidor surrenders
May 8	Battle of Coral Sea
May 12	Russia opens offensive against Germany
May 20	First 1,000-bomber raid (against Cologne)
June 2–6	Battle of Midway

June 11   Free French establish their military reputation at Bir Hakeim

June 21   Tobruk falls to Rommel's Afrika Korps

June 28   Germany opens offensive against Russia

August 7   U.S. Marines land in Guadalcanal

August 9   Indian Congress Party opens civil disobedience campaign

September 7   Australian and U.S. troops defeat Japanese near Milne Bay, New Guinea

September 16   Battle of Stalingrad begins

November 8   Operation Torch begins

November 13   British retake Tobruk

November 26–27   Anti-Fascist Council of Peoples' Liberation of Yugoslavia first meets in Bihac

1943

January 11   The United States and Britain give up extraterritoriality in China

January 14–24   Casablanca Conference, Symbol

February 2   Von Paulus surrenders at Stalingrad

April 19   Warsaw ghetto uprising begins

April 26   News of Katyn Forest massacre announced

May 11–25   Second Allied Washington Conference, Trident

May 12   Axis forces driven from North Africa

May 15   Stalin disbands Third International

May 24   Dönitz withdraws U-boats from the Battle of the Atlantic

May 27   National Council of the Resistance (France) forms

June 2   French Committee of National Liberation forms

July 5   Battle of Kursk begins

July 10   Allies invade Sicily

July 24   Hamburg air raids begin

July 25   Badoglio becomes prime minister of Italy

August 17–24   First Quebec Conference, Quadrant

September 2   Britain and the United States invade Italy

September 8   Italy surrenders

September 9	Committee of National Liberation (Italy) forms
October 10	Moscow Conference with Hull, Eden, and Molotov opens
November 23–25	Cairo Conference, Sextant
November 28–December 1	Tehran Conference, Eureka
December 3–7	Continuation of Cairo Conference

1944

January 16	Eisenhower becomes Supreme Commander, Allied Expeditionary Force
January 22	Anzio landings in Italy
March 20	Germany occupies Hungary
April 17	Japan opens offensive against China
June 4	Rome is liberated
June 6	Normandy invasion begins
June 13	Germans use first V-1 bombs
June 19	Battle of the Philippine Sea begins
June 23	Russia opens Operation Bagration, summer offensive against Germany; Japanese offensive in Burma defeated
July 1	Bretton Woods Conference opens
July 20	Assassination attempt on Hitler
August 1	Warsaw uprising begins
August 21	Dumbarton Oaks Conference opens
August 23	Romania surrenders
August 25	Paris liberated
September 4	Second Russo-Finnish war ends
September 8	Germans use first V-2 rockets
September 12–16	Second Quebec Conference, Octagon
September 17	Operation Market Garden opens
October 9	Stalin and Churchill agree on the percentage of their relative influence in eastern Europe
October 20	Belgrade liberated; the United States invades the Philippines

October 21	Battle of Leyte Gulf begins
November 7	Roosevelt reelected to fourth term
November 24	B-29 raids on Japan begin
December 16	Battle of the Bulge opens

1945

January 12	Russia opens winter offensive against Germany
January 17	Russians occupy Warsaw
February 4–11	Yalta Conference, Argonaut
February 13	Dresden air raids begin
March 9	The United States begins incendiary campaign against Japan
March 22	Arab League formed
April 5	Suzuki becomes prime minister of Japan
April 12	Roosevelt dies; Truman becomes president
April 19–25	Partisans lead insurrections in northern Italy
April 23	Russians enter Berlin
April 25	United Nations Conference opens in San Francisco; American and Russian soldiers meet at Torgau on the Elbe River
April 30	Hitler commits suicide
May 2	German army in Italy surrenders
May 7	Germany surrenders unconditionally
May 8	V-E Day
July 16	Potsdam Conference, Terminal; first atomic bomb exploded at Alamogordo, New Mexico
July 26	Potsdam Declaration; Labour Party wins British elections
August 2	Potsdam Conference ends
August 6	Atomic bomb is dropped on Hiroshima
August 8	Russia declares war on Japan
August 9	Atomic bomb is dropped on Nagasaki
August 14	Japan surrenders
August 17	Sukarno proclaims Indonesian independence

September 2   Japan signs surrender terms; Ho Chi Minh proclaims Vietnam-
ese independence

October   Pan-African Conference meets in Manchester, England

WORLD WAR II
EXPLAINED

German Offensives and Territorial Changes in Europe, 1939–1941

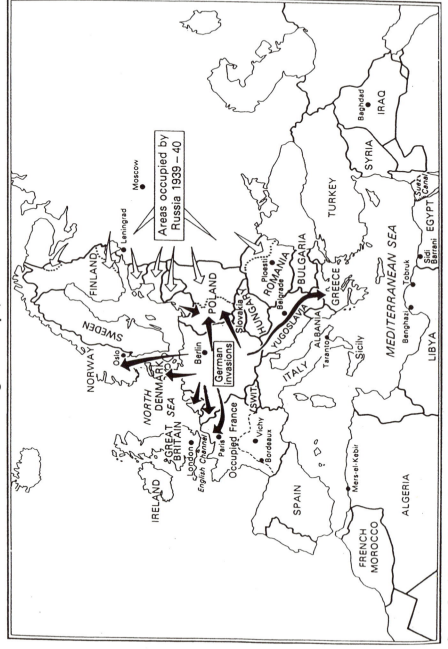

Source: Loyd E. Lee, *The War Years: A Global History of the Second World War* (Boston: Unwin Hyman, 1989). Used by permission of Routledge.

Allied Offensives against Japan, 1942–1945

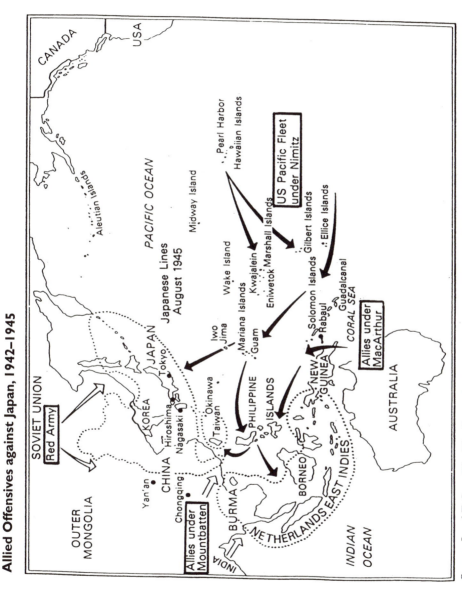

Source: Loyd E. Lee, *The War Years: A Global History of the Second World War* (Boston: Unwin Hyman, 1989). Used by permission of Routledge.

The Defeat of the Axis in Europe, 1944–1945

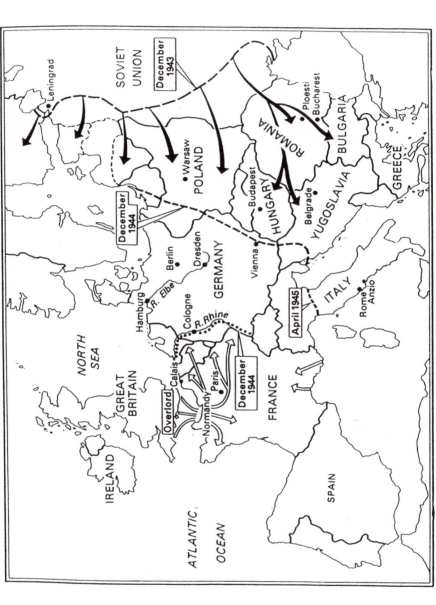

Source: Loyd E. Lee, *The War Years: A Global History of the Second World War* (Boston: Unwin Hyman, 1989). Used by permission of Routledge.

I

An Overview of the War

More than a half century ago the Third Reich collapsed from the force of Allied armies, and Japan surrendered on the U.S.S. *Missouri* in Tokyo harbor. Yet, since V-E and V-J days, writing about the war years has continued to expand. Because so much of the present geopolitical (geographic, economic, demographic, and political) framework was a product of World War II, the war remains the touchstone for understanding the modern world. Such understanding entails more than attention to military and political affairs. World War II changed societies, recast intellectual assumptions, altered racial and gender relations, and more. Some old questions, especially on military strategies and the conduct of campaigns, have been largely resolved. New ones of gender, race, the relationship of European imperialism to former colonies, and of culture and religion have emerged. The end of the Cold War and the collapse of the Soviet Union have also changed our perspective on the meaning, even the conduct of the war.

The term "Second World War" was coined soon after the First World War, but it did not gain currency until after 1939. Initially, the European war that broke out in September 1939 was called the War of 1939. That became inadequate when war spread to western Europe and then to the Mediterranean and North Africa in 1940. When Germany attacked the Soviet Union in 1941, the Soviets called it the Great Patriotic War, without clearly identifying warfare elsewhere as part of their struggle. When the European conflicts merged with the East Asian war with the Japanese attack on Pearl Harbor and invasion of southeast Asia, a true world war was under way. The United States and the British Commonwealth and Empire linked warfare in Europe and the Mediterranean with that in China and the Pacific.

An understanding of the origins of the war and the course of events during the war is of intrinsic historical interest. It is also necessary for comprehending the meaning of the war on human civilization and its impact on later generations.

THE ORIGINS OF THE WAR IN EUROPE

In a real sense the origin of the world war has a simple explanation. Adolf Hitler, named to the Reichs Chancellorship in 1933 at the urging of conservative opponents of the German Weimar Republic, viewed history as racial conflict in which war played a central role. To Hitler the coming war meant survival against Jews, and it meant German expansion of territory for sustained, healthy growth (*Lebensraum*). Hitler wanted war. He saw it as necessary to realize his own and Germany's greatness. The exact measures, diplomatic and otherwise, he took to reach that goal are not simple. They rested on bluff and obscuring his real aims from many of his domestic supporters. They relied on deceiving European diplomats and statesmen into thinking that he was a German nationalist interested in restoring Germany to its earlier imperial glory and revising the Treaty of Versailles.

By the 1930s the moral basis of the post–World War I European peace had been undermined inside and outside Germany. Revisionists argued that the Treaty of Versailles of 1919 wrongly charged Germany with the guilt of beginning "the Great War," World War I. Many believed it was a punitive peace, responsible for Germany's domestic political and economic problems, and that it violated the principle of national self-determination. Only its revision in Germany's favor would set matters straight.

The weakness of the international order was not the injustice of the Versailles Treaty, nor Hitler's obsessive racism. The treaty left Germany as a unified state, and reparations were largely balanced by American loans. The so-called war guilt clause (article 231) appeared in other treaties of Paris signed with Austria, Hungary, Bulgaria, and Turkey. No one laid responsibility on them for the war.

The critical fact was that the international system after 1919 was fundamentally weaker than that before 1914. And the international order of 1914 had not prevented war. Britain and France were victors in the Great War, but both faced increased imperial unrest from nationalists throughout Asia and much of Africa. And after 1919 they had fewer resources to meet the new challenges. In addition, the United States withdrew into diplomatic isolation, unwilling to support the peace in Europe. The communists in the Soviet Union, in the throes of revolution, interpreted the postwar tensions as the last stage of imperialist capitalism from which they would be the beneficiaries. The Soviet Union did in time turn to collective security and support for the League of Nations, but it remained an international pariah with limited credibility.

Most importantly, however, eastern Europe was no longer divided among the four great prewar empires. World War I had swept the Habsburg, the Hohenzollern, the Romanov, and the Ottoman empires from history. The remnant of the Hohenzollern empire, the Weimar Republic, was still largely intact. It was flanked on the east by 12 militarily weak states stretching from Finland to Greece, most with territorial or ethnic claims against their neighbors. Eastern Europe provided no effective barrier to the spread of German influence, whether by force or by trade and culture. For Britain and France, their imperial role took precedence over eastern Europe. The Soviet Union in its own way was as isolationist as the United States. German domestic political weakness rather than external barriers largely restrained German assertiveness in central and eastern Europe.

The steps traditionally ticked off as the Nazi road to war largely confirm these facts: 1933, German withdrawal from the League of Nations; 1935, rearmament; 1936, military occupation of the Rhineland; and 1938, annexation of Austria. These were all accomplished with a combination of promises and threats rather than military force, all under the guise of realizing the principle of national self-determination and undoing the terms of the Versailles Treaty.

In the summer of 1938 Hitler attempted to instigate a war with Czechoslovakia. He rued the day when the British prime minister Neville Chamberlain, supported by the French, the Italians, and the Hungarians, seized the opportunity from him by forcing the Czechoslovak government to cede borderlands of predominantly ethnic Germans to the Third Reich. The lessons of "appeasement" at Munich, as this policy was called, are complex. But neither Chamberlain nor the French premier Édouard Daladier had domestic support for war. Their defensive military posture made military intervention on behalf of Czechoslovakia difficult. The British and French would have to confront Hitler alone, as they in fact did the next year when the Germans invaded Poland. By that time, the destruction of Czechoslovakia in March 1939 and naked aggression against Poland in September clearly showed that Hitler was not acting in the interests of national self-determination. German propaganda rang hollow, lacking all credibility.

THE BEGINNING OF WORLD WAR II

Geographically, the defense of Poland was most difficult. German troops surrounded the country to the north, west, and south. There was no point of natural defense. In the unexpected and shocking Russo-German Non-Aggression Pact of August 23, 1939, Soviet premier Joseph Stalin had joined Hitler to isolate Poland (while also secretly agreeing to partition the country) and to make Poland's defeat inevitable. The German army and its Panzer tanks smashed into Poland on September 1, unleashing blitzkrieg (lightning war). The Poles fought heroically against overwhelming odds. Britain and France declared war on Germany, the only countries to do so during the war without themselves being attacked. But they had no plans to come to Poland's immediate aid.

Hitler wanted Poland's rapid defeat for its psychological impact both at home and abroad. Nowhere in Europe was there enthusiasm for a repetition of 1914. Hitler got his wish. Mechanized forces, backed by 1,700,000 men, broke through Polish lines, isolating pockets of troops, quickly to reduce organized resistance. Warsaw surrendered on September 27. Polish soldiers became prisoners of war, but a few went into hiding or escaped abroad with the government. Poland as a state ceased to exist, except in exile.

Simultaneously, the racist and biological reshaping of Europe started. Euthanasia of several tens of thousands of insane, senile, and invalid Germans began. Massacres of Jews, Polish intellectuals, and priests occurred, and the establishment of ghettos spread throughout Poland.

THE WAR IN WESTERN EUROPE, 1940–1941

French preparations for a conflict with Germany were not premised on defending an eastern European ally. Rather, the French chose a defensive posture. French strategists concluded from World War I that a defense behind machine guns, trenches, and underground bunkers was far superior to any offense or striking capacity elsewhere. They thus built an elaborate series of fortifications, the Maginot Line, along the Franco-German border. Often ridiculed, it was in fact not breached. It forced the Germans to invade through Belgium, a much narrower front that the French thought they could defend.

Hitler's aim in destroying Poland was to eliminate Anglo-French opposition to German hegemony (influence and authority) in eastern and central Europe, the first stage in his design for world domination. Elated by his success, Hitler ordered an immediate invasion of western Europe, but the German General Staff, realizing the strengths of the French army, managed to postpone the invasion until 1940.

Meanwhile, in a separate operation, Germany occupied Denmark and invaded Norway on April 9, 1940. France and Britain sent forces to aid the Norwegian resistance, but were soon forced to withdraw. This setback led to Chamberlain's resignation and Winston Churchill's appointment as prime minister.

Luckily for Hitler, the delayed invasion in the west provided an opportunity to revise the army's war plans. The new strategy was to draw French armies and the British Expeditionary Force into Belgium, to sweep behind them with concentrated Panzer divisions from the Ardennes—a wooded region with deep ravines—and cut them off from their supplies and communications. The surprise attack came on May 10. Exactly how to explain the events of the next few days remains contested. But the results are not. One third of a million Allied soldiers were surrounded on the coast at Dunkirk, most of whom were evacuated to England. Benito Mussolini now brought Italy into the fray, eager to sit among the victors at the coming peace conference. The next week, with German armies pointing southward, Henri Pétain, World War I hero and new head of the French government, asked Germany for an armistice. The armistice did not bring peace. The British continued the war, fighting the Germans alone for the next year, and resistance movements began to spring up in German-occupied countries.

Victory over France was achieved at little cost and great speed. The French army collapsed, and the Germans entered Paris in triumph on June 14. Hitler and the Germans appeared to have supremacy in Europe, but they needed to persuade the British to end the war and accept the new geopolitical map Germany had forged in Europe. As encouragement, the Germans prepared for an invasion. The Luftwaffe needed to destroy the British Royal Air Force (RAF), but unprepared for Hitler's grand designs, the Luftwaffe lacked a strategy and a seasoned organization for an air war over Britain. Although British victory was never certain, the RAF's Fighter Command had several advantages. It had a centralized defense command based on a coastal radar system and radio ground control. It enjoyed increased production of aircraft during the battle. With the fighting above British airspace, pilots had maximum airtime and could be rescued. Most importantly, in Sir Hugh Dowding the British had a commander who knew how to link various elements of defense into an effective whole.

The Battle of Britain lasted from mid-June through mid-September, 1940, though Germany's main attack came in August. Target selection was confused and frequently changed. It never concentrated on the radar chain, a key factor in Britain's success. Meanwhile invasion plans stalled as the navy and the army disputed the details. In any case the invasion could not take place until the RAF was destroyed. On September 7 the Luftwaffe turned from attacking the RAF to bombing London, in hopes of leveling the city and undermining British morale. After massive raids against an effective defense, the Germans ended the battle the next week, though air raids continued for the next few months.

THE MEDITERRANEAN AND NORTH AFRICAN WAR

While the Luftwaffe pounded Britain, Italy expanded the war in North Africa by invading British Somaliland in July and Egypt in September 1940. Then in November Mussolini struck at Greece from Albania, but without success. In early November the British sank much of the Italian fleet at Taranto by air in a night raid, in a surprise attack that showed the vulnerability of battleships to air power and inspired the Japanese plans for Pearl Harbor. It also turned the naval balance in Britain's favor. Hitler was furious. Germany now ran the danger of both British and Soviet intervention in the Balkans, which would threaten Germany's meager oil supplies from Romania. Worse, a Balkan fiasco might jeopardize planning for Operation Barbarossa, the attack on the Soviet Union, scheduled for spring 1941.

To secure Axis power in the region, Hitler sent Erwin Rommel with the Afrika Korps to North Africa. They nearly drove the British out of Libya. In April 1941 the German army occupied Yugoslavia and invaded Greece, destroying its army and forcing British withdrawal. The offensive continued with a startling German airborne invasion of Crete in May. Such successes spread German resources thin. The approaching invasion of the Soviet Union left the Germans unable to consolidate their position in the eastern Mediterranean.

THE WAR AT SEA

The German navy was not prepared to challenge the British at sea in 1939. Aside from a few raids on merchant shipping, the battle of the Atlantic began in earnest in 1940 after the Germans stationed submarines on the French coast. Submarine commander in chief Karl Dönitz used radio to control the U-boats, enabling them to locate and converge more effectively on shipping in the narrow English channel. The British originally intended to rely on the new technology of sonar (asdic), but they had to revert to convoys as in World War I to protect their shipping. Lengthening nights of late 1940 gave Britain a reprieve, but losses increased the next spring. In May 1941 the Kriegsmarine tried surface attacks on merchant ships, principally with the new battleships *Bismarck* and the *Prinz Eugen*. They did some damage, but they also invited British reprisals. The British navy chased the *Prinz Eugen* to France where it remained bottled up along with other capital ships for the rest of the war; and in May 1941 they sank the *Bismarck* in the last great surface-to-surface naval battle in the Atlantic.

Earlier the same month, the British captured a U-boat with its Enigma machine and its enciphering instructions, enabling them to read German naval messages. The effect was dramatic, and critical in the war for control of the Atlantic. But it took time for the British, and then the Americans, to capitalize on their knowledge of the German codes. Declaration of war on the United States in December 1941 extended U-boat attacks to the unprepared eastern North American coast. Increased submarine production further aided the Germans. The Allies suffered their worst merchant ship losses in 1942.

By 1943, however, the tide turned permanently in the Allies' favor. A steadier supply of intelligence, escorts armed with radar, near complete air cover of the North Atlantic, plus more-experienced crews all contributed to force the Germans from the North Atlantic. German raids continued elsewhere around the world, but the critical link between North America and Europe remained secure. The improved U-boats of 1945 came into production too late to affect the course of the war.

THE RUSSO-GERMAN WAR, 1941

Hitler's abiding goal was Lebensraum in the east. In December 1940 he ordered preparations for Operation Barbarossa against the Soviet Union for the next spring. The Balkan and North African hostilities intervened, but planning continued for a "swift campaign." In contrast to previous campaign plans, the strategic objectives for Barbarossa were never clearly defined.

On June 22, 1941, the Germans invaded the Soviet Union. The scale of the invasion dwarfed all military campaigns before and since. Over 3,500,000 German and other Axis troops, some 3,500 tanks, and nearly 3,000 aircraft spread over a front 1,300 miles long, which increased in width as it advanced. Rapid tank sweeps through and behind enemy lines were initially as successful in Russia as they had been in western Europe, and the Luftwaffe achieved air supremacy. Soviet commanders and their forces reeled under the impact, neither expecting an invasion at that time nor in that strength. By mid-July the German High Command surmised that the war was over. Meanwhile, a war of annihilation and extermination was under way as captured Red Army political commissars, Jews, and selected Soviet leaders were summarily killed.

But the German advance stalled, and the Soviet military recovered. Some losses of personnel and equipment were made good by bringing in fresh troops from the east, while the vastness of the country denied the Germans the destruction of the Red Army they needed for victory. Stalin relaxed communist propaganda in favor of defense of the Motherland.

In August 1941 Hitler turned south toward the Ukraine and north toward Leningrad. Then in September he launched a new operation, Typhoon, against Moscow. By this time the Soviets knew that Japan had decided on war with the Western powers, not with the Soviet Union. This allowed the transfer of fresh troops from Siberia. These, along with Soviet fighting skills, determined resistance, and new equipment stopped the German advance before Moscow. On December 6 a Soviet counteroffensive led by Georgii Zhukov drove the Germans back. Barbarossa had failed. The German army had to organize a new campaign for 1942.

THE JAPANESE AND ASIAN BACKGROUND TO THE PACIFIC WAR

The East Asian and Pacific war had its origins in Japan's quest for economic domination of China. The decision for war against Britain, the Netherlands, and the United States in 1941 was not part of a coordinated effort with other Axis powers, though it was in response to what looked like a changed military balance in Germany's favor. The European and Asian conflicts were not directly related, though Germany and Italy's declaration of war on the United States following the attack on Pearl Harbor gave that impression. Only the United States conducted major campaigns in both the European and Pacific theaters.

The worldwide depression beginning in 1929 denied Japan much needed trade and tipped the political scales within the country to supporters of expansion, primarily in the military. In 1931 the Japanese army in Korea, a Japanese colony, occupied Manchuria on its own initiative and conspired to bring north China into its orbit. When the League of Nations condemned the Japanese attacks, the Japanese withdrew from the organization. Contemptuous of Western weakness, the Japanese threatened European interests in Asia. They promised a "greater east Asian Co-prosperity sphere" under Japanese control in a seeming bid to throw off European rule in favor of Asian unity. Japan's need for natural resources and its highly developed sense of cultural superiority, however, drove Japanese ambitions in Asia.

In 1937 the Japanese army in Manchuria launched a campaign against China, which the government in Tokyo backed for fear of retaliation by radical nationalists if it did not. Japan steadily fell into a quagmire that it could not win and from which it had no will to extricate itself. Chinese resistance was ineffective, but the country's huge size and difficult terrain prevented its conquest.

At the same time, Japan confronted Soviet forces in Manchuria, suffering defeat at Nomonhan (Khalkhin-gol) in August 1939. Little noticed outside of East Asia, this defeat cautioned the Japanese Army against tangling with the Soviet Union. A cease-fire in September 1939 led to a ten-year neutrality pact in April 1941.

THE JAPANESE AND AMERICAN ROAD TO WAR

Disturbed by Japanese expansion in China, Washington lent the Chinese nationalist leader Chiang Kai-shek diplomatic support and limited military aid. Frustrated, Japan moved to occupy China's Pacific coast and cut the country off from the outside world. These measures coincided with the German occupation of western Europe, which shut off French Indochina (today's Vietnam, Laos, and Cambodia) and the Netherlands Indies (Indonesia) from their metropolitans. If Britain fell, it looked as if Germany and Italy would be the beneficiaries of the European empires in Asia.

American intentions were unclear, but the promise of independence to the Philippine Islands for 1946 and the absence of significant military investment indicated American acquiescence to Axis expansion. In anticipation of a change in the world order, Japan declared a New Order in East Asia in June 1940. This was followed by the Tripartite Pact of September 1940 in which Japan, Germany, and Italy each recognized the others' "spheres of influence." The pact was also intended to warn off the United States. It had the opposite effect.

As Japanese-American negotiations dawdled, Japan continued its southward advance, occupying all of Indochina in the summer of 1941. Washington responded by an embargo on trade, most importantly on oil, and freezing Japanese assets. As Japan's most important trading partner, the United States thought to pressure Japan to back down. Instead, it led to a decision for war before the lack of oil could cripple Japan's military capacity.

The Japanese campaign against the Western powers fell to the navy, one of the world's best prepared and trained peacetime navies. Although Japan had battleships, including the superbattleships *Yamato* and *Musashi*, its real strength lay in its carrier fleet and its pilots. Their "Long Lance" torpedo was the most effective of the war.

JAPAN DECIDES ON WAR

Initial Japanese plans called for severing American lines of communication to the western Pacific and occupying all of southeast Asia in order to establish a line of defense stretching from Burma in the west through Netherlands Indies, New Guinea, and the Solomon Islands to the Gilbert, Marshall, and Wake Islands. The attack on Pearl Harbor was a bold attempt to weaken the American fleet long enough for Japan to conquer and mobilize resources or, perhaps, even to dispirit the United States into accepting Japan's new empire.

Even though the Pearl Harbor raid on Sunday morning, December 7, 1941, achieved complete surprise and met limited resistance, it was a strategic mistake. The battleships sunk were relics of a previous naval age. The American carriers were not in port. The valuable fuel tanks (enough for most of the U.S. Navy's 1942 operations) remained intact. Most importantly, the attack united Americans solidly behind the war effort and for the total defeat of Japan.

Elsewhere, the Japanese marched from triumph to triumph. Pacific islands were taken. Borneo was attacked. Singapore, the bastion of European power in Asia for over three centuries, fell February 15, 1942, portending the end of the British Empire. Days later, Allied naval forces in the Java Sea were annihilated. The Japanese overran the Philippines in early 1942, humiliating the Americans and their Filipino comrades. Douglas MacArthur, in command of their defense, left in March 1942 for Australia, pledging "I shall return." The only bright story for the Americans was the Doolittle raid, air strikes launched from the aircraft carrier U.S.S. *Hornet* against the Japanese homeland in April. The attacks did little physical damage, but they suggested Japan's vulnerability and buoyed American spirits.

With opposition cleared, the Japanese navy prepared to take on the Australians at Port Moresby in New Guinea. This led to the Battle of the Coral Sea in early May 1942. Coral Sea opened a new era in modern war. For the first time in naval history, neither fleet sighted the other; rather, the carriers launched planes to attack the enemy. American losses were heavy, but Japan abandoned the invasion of Port Moresby.

THE PACIFIC WAR IN 1942

Flush with success in much of the region, the Japanese navy prepared an elaborate attack on the American-held island of Midway to extend Japan's defensive perimeter and force the U.S. Navy to a conclusive battle. It now faced a revitalized foe. The new U.S. Commander in Chief, Pacific, Chester Nimitz revamped American intelligence, enabling it to discern Japanese intentions in advance of the June 4 attack. Even so, the Americans still needed skill, considerable luck, and Japanese mistakes for their decisive victory at Midway. The Japanese lost four aircraft carriers and many of their trained pilots.

Victory at Midway did not result from an overall strategic plan or American rearmament. The two-ocean navy program authorized by the U.S. Congress in 1940 was not yet in full force. A final strategy had yet to be developed for the defeat of Japan. In addition, Washington had agreed with the British in January 1941 that in the event of American involvement in the war in Europe and in a war against Japan the United States would make the defeat of Germany its priority.

Ironically, the postponement in 1942 of a direct assault on the European continent in favor of landings in North Africa opened the way for an American counteroffensive in the Solomon Islands in August, with the island of Guadalcanal the main objective. Initially a costly disaster for the U.S. Marines, the Guadalcanal campaign thwarted Japan's southern advance and laid the basis for Allied naval and army campaigns of 1943.

THE ANGLO-AMERICAN ALLIANCE

Roosevelt pursued a cautious policy toward Britain in 1940. Running for a third term as president, he was up against the strength of isolationist opinion. The Neutrality Acts, passed to keep the United States out of another World War I, forbade trade with countries at war, but Congress modified them in 1939 to permit American firms to sell supplies on a "cash and carry" basis—that is, only for cash and without the involvement of American shipping.

Roosevelt believed that it was in the United States' interest to save Western democracies and check Germany, but the question was how to do so without angering already leery, and still powerful, isolationist forces in the United States and without triggering a German attack on the United States. Events in Europe forced America's hand.

In late summer 1940, as Britain braced for German invasion, Washington leased 50 World War I destroyers to the British in return for 99-year leases on bases in the Caribbean and the northwestern Atlantic. The "destroyers for bases" deal served to help the British while it also seemingly kept the war away from "American waters." After Roosevelt's reelection in November, Churchill pressed him for further aid. Britain could not continue to pay cash for supplies because its gold reserves and other financial resources were running low. In response, Congress in March 1941 passed the Lend-Lease Act, which authorized the president to supply goods and services to countries at war whose defense he deemed in American interests. By war's end over $40 billion of equipment, food, oil (two thirds of the world's supply), and services went to Britain, the Soviet Union, the Free French, China, and more than 30 other nations under Lend-Lease.

Lend-Lease's importance extended beyond diplomacy and winning the war. A thorough public debate moved the United States away from isolationism. In implementing Lend-Lease, the Americans insisted on Britain opening its Commonwealth and Empire to American producers. It also laid the basis for a new worldwide free trade system negotiated at the Bretton Woods conference of 1944 and in other agreements to increase international economic cooperation.

MOBILIZING THE HOME FRONTS FOR WAR

All belligerents mobilized their societies and economies for war, and even neutral countries that hoped to stay out of the conflict shifted resources to meet economic demands of a world at war. The degree of mobilization, however, varied greatly because of factors such as the length of active participation in the war, access to raw materials, the nature of the country's political system, and the level of its population's education and skills.

Social mobilization depended in part on film and radio. All governments used propaganda to reinforce commitment to the war effort from soldiers and civilian workers. Propaganda worked best when it confirmed already held opinions and corresponded to individuals' experience. Joseph Goebbel's Nazi Ministry of Propaganda and Enlightenment was undermined by the declining standard of living in Germany, especially after 1942. News about the disastrous losses at Stalingrad in January 1943 eventually had to be reported. Most successful was the British Broadcasting Corporation. It expanded its services, vastly expanding its overseas foreign language broadcasting. It relaxed its highbrow programming and offered a more popular fare. The BBC double-checked its news reports for accuracy, and gained a reputation for reliability, becoming respected at home and abroad. In the United States, radio, Hollywood films, and newspapers churned out anti-Axis propaganda and helped make the entire wartime experience a "good war" for Americans. In cartoons Bugs Bunny and Mickey Mouse did their part to sock it to the Axis.

After the French catastrophe of 1940, the British government conscripted workers, including women, as well as property, for the war effort. Britain mobilized a greater percent of civilians for war production than any other belligerent. Rationing eliminated unnecessary consumption. The expansion of war production reached its limit by 1944, when unemployed labor was reduced to its minimum and shipping constraints in preparation for the invasion of France reduced the importation of raw materials and nonessential manufactured goods.

The empire also proved a great source for labor and war materials. Imperial mobilization in India, for example, led to an extension of industrialization and in the Middle East to an expansion of the economic infrastructure. In African settler colonies such as Kenya, the Rhodesias, and South Africa, white farmers prospered from the demand for agricultural products. In west Africa the demand for raw materials and manufactured goods brought increased prosperity.

Politically, mobilization came at the cost of concessions to local nationalist elites. Nationalists throughout the empire appealed to references to national self-determination in the Atlantic Charter issued by Churchill and Roosevelt in August 1941. The aim of the 1942 Quit India movement led by Gandhi was to force the British out. It failed and temporarily weakened the Indian Congress party when the British threw thousands into jail, but it also showed that London could not dictate the terms of wartime cooperation. The war increased the strength of the Muslim League in India, making it a major factor in national politics. In both east and west Africa, nationalist parties benefited from the British need to expand production and recruit troops and labor. In the settler colonies the war strengthened the political clout of whites, while paradoxically also undermining European power to control events.

It was believed in 1940 that Germany already had a total war economy. In fact, though Germany rearmed in the late 1930s, civilian consumption reached its peak in 1942. Believing that World War I was lost in part on the home front, Hitler wanted to avoid making heavy demands on the German consumer. A large part of German military equipment and supplies in the early years of the war came from seizing that of defeated countries, especially Czechoslovakia and France. After 1940, occupied countries made significant contributions to the German war effort, as did Soviet provisions from 1939 until June 1941.

The failure of Barbarossa, however, forced a change. Germany lacked a unified war mobilization plan until Hitler appointed Albert Speer minister for armaments and munitions. Central planning, the setting of priorities, better management, and reducing nonessential production were at the heart of the new "total war" effort. It also included the exploitation of foreign resources and the employment of nearly 2,000,000 prisoners of war and 7,000,000 forced laborers recruited throughout Europe, plus concentration camp captives.

The United States never centrally managed its economy. Congress, after 1940, was willing to spend, but the divided military establishment (separate Departments of War and Navy) led to conflicts of the allocation of personnel, raw materials, and war production. Roosevelt solved problems in the economy by establishing new agencies, a practice compounding rivalries and inefficiencies. Restraints on big businesses were reduced, and corporate officials went to Washington to work for the government while favoring their own firms. With money to spend and a skilled workforce to hire, there was plenty of opportunity for all, with profits and wages rising. Unemployment fell, and African Americans and women joined the industrial workforce in greater numbers than before.

Roosevelt's promise in 1940 to produce 50,000 airplanes was greeted by disbelief. By 1945, Americans had manufactured over 300,000. Shipyards constructed over 60,000 vessels, including 27 aircraft carriers and 111 escort carriers. From a 1940 base of 100, the real gross national product soared to 159 in 1944; the percent of gross domestic product devoted to war rose from 1.0 in 1939 to 41.5 in 1944. American worker productivity increased to the highest in the world. Macy's department store in New York City had its largest sale in history to that date on the third anniversary of Pearl Harbor. War brought economic destruction to Europe, China, and Japan, but in the United States it brought prosperity and leadership of the world's capitalist economies.

COLLABORATION AND RESISTANCE

Within Axis-occupied territories, some people collaborated with the enemy, others resisted. Most were bystanders, or attempted to be bystanders. Collaborators had several motives for cooperating with the enemy. Some shared the occupier's ideology. This was easier to do in western Europe where the German administration was in military hands and was less racist in practice, except in its application to Jews. In Asia, some believed Japanese propaganda calling for an expulsion of the Western imperialists and the formation of a Pan-Asian bloc led by Tokyo. Some collaborators were opportunists; others believed that Axis triumph was inevitable and irresistible. Still others argued that resistance would only make a bad situation worse and that collaboration ameliorated the conditions of life.

Collaboration in eastern Europe was near impossible. Poland disappeared as a state, as would the Soviet Union had Germany won the war. Everywhere, the Nazis intended to replace local Slavic populations with German colonists. In western Europe, Hitler preferred to work with traditional elites in order to avoid domestic conflict and to maximize each country's contribution to the German war machine. Thus, Vichy leaders like Pétain and Pierre Laval were favored over any of the many French fascist leaders, however much they mimicked their German counterparts.

In Asia, collaborationists came from nationalist leaders eager to throw off European colonialism. Some were successful, most were not. Wang Chingwei, for example, left Chiang's Nationalist Party with the hope of leading a reformist, independent movement. He found, however, that the Japanese military dominated his Nanjing-based government. In the Netherlands East Indies, Achmad Sukarno worked with the Japanese and was promised independence in 1944. He led the postwar struggle against the Dutch to become Indonesia's first president. The Indian nationalist leader Subhas Chandra Bose turned first to Nazi Germany, then in 1943 to Japan. He led the Indian National Army (INA), but it failed to win significant support within India, and suffered defeat with the Japanese in Burma.

Resistance to Axis occupation developed slowly. In some countries, such as Norway, Denmark, and the Netherlands, resistance centered on collecting intelligence about the Germans and assisting the anti-German war effort. In others, such as France, Yugoslavia, and Poland, resistance took on strong political overtones. By 1943 the French resistance succeeded in uniting a diverse group of individuals around a reformist political platform with Charles de Gaulle as its head. In Yugoslavia, the communists under Tito's leadership dominated the resistance and became the liberators of the country. In Poland, an extensive "secret state" kept alive Polish sovereignty and national identity. Conservative and anti-Russian, it failed to become the basis of a postwar government when the Red Army occupied the country and installed a pro-Soviet government.

The military significance of resistance is disputed. In Yugoslavia, the resistance played a major part in the liberation of the country. In France, the armed *maquis* assisted the Allied invasion by harassing German military units behind the line. In Italy, the resistance played a similar role in 1944 and 1945. Resistance also took the form of demonstrations, sabotage, strikes, and noncooperation. Less dramatic than armed resistance, such resistance provided an important moral response to occupation, and participation in such forms of resistance mobilized a wider array of men and women against the occupiers.

THE GRAND ALLIANCE

The Grand Alliance of the United Kingdom, the United States, and the Soviet Union was based on their common enemy, Germany, rather than on an agreed-upon common program. Because of the requirement in the American Constitution that the Senate approve all treaties, Roosevelt avoided making formal commitments to either Britain or the Soviet Union. There were, however, statements of principle, such as the Atlantic Charter of August 1941, announced by Roosevelt and Churchill after their first meeting. It provided for world free trade, the principle of self-determination, and promises of a system of general security. The United Nations Declaration of 1942 reaffirmed the Atlantic Charter and committed its signatories to the defeat of the Axis in defense of life, liberty, independence, religious freedom, and human rights. At the Casablanca conference in January 1943 Roosevelt announced the policy of unconditional surrender, that is, the complete and unqualified defeat of the Axis powers and the takeover of their national sovereignty by the Allies. Churchill and Stalin agreed.

At the Tehran conference of November 28–December 1, 1943, the heads of the three major allies met for the first time. There the Western Allies committed themselves to an invasion of France in May 1944. Stalin indicated that the Soviet Union would join in the war against Japan after the defeat of Germany. "The Big Three" also agreed that the eastern borders of Germany were to be moved westward, compensating Poland for territory lost to Ukraine with land in the west. Finally, the basic structure of the future United Nations organization was agreed upon, especially the veto power of the permanent members of the Security Council.

THE NORTH AFRICAN THEATER AND
THE BATTLE FOR STALINGRAD

The year 1942 proved the military turning point of the war. Operation Torch, a substitute second front in Europe, opened on November 8, 1942, in North Africa. Marred by confusion, this first campaign in the European theater by the United States army marked the beginning struggle to liberate Europe in the west. In Libya the British pushed the Afrika Korps back across the Western Desert to join the Allied armies coming from Algeria. On the eastern front, the German siege of Stalingrad turned into a major defeat after the Red Army's counterattack in November. The German Sixth Army was forced to surrender with a loss of more than 200,000 men. The loss of men was more than Germany could replace.

The Anglo-Americans invaded Sicily in July 1943 and the Italian mainland in September. Concurrently, the Soviets repulsed the Germans at Kursk, the greatest tank battle of the war. Although the war lasted two more years, Germany never recovered the initiative. Its resources of men and matériel diminished while those of the Allies increased.

COMBINED BOMBER OFFENSIVE

In 1942 the British Bomber Command, led by Arthur T. Harris, abandoned daytime target bombing in favor of nighttime area bombing. Unable to hit precise objectives, the idea was to "dehouse" the Germans through massive attacks of residential areas. Bomber Command became an effective force in 1942 and levied devastating night attacks on Ruhr industry in 1943. It unleashed the world's first firestorm on Hamburg in July when it bombed with high explosives and incendiaries by night and the Americans bombed by day.

The United States Eighth Army Air Force under Ira C. Eaker stuck with daytime bombing, with B-17s flying in close formation to provide mutual defense. The effects were devastating on both sides. The 1943 attacks on the Schweinfurt ball-bearing industry, for example, were effective, but the cost in American planes and crews led to their temporary suspension. Germany, however, had to invest increasingly in costly air defense and in dispersal of the war economy.

After the summer of 1943 the Allies controlled the air over Europe to prevent the Luftwaffe's recovery. The loss of crews and planes was enormous, however, and German morale did not break. With ever-increasing numbers of bombers and the introduction of the P-51 fighter plane to accompany them over Germany, the Americans turned the tide. After May 1944 the Allies had air superiority for the rest of the war.

The morality and effectiveness of strategic bombing remains controversial. Indiscriminate attacks on civilians intensified the barbarities of mid-century warfare, yet it was civilians who turned out the necessary sinews of war. It is hard to prove decisively the importance of strategic bombing in winning the war. What can be said is that those who believe it could have won the war without ground troops are few in number.

THE INVASION OF WESTERN EUROPE

By agreement at the Tehran conference, the Soviets and the Western Allies opened new campaigns in late spring 1944. The massive Operation Bagration achieved surprise against the German Army Group Center, remarkable in that the Soviets brought more than a million men, plus more than another million in reserve, along with a huge array of tanks, artillery, and aircraft. By the end of July the Red Army was on the outskirts of Warsaw. This Soviet advance overshadowed in size the better known Normandy invasion, Overlord, of June 6, 1944.

Preparations for a cross-channel invasion had been in progress for over two years, growing in complexity and detail at each stage. The Americans originally wanted it in 1942, and then again in 1943, but the British steadfastly refused to be drawn into a premature invasion that could very well bog down like the trench fighting of World War I. Postponement may have been the wise choice, but the delay also gave the Germans more time to prepare a defense. It also soured relations between the Soviets and their Western Allies.

By 1944 the landing craft, the logistical support, two artificial ports, an undersea pipeline, and the trained men were in place. Deception prevented the Germans from discovering the location of the landings or the numbers of troops involved. On June 6 men landed on Normandy beaches in the greatest amphibious assault in history, some 150,000 men the first day, over 5,000 ships. Operations did not go as planned. Target dates were missed, the terrain proved difficult, and the Germans resisted tenaciously. Yet the stream of supplies and men continued as the Allies poured men and resources into the operation. In early August a breakthrough finally came, and Paris was liberated on August 25.

Overlord's supreme commander, Dwight D. Eisenhower, arrived on the continent to take direct command on September 1. A dispute developed over whether to pursue a broad front against the Germans or to launch a single thrust into Germany. British general Bernhard Montgomery advocated the latter, with himself in command. His plan, Market Garden, was approved and launched. But it failed to capture bridges across the Rhine. The Germans renewed their strength and delayed the fall of the Third Reich from autumn 1944 to April of the next year. In mid-December, the Wehrmacht even managed a counterattack in Belgium in the Battle of the Bulge. An embarrassment to Allied commanders who failed to take heed of intelligence warnings, this last Western foray by Hitler did nothing except waste lives.

THE YALTA CONFERENCE

Preparing for the windup in the European war, the near victorious Allies held a summit from February 4 to February 11 at Yalta, a Crimean resort on the Black Sea. Because the German military defeat was assured, the conference devoted its attention to political concerns. Among the most important were the future of Poland and Germany, the Soviet Union's participation in the war against Japan, and the establishment of the United Nations.

Poland was the most intractable problem. Britain had gone to war for its defense, yet the Soviets had recognized the procommunist, pro-Soviet Lublin Committee as the provisional government of the country. The Soviets were the sole military power in Poland, and laid claim to the boundaries settled upon in 1939 with Germany. In compensation for the loss of eastern territory, Poland was to receive German territory. Stalin and his foreign minister, Vyacheslav Molotov, promised to make efforts to bring communist and noncommunist Poles together in a reorganized government, but little was done to implement that decision. Privately, both Churchill and Roosevelt conceded Soviet dominance in Poland and eastern Europe. They could hardly ignore the fact of the Red Army's power there, not the Soviet Union's "legitimate interest" in establishing "friendly governments" on its borders.

Yalta planned the occupation of Germany, with the major Allied powers, now enlarged to include France, administering military zones of occupation. The unity of the country was to be maintained and Berlin jointly occupied. Similar arrangements were made for Austria. Other questions such as reparations and war crimes trials were discussed but left unsettled.

Most important for the United States was a Soviet reaffirmation of a declaration of war against Japan, because the bulk of Japan's army was in Manchuria and China. How the war in Asia would end was not yet clear. American military planners wanted to avoid an invasion of the Asian mainland, and were willing to make concessions to Stalin on behalf of the Chinese (who were not consulted) in order to achieve Soviet cooperation.

The establishment of a United Nations Organization was also high on Roosevelt's goals. He believed that if the four "policemen" of the world—Britain, the Soviet Union, China, and the United States—cooperated, then the basis for world peace could be established. Because the Soviet Union would be in the minority in a world organization, Stalin's acceptance of the UN represented a major achievement for the American president. That the Soviet Union got three seats in the General Assembly—one each for Russia, Belarus (then Byelorussia), and Ukraine—needed to be balanced by U.S. influence over the Latin American republics.

While the statesmen met at Yalta, in the east the Red Army opened its last final fronts against the Third Reich. By February it was within forty miles of Berlin. Revenge was the order of the day, with looting, raping, and murder of German troops and civilians alike. Brutal as "liberation" was, the Germans were reaping the whirlwind sown by their own racist and ideological campaigns.

British and American advances in the west were much less costly, and for that reason more rapid. Hundreds of thousands of prisoners were taken. In many places, the Allies faced only token resistance. On April 25, Soviet and American troops met at Torgau on the Elbe. A few days later, April 30, Hitler committed suicide with his mistress and the Goebbels family in his Berlin bunker. The thousand year Reich had only recently celebrated its twelfth birthday, but not before leaving a trail of death, genocide, and destruction unparalleled in the bloody annals of human civilization.

THE PACIFIC WAR

The Pacific War remained primarily an American affair. The United Kingdom long had vital interests there, but the burden of war, and the material and military ascendancy of the United States, made a British reassertion of imperial control unlikely. The same was true of France and the Netherlands in Indochina and the East Indies.

The major issue for Washington was the dispute between the Army's Douglas MacArthur and the Navy's Chester Nimitz over the strategy to defeat Japan. MacArthur wanted to advance from the Solomon Islands through New Guinea to Rabaul, Japan's principal naval and air base on southeast Asia, and then on to the liberation of the Philippines. Because the new U.S. Navy was still being built in early 1943 and Washington was committed to the defeat of Germany before that of Japan, MacArthur was able to take the lead, along with William F. Halsey, then Commander of South Pacific Forces and Area, in advancing on Rabaul. It was neutralized by the end of 1943.

Meanwhile, the American submarine campaign against Japanese shipping swung into full force. After mid-1943 more aggressive search-and-kill operations, improved torpedoes, and effective intelligence brought commerce between southeast Asia and Japan to a near halt by the end of 1944.

Ernest J. King, commander in chief of the United States Fleet, won support in spring 1943 for a central Pacific campaign across a chain of Islands from Tarawa in the Gilberts to Okinawa. With the spectacular increase in U.S. naval capacity (one new fleet carrier per month plus a vast number of support craft), the balance of naval power tipped decisively in Allied favor, allowing the president and the Chiefs of Staff to approve both the Navy's and MacArthur's strategic campaigns. Indeed, the force was so strong that it was maintained indefinitely at sea, with William Halsey's Third Fleet alternating with Raymond Spruance's Fifth Fleet between planning in Pearl Harbor and carrying out operations at sea.

THE PACIFIC CAMPAIGNS

Fighting in the Pacific was unusually bloody. Each invasion grew in size and in number of casualties. By August 1944, the Marianas were in American hands, and bases were being constructed for the B-29s to launch bombing raids on Japan. The June Battle of the Philippine Sea opened the way to the invasion of the Philippines in October and history's greatest naval engagement, the confused battle of Leyte Gulf. The Japanese navy attempted to destroy American forces landing on Leyte, introducing the kamikaze suicide missions during the battle. Mistakes were made all around, but the struggle ended with the complete defeat of the Japanese. Fighting on the Philippines continued until the next summer.

B-29s began bombing Japan in November 1944, but with little success, in part because of Japanese early warning stations on Iwo Jima, midway between the Marianas and the Japanese home islands. A desperate fight for the island in February and early March cost nearly 6,000 Marines' lives and almost all of the 21,000 Japanese there. On April 1 the struggle for Okinawa began with the largest American amphibious fleet assembled to that date. When the island was finally conquered, some 70,000 Japanese troops had died plus even more civilians. The Americans suffered 65,000 casualties, with more than 10 percent killed. Kamikaze attacks from the autumn of 1944 on and a Japanese willingness to sacrifice life indicated that the invasion of Japan would be even more costly.

Meanwhile, strategic bombing took a new, more deadly turn when Curtis LeMay, who took command in January 1945, had the B-29s attack at night with incendiary bombs and at low altitudes. On March 8 they ignited a firestorm over Tokyo, killing more than 80,000 and destroying the city center. The bombing continued, as fast as bombs could be delivered. Soon there were few targets left. Japan's major cities had been badly damaged.

By July, Japan was more than defeated: submarines and mines had cut off supplies from overseas; industry was prostrate; the navy was rendered useless; Japan had no air defense. Although there were some changes in Tokyo—Suzuki Kantaro, an advocate of peace, became prime minister in

April—there were few signs of surrender. Militarists opposed anything other than death in defeat, and others hoped that the cost of an invasion of the home islands would cause the Americans to accept a negotiated surrender. On July 26, the United States and the United Kingdom issued the Potsdam Declaration, insisting on Japan's unconditional surrender, though deliberately remaining silent on the troublesome question of the future status of the emperor.

By that date the Manhattan Engineer project to develop and produce an atomic bomb had come to fruition with a successful test on July 16, 1945. When no clear answer to the Potsdam ultimatum came from Tokyo, President Harry S Truman authorized the dropping of the two available atomic bombs to end the war and, Truman later insisted, to save up to a million American casualties by avoiding a land invasion of the Japanese home islands.

Whether the bombs were necessary and why they were used has been much debated. Recent research indicates that fanatical resistance would have made an invasion of Japan costly, probably killing more Japanese than the two attacks on Hiroshima and Nagasaki on August 6 and 9. Using the bombs to achieve military victory in Europe or Asia had always been assumed. Only a rapid Japanese surrender could have led to a decision not to use them.

EPILOGUE

Four weeks later the formal Japanese surrender aboard the U.S.S. *Missouri* ended the greatest human catastrophe of all time. In the process much was changed: Europe lost its central position in world history and was soon divided. The remembrance of the Holocaust will mark a major turning point in human history. European empires were weakened and began to dissolve. The Soviet Union, however temporarily, became an assertive world power. The United States became the globe's strongest economic and military power. Jet planes, rockets, global communications, and unprecedented world trade as well as the less desirable nuclear weapons and genocide opened a new world where the markings of the past gave inadequate and unclear guidance for the future.

2

The Grand Alliance of the United Kingdom, the United States, and the Soviet Union

Allied diplomacy during World War II differed from the diplomacy of earlier wars in that statesmen relied on more frequent, more direct communication, often by telegraph, radio, or telephone. From September 1939 to April 11, 1945, Prime Minister Winston Churchill sent more than 1,000 messages to President Franklin D. Roosevelt and received nearly 800 in return. Over 400 communications passed between the prime minister and Marshal Josef Stalin, and nearly 300 between Stalin and the president.

These three—the "Big Three" as they were known—also met face to face more often than previous wartime leaders. Safer, long-distance air travel facilitated summit meetings while also allowing the heads of government to return home quickly to manage domestic politics. Churchill traveled the most. He and Roosevelt met on seven different occasions. He flew to Moscow twice, in August 1942 and again in October 1944. Handicapped by the crippling effects of polio, Roosevelt traveled to the Old World only three times. Stalin feared to fly. He refused to leave territory not under control of the Red Army, whose commanders he kept under strict supervision.

The Grand Alliance of the United Kingdom, the Soviet Union, and the United States was neither predictable nor was it based on deeply held common interests. It has often been faulted for leading to the Cold War rather than realizing its often expressed high ideals. Although Cold War tensions dominated the half-century of the postwar world, this view overlooks the Alliance's primary achievement: victory over the Axis powers. The defeat of the Axis was not inevitable, nor was the complete crushing of the dread regimes of the Axis leaders. Whatever the defects of the Allies' postwar set-tlements, the Axis alternatives of racism, exploitative imperialism, and militarism would have been much worse. The Big Three's triumph over Fascist Italy, Nazi Germany, and Imperial Japan fully warrants the designa-tion "Grand Alliance."

1939–1941: FORMING THE GRAND ALLIANCE

In 1939 the interests of the British Empire and Commonwealth, the United States, and the Soviet Union differed significantly from one another. There may have been growing sympathies between the two English-speaking democracies, but the United States was isolationist, its primary competitor in foreign trade was Britain, and many of its people were hostile to the British Empire (such as Irish Americans and anticolonialists) or indif-ferent to its fate (as in the Midwest).

Great Britain ruled territory covering a quarter of the globe. At a time of rising nationalism within its colonies and worldwide depression, its mili-tary obligations far exceeded its ability to provide for adequate defense. When a negotiated settlement with Hitler failed in 1939, London went to war, along with Paris the only governments to go to the defense of a third country without themselves being attacked. After Stalin allied with the Ger-mans and France fell to the Wehrmacht, Britain's only hope to defeat the Third Reich was American entry into the war or a German invasion of the Soviet Union. Air and naval power might defend the country; it could not defeat the Wehrmacht.

Stalin's foreign policy goals are unclear. Suspicious of the British and French, whose appeasement at Munich suggested that they were giving Hit-ler a free hand in the east, Stalin signed a Non-Aggression Pact with the Nazi regime days before the invasion of Poland. Between then and the end of 1940 Stalin annexed the Baltic states, half of Poland, and other lesser ter-ritories as security against the Germans. All of this bought precious little time when the German onslaught began in June 1941.

The formation of the Grand Alliance owed much to Hitler and the Japa-nese. The Churchill government refused to strike a deal with Berlin. By in-vading the Soviet Union, Hitler gave London a much needed ally. The Japanese government, thinking in late summer 1941 that the Germans were near victory in Europe, decided to conquer southeast Asia. This would iso-late China, deliver up the rich resources of the Dutch East Indies needed by Japan, and drive out the British. This also meant war with the United States. Thus, the attack on Pearl Harbor and other American territories in the western Pacific sealed the bonds of the Grand Alliance. Three days later, Hitler declared war on the United States.

Between September 1939 and December 1941 the United States gave ever-increasing assistance to the British, though not enthusiastically and at a price. Roosevelt was inclined to play a more active international role, but feared the strength of isolationist opinion in Congress and among the electorate. When the war began, he persuaded Congress to open up American markets to Britain and France if they paid for purchases in cash and carried them in non-American vessels. In the following year the American public engaged in one of the greatest debates in the history of the republic. Opponents of intervention argued that American security was best maintained by armed neutrality and keeping aloof from European entanglements. Outright pro-Axis sentiment was weak; many isolationists believed that Great Britain and France could restrain the Germans in Europe and that a negotiated settlement could be found in Asia. The fall of France in May-June 1940, the Battle of Britain, and the signing of the Tripartite pact by Germany, Italy, and Japan in September revealed those ideas as baseless.

Although the president pledged during an election campaign of 1940, that the country would not go to war he also supported the creation of a two-ocean navy, pushed for the introduction of a peacetime draft, and brought internationalist Republicans into his administration. He showed his belief in British survival by "lending" 50 World War I destroyers to Britain, in return for 99-year leases on seven Caribbean and North Atlantic bases, and by allowing arms shipments to the British.

When Churchill informed Roosevelt of Britain's impending bankruptcy in November 1940, the president responded by proposing the Lend-Lease legislation to Congress. Passed in March 1941, it granted him extensive authority to commit American arms, equipment, and services to other countries whose security he considered vital to the defense of the United States. The legislation may have been, in Churchill's words, an "unsordid act," but it also became a vehicle for the United States to dismantle British imperial preferences. These were special arrangements giving trade advantages to members of the Commonwealth and Empire. Their abolition was intended to expand American trade opportunities. In addition, the extension of Lend-Lease aid to countries around the globe opened them up to postwar American military and commercial influence. Several months after the German invasion of the Soviet Union, the president authorized Lend-Lease shipments to it as well. He wanted assurance that the U.S.S.R. would survive. After 1941 he continued sending aid in order to guarantee Moscow's future cooperation.

The United States lent military and economic assistance to Axis victims. It also contributed to a propaganda campaign extolling American liberal ideals. At the first summit between Roosevelt and Churchill off the coast of Newfoundland in Argentia Bay, in August 1941, they agreed to the Atlantic Charter. The Charter renounced any territorial aggrandizement, opposed "territorial changes that do not accord with the freely expressed wishes of the peoples concerned," and affirmed the principles of national sovereign rights and self-government. In advocating equal access to world trade and raw materials for all nations, it stated an American goal. Other expressions of American liberalism are found in freedom of the seas, international economic cooperation, an anticipation of a system of general security, and a hint of anticolonialism. After returning to London, Churchill explained to British critics who thought he conceded too much for American support that restoring national self-determination only applied to Axis annexations, not to the colonies of the British Empire.

The Atlantic Charter was designed to woo liberal and internationalist opinion in Britain, the United States, and throughout the world. It intended to encourage resistance within Europe, but it also spurred nationalist leaders throughout Africa and Asia to petition for national independence.

THE ALLIANCE IN 1942

Militarily, 1942 began as a year of Axis expansion, but ended as a year of Allied recovery. During the same period, in spite of bouts of quarreling and mutual suspicions, Allied leaders began sorting out various proposed strategies for the defeat of the Axis.

The year began auspiciously with the United Nations Declaration. Based on the Atlantic Charter, it was agreed to by China, the United Kingdom, the United States, and the Soviet Union, and in succeeding weeks by 22 other countries recognized as cosigners. The declaration promised membership to future nations that rendered assistance to the defeat of the Axis powers. By the end of the war 19 other countries had signed.

During most of the year, Britain and the Soviet Union stood at the lowest point of national power. Erwin Rommel drove the British back across the North African desert (for which he became Germany's youngest field marshal); Japan seized Singapore and Burma and threatened India and Australia. Renewed and reorganized, the Wehrmacht advanced into southern Russia and the Caucasus. The loss of Allied merchant shipping in the battle of the Atlantic reached its peak. The Arctic convoys to the Soviets were suspended during the summer. Only the Americans had options. Their rearmament was in its early stages. They could still choose when and where to fight. However, because they were not yet in the fight, they were in no position to dictate strategy. Until they were, their first need was to keep the alliance together.

The United Nations Declaration came during the Arcadia conference, the second meeting of Churchill and Roosevelt. At this same conference, they reaffirmed an agreement of the previous January that in case of American involvement in a war against both Germany and Japan, the defeat of Germany would have priority. Although many isolationists and the U.S. Navy opposed the policy, Roosevelt maintained the commitment throughout the war. Arcadia also decided on the full rearmament of Britain in close coordination with American rearmament. It established a Combined Chiefs of Staff (CCS). The CCS met weekly in Washington or at later summit conferences, with the U.S. Joint Chiefs of Staff and the British Chiefs of Staff as members. It directed operations in the Mediterranean and European theaters, and the Atlantic, with supervisory authority over other theaters. This was the first time in history two great powers so closely integrated their military efforts.

The Allies' first flush of working together soon yielded to suspicions. Stalin's 1939 deal with Hitler might be repeated. American pledges to the European war might erode. The British refusal to support a second front in western Europe in 1942 upset the Americans and fed Stalin's fear that the Westerners wanted the Germans to weaken the Red Army and leave Europe to British domination. The suspension of convoys struck the Soviets as overly cautious.

The British refused to acquiesce to Stalin's insistence on recognition of his 1939 and 1940 annexations, but a treaty was signed in May 1942 in London by the British Foreign Secretary Anthony Eden and Vyacheslav Molotov, the People's Commissar of Foreign Affairs. It renounced an armistice or peace with the Axis without mutual consent. It also provided for mutual aid in the war against Germany and for postwar cooperation.

In the same visit, Molotov demanded a second front in Europe. By that time, British strategists had convinced Churchill not to support such an invasion. Churchill refused Molotov, who proceeded on to Washington where Roosevelt promised what Churchill had denied.

The next month, while in Washington for a third conference with Roosevelt, Churchill learned of the Afrika Korps' capture of Tobruk in Libya. He suggested an invasion of North Africa to relieve the British 8th Army and appease the Soviet request for an Anglo-American campaign against the Germans. The U.S. Army Chief of Staff George Marshall vigorously objected. The army considered North Africa militarily peripheral and a diversion from the strategy of striking directly at Germany. Disregarding that advice, Roosevelt as commander-in-chief ordered the army to campaign in North Africa (Operation Torch) before the end of the year.

Operation Torch opened on November 8 but failed to advance as rapidly as planned. In order to minimize the killing, General Dwight D. Eisenhower negotiated a cease-fire with Admiral Jean Darlan, commander of the Vichy armed forces. Darlan, however, was a collaborator with the Nazis. Eisenhower's "deal" suggested that the Americans were not committed to the war as a war against fascism and that they might arrange armistices with Axis authorities. Meanwhile the campaign in North Africa continued.

Roosevelt and Churchill, wishing to take advantage of the liberation of occupied territory, decided to hold a conference at Casablanca in Morocco early in 1943 at which they would also deal with the new political and military problems presented by the delay in driving Germany and Italy out of Africa. Stalin was invited but chose not to attend.

1943: THE GRAND ALLIANCE CONSOLIDATES

Militarily, 1943 began as favorably as 1942 had started disastrously. The British had routed the Germans at El Alamein in November, and the Red Army tightened its noose around the German 6th Army at Stalingrad; the Americans foiled the Japanese at Midway in June and in Guadalcanal that same autumn. Through mid-1943, the Allied advances continued, but without sharing one prevailing purpose. Of course, they wanted the complete defeat of the Axis as quickly as possible with the least cost in lives and resources. This last objective was unattainable; indeed, during the last two years of the war the killing and destruction accelerated. They began, however, to try to settle postwar matters before the war ended and while the alliance was vital. This would avoid disagreements such as those among the victors of World War I, which sowed the seeds of failure for the 1919 Paris treaties.

The Casablanca conference opened on January 14. The president, the prime minister, and their staffs met for ten days. They set up a Combined Bomber Offensive, giving priority to demolishing U-boat construction sites and strategic points such as the aircraft industry, ball-bearing factories, and oil refineries. They brought General Charles de Gaulle together with their choice for Free French leadership, General Henri Giraud. Although American military planners opposed extending the war in the Mediterranean to Italy, the British planning staff demonstrated that there were insufficient men and supplies to open a second front in France in 1943. That being the case, the invasion of Sicily in 1943 was approved, a decision much resented by some American officers.

Casablanca is primarily remembered, however, for Roosevelt's press conference at which he enunciated the policy of unconditional surrender. Churchill and Stalin were not enthusiastic about the idea, although both endorsed it and later reaffirmed their approval. Unconditional surrender was not mentioned in the official communiqué of the conference. In August, it made negotiations to take Italy out of the war more difficult, and it may have prolonged the war, especially in the case of Japan.

Allied motives behind the policy of unconditional surrender are not entirely clear. In part, it reassured public opinion, especially among the resistance movements, that this was indeed a war for the principles of the Atlantic Charter and that there would be no more "Darlan deals." It confirmed that none of the Allies would seek a separate peace. It also laid to rest the fear that a Germany not completely subjugated might revive the post–World War I myth that it had not been defeated but was "stabbed in the back" by traitors at home.

Churchill and Roosevelt met twice during the following spring and summer, in Washington (Trident) in May and in August at Quebec (Quadrant). In Washington they reconciled their differences over strategy in Europe, but showed different goals in Asia. Churchill wanted to restore Burma, Malaya, Singapore, and Hong Kong to the empire. Roosevelt wanted none of that; he even publicly expressed sympathy of the Indian nationalist demands for independence. Citing insufficient resources, the United States withdrew its support for an invasion of Burma. The president also opposed Churchill by insisting on China joining the alliance as one of a "Big Four." The Americans believed that the defeat of Japan required military bases in China, the site of the bulk of the Japanese army.

The Americans agreed at the Trident conference to the British proposal to invade Italy that fall. When the Italian campaign stalled later that year, however, they refused to reconsider the decision for a second front in France in 1944. Finally, the United States gained CCS approval to send sufficient forces to the Pacific to keep its newly won initiative. In spite of its Germany-first commitment, at no time did the United States have more personnel in the European theater than in the Pacific.

The Quebec conference also took up the possible use of an atomic bomb being developed as a supposedly joint effort. The Americans and the British agreed not to use it against one another, nor against a third nation without the other's consent. They would not share nuclear information with a third party without the other's consent. Roosevelt's promise to share fully information on the atomic project with the British was not, however, implemented.

Although not a summit meeting, the foreign ministers of the Allies met in a third Moscow conference in October 1943 to prepare for the first Big Three summit in Tehran later that year. They decided upon an Advisory Council for Italy with France and the Soviet Union as members, but left the military administration of Italy to a local Anglo-American Control Commission. This established the precedent that liberated countries would be administered by occupying armies. The foreign ministers also issued a Four-Power Declaration (China being the fourth power, even though its foreign minister was not present), which reaffirmed the principle of unconditional surrender, the United Nations Declaration, and the need to establish an international organization to maintain the peace. They also issued the "Allied Declaration on German Atrocities" that war criminals would be prosecuted in the country in which the atrocities were committed.

In late November, Churchill and Roosevelt met in Cairo where they agreed that an American would command Operation Overlord. The original choice was General George Marshall, but upon later reconsideration Roosevelt decided that Marshall's presence in Washington was indispensable and appointed Dwight Eisenhower instead. Roosevelt also met with Chiang Kai-shek and again in December after the Tehran conference because Churchill and Stalin refused to admit him into the discussions held at Tehran starting November 28.

The Big Three first met in Tehran because of Stalin's insistence on staying within a Soviet sphere of military communications. To secure Iran's oil output for themselves and transportation links needed for the shipment of lend-lease aid, British and Soviet troops occupied the country in August 1941, with Tehran straddling the two occupation zones. Thus, Tehran was something of a neutral location, but it required an extraordinary journey for Roosevelt.

Roosevelt was eager to meet Stalin and establish the close personal relationship he believed necessary to assure successful negotiations among subordinates in the coming months. It also would lay the basis for postwar cooperation. In doing so, he set a precedent for all future American presidents. He also wanted to undercut Churchill's role as a mediator and disabuse Stalin of the idea that he and the prime minister were ganging up against him. Stalin however, was largely an unknown factor. Only a few of Roosevelt's trusted advisors—such as Averell Harriman, recently appointed ambassador in Moscow, and Harry Hopkins—had met him.

When the president arrived in Tehran, Stalin suggested that he stay at the Soviet embassy to avoid the dangerous transfers back and forth to the American embassy. Tehran was unsettled and no doubt teemed with Axis agents. The president's security officers agreed, and Roosevelt spent the next three days as Stalin's guest. These arrangements made it possible for them to meet together. They also irritated Churchill, who was ill and already worried by growing American military predominance in Europe. Stalin's and Roosevelt's comments on the future of the British Empire further distressed the prime minister.

Stalin stalled meeting jointly with Churchill and Roosevelt in order to negotiate from strength. Although there was much more fighting ahead, the Red Army was on the advance while the German army held the Western Allied armies at bay in Italy. The conference did business, but interrupted it with dinners and relaxation. On one occasion, Stalin's confidence showed in his toasting the British Conservative party; Churchill responded by drinking to the proletarian masses. Roosevelt gave a "rainbow" speech, lauding the differences among the peoples of the alliance. The conviviality ended when Stalin suggested that the solution to the German problem was to shoot 50,000 German officers. The president attempted to turn the idea into a joke—perhaps 49,000—or 48,000? Disgusted, Churchill left the table.

During the first session, Stalin announced that he would declare war on Japan within three months of the defeat of Germany. This relieved Roosevelt and his military advisors; it would make a costly American invasion of China unnecessary. In return for this promise, the president and the prime minister promised Stalin a warm-water port in China.

Much of the conference dealt with the second front in western Europe. Churchill reiterated schemes for continued operations in the Mediterranean, but Stalin and Roosevelt refused to yield. France would be invaded in May of 1944, with a second assault in southern France. The Soviets promised a coordinated offensive from the east, Operation Bagration, the war's largest single campaign. These agreements were good news, for they guaranteed the military cooperation of the Allies for the duration of the war.

The Tehran conference was overshadowed by the one held fourteen months later at Yalta, but it was less contentious and laid the groundwork for later agreements. The three great powers accepted Roosevelt's ideas on a United Nations organization, with the Big Four as the "policemen" of the world responsible for keeping the peace. The president intended to disarm all other nations, allowing each only enough men in arms to guarantee domestic security. The president's corollary was opposition to regional security arrangements and spheres of influence such as Churchill and Stalin preferred. But they agreed on establishing an international organization and authorized American leadership in preparing a proposal.

Although postwar Germany was not the Allies' only problem, it was central. There was strong sentiment for dividing Germany (dismemberment was the word used at the time) and restoring the loose confederation of independent states it was before 1870. This, however, would leave the Soviet Union as Europe's leading military power. A weak (and perhaps demilitarized) France facing a divided Germany was not a good alternative. And Roosevelt followed his own reading of American history by announcing that American troops would be withdrawn from Europe two years after the conclusion of hostilities.

The most difficult discussions entailed the future of Poland. Britain went to war in defense of the Poles. Churchill acknowledged Soviet claims to the eastern half of prewar Poland; in fact, the post-1939 frontier resembled the Curzon line proposed by a British foreign secretary in 1920 but not implemented. The prime minister helped arrange a Polish-Soviet Treaty in 1941, but the two severed relations when news of the Katyn massacre surfaced in 1943. The Polish government-in-exile in London feared the Russians as much as communism and hoped against all odds that Poland would liberate itself and remain free of Soviet domination. Both Churchill and Roosevelt knew that that was unlikely and that Stalin's demand for security against a future German invasion required a friendly government in Warsaw. For a hundred years before World War I, Poland was a part of the Russian empire. It would resume that role again. In compensation for losses in the east, Churchill supported Polish annexations of German territory as far west as the Oder River.

With Tehran behind them, the Allies prepared for the final assault on the Third Reich. Differences in strategies and goals remained, but on the whole, the main outlines of the postwar settlement were becoming visible. Clearly, the Soviet Union would emerge as a major player in European, and perhaps Asian, affairs. If Roosevelt's plans worked out, the U.S.S.R. would be an international player for peace.

American power grew steadily every day, but at the end of 1943 its postwar role was less predictable than that of the Soviet Union. Whether the U.S. economy could power a worldwide recovery was not clear. American military strength grew by leaps and bounds, but its new headquarters in Washington across the Potomac River, the Pentagon, was built for temporary occupancy. The politics and the technologies that would propel Americans into global leadership still lay in the future. What was most certain after Tehran was the decline of British power. Americans largely dictated 1944 military operations. Wartime production peaked; there were no more reserves. American lend-lease and credits sustained the economy, while Commonwealth countries were weaned on American largesse and colonies lodged their own demands for independence.

1944

Nineteen forty-four was the year of Allied victories. The Normandy invasion, although stalled at first, liberated Paris by the end of August and advanced into Belgium. From the east, the Red Army crossed the Vistula and swept into Romania in August and then Hungary to finish the year within 50 miles of Berlin. A German resurgence late in the year prevented the collapse of Germany, but no one, probably not even Hitler, continued to believe in the triumph of the Third Reich. Many German leaders, in fact, prepared to face its destruction.

There were no summits in 1944. Churchill met once with Roosevelt in Quebec (September) and once with Stalin (October). Two less well-known conferences, at Bretton Woods and Dumbarton Oaks, had great significance for the postwar world, but none of the Big Three attended.

Informed opinion in the early 1940s attributed economic conflict as the cause of war. To avert a third world war, the postwar world needed to ease and expedite international trade. By the end of 1943, the world trade system had greatly changed. The unprecedented expansion of the American economy made it the center of international commerce and its dollar the premier currency. The economies of Latin American countries also rapidly grew, as did those of India and the British Commonwealth. International trade also depended on a stable system of currency exchange. The gold standard had provided the basis before World War I, and briefly in the late 1920s. As the Great Depression of the 1930s spread, every country, including the United States, abandoned the redemption of currency in gold.

The Bretton Woods conference (July 1–22) was called to solve these problems. Backed by the eminent British economist John Maynard Keynes and Harry Dexter White, assistant U.S. treasurer, representatives from 44 countries met in New Hampshire in July. They outlined the International Monetary Fund (IMF) and an International Bank for Reconstruction and Development (World Bank). The IMF was designed to establish international monetary stability. That would facilitate trade but also restrain the ability of governments to regulate their economies.

For this reason, conservatives in the British government opposed it as an infringement on the empire. The Labour Party also disliked the Bretton Woods agreement. It wanted to extend social benefits to all British citizens and economically develop the colonies, neither of which fit easily into the IMF. When Labour came to power, the British government was bankrupt and it had no choice but to join the American-led system. The IMF began to function in December 1945. The Soviet Union sent an observer to Bretton Woods, but because its currency was inconvertible and prices inside the U.S.S.R. were not set by market demand, it rejected membership.

The conference to plan the United Nations met at Dumbarton Oaks (August 21–October 7), in Georgetown, Washington, D.C. Though not accepting all of Roosevelt's ideas, the conference laid the basis for the United Nations organization approved by the Big Three at Yalta and later by all members at San Francisco. The conference modified Roosevelt's idea of "four policemen" by making them permanent members of a security council charged with keeping the peace. The four permanent members (France was added later as the fifth) would have veto power over the council's actions. The British accepted the idea that a permanent member could not veto any action in which it was a party. Neither the United States nor the Soviet Union accepted it.

A General Assembly would represent all members, each with an equal vote, although who would be eligible for membership and voting was unclear. The Soviet Union wanted sixteen votes, one each for the sixteen constituent "republics" making up the U.S.S.R. The British Commonwealth included several independent dominions, while the United States had several client states in Central America. Such geopolitical facts added to the initial confusion about allocating membership and voting rights.

Churchill and Roosevelt met in September in Quebec when the collapse of the Third Reich seemed imminent. They discussed British participation in the Pacific war, but concentrated on the future of Germany. Henry Morgenthau, the U.S. Secretary of the Treasury, presented his plan for postwar Germany. He would deindustrialize the country, destroying its war-making capacity. This idea of "pastoralization" ran counter to other plans for European recovery. An agricultural Germany in the heart of Europe would thwart the continent's economic development; it would be a permanent international liability. The plan was leaked to the *New York Times* in November, and subsequently rejected by both Roosevelt and Churchill. It resurfaced, however, in the American Joint Chiefs of Staff 1067 order for the military administration of the American zone of occupation in Germany.

With the defeat of Germany assured by the autumn of 1944, Churchill grew more concerned about Moscow's domination of eastern Europe and arranged to meet Stalin in October. American representatives attended some sessions, but only Churchill and Stalin were present (except for translators) at their notorious exchange over the relative influence each should have in the liberated countries of eastern Europe. Churchill jotted on a sheet of paper his division of influence in the Balkans—Romania: 90 percent influence to Russia, 10 percent to others; Greece: 90 percent influence to Great Britain, 10 percent to Russia; Yugoslavia and Hungary: 50 percent for each; Bulgaria: 75 percent to Russia, 25 percent to others. In his history of the war Churchill related that he and Stalin decided not to keep the note.

Would the United States agree? Roosevelt disliked the idea of regional blocs of influence, but the United States had limited influence in the area. He eventually went along, although the division of Hungary and Yugoslavia proved premature. Tito cleared the Red Army from Yugoslavia, while Hungary came completely under Soviet control.

YALTA AND THE BEGINNING OF THE COLD WAR

Stalin, Roosevelt, and Churchill met for the second and last time together at Yalta in February 1945. Having won reelection for an unprecedented fourth term, Roosevelt was secure at home. He now hoped to establish a firm relationship with Stalin and secure the peace for the next generation. Churchill was less sanguine. British power was ebbing, and Roosevelt was reluctant to form a common front against Stalin. He also stuck by his commitment to the United Nations and to China's role as a great power.

The defeat of Germany was assured by 1945. Thus, the issues at Yalta concerned the postwar settlement: the administration of Germany, reparations, Poland, Russian participation in the war against Japan, and the United Nations organization.

The European Advisory Commission established in 1943 to plan for the occupation of Germany and its Axis allies proposed three zones of military occupation, with Berlin to be jointly occupied. The same arrangements were made for Austria. At Yalta, this was altered to make a zone for France from parts of the American and the British zones. There was much discussion of the dismemberment of Germany, but the idea was rejected in favor of keeping Germany as an economic unit, in order to collect reparations and to rebuild European economies.

Both Roosevelt and Churchill had come to believe that extracting reparations from Germany would create unnecessary problems and detract from the reconstruction of Europe. Stalin, however, wanted reparations to rebuild the Soviet Union. The conference agreed in principle on a total of $20 billion to be taken in kind, with half to go to the Soviets.

The future of Poland was the primary topic at Yalta. Stalin already had recognized the Soviet-backed Lublin Committee as the government. Churchill and Roosevelt hoped to add representatives from the London government-in-exile. The best Stalin would do was to promise free and open postwar elections, but he would not agree to international supervision. Churchill realized that the promise was worthless, but Roosevelt needed it to make the overall Yalta agreements palatable to Americans of Polish descent. On the topic of Poland's borders, Churchill and Roosevelt agreed to the Curzon line as Poland's eastern border but did not accept a western boundary at the Oder and western Neisse Rivers.

Roosevelt's primary interests at Yalta were Soviet agreement to the United Nations organization and its entrance into the war against Japan. An effective United Nations was essential for the future of peace. The defeat of Japan required, it was still assumed, the defeat of Japan's armies in China. Stalin accepted a compromise on the United Nations' Security Council whereby a permanent member could veto actions taken, but not the discussions. Churchill and Roosevelt also agreed to recommend separate membership and voting power for Belarus and Ukraine in the General Assembly.

For the American public, the Declaration on Liberated Europe became the touchstone for decisions taken at Yalta. It promised free elections and democratic governments in all liberated countries. Because it violated their percentage agreement made the previous October in Moscow, Churchill and Stalin viewed the declaration more or less as American window dressing. Roosevelt may have seen it the same way. But for consumers of the heady idealism of wartime propaganda shielded from the compromises of the real Yalta, the declaration elicited unrealistic expectations. The Red Army had four times the number of troops as the Western Allies in Central Europe. Americans were war weary; Roosevelt thought that all American troops would have to be withdrawn within two years. The president's deteriorating health may also have been a factor in his agreeing to this, but that cannot be known for certain.

Between February and his death in April, Roosevelt expressed concern about Soviet suppression of noncommunists in eastern Europe. Moscow installed procommunist governments in Romania and Bulgaria. Tito ignored the noncommunist members of his coalition government. Politics in other Eastern countries seemed headed in the same direction. This bode ill for postwar Allied unity.

Critics of the Yalta agreements blamed the president as naïve, or duped by closet communists among his advisors, or too ill (or drunk) to govern. Roosevelt shares some blame for this. He knew of Stalin's ambitions and that he drove hard bargains, but the president had not prepared the public for compromise or for understanding the limits of American power. His motive may have been to unite Americans behind his broader program of Soviet participation in the United Nations and in the war against Japan. The effects of peace and drawing Moscow into a network of treaty agreements took priority over conflict. Whatever the case, Roosevelt did not even confide in his vice president, Harry S Truman. Truman entered the White House upon Roosevelt's death on April 12 knowing little more than what he had read in the newspapers.

Churchill, who had been eager in late 1944 to secure agreement for spheres of influence in Europe before British military power dwindled further, at Yalta and after tried to push Anglo-American influence further east. He wanted Eisenhower to advance toward Berlin and into Czechoslovakia rather than adhere to Yalta agreements that these were Soviet operational areas. Eisenhower instead directed Anglo-American efforts into German areas that he knew had been assigned to them. Washington backed him. After Yalta Roosevelt demurred from Churchill's suggestions to be tougher on Stalin, fearing that they would split the alliance and give the appearance of a joint Anglo-American scheme to deprive the Soviet Union of the fruits of victory. On the other hand, he was dismayed at the Soviets' behavior in Poland. The day before his death Roosevelt told Churchill that he would minimize the general Soviet problem as much as possible, but still cautioned firmness.

POTSDAM

The Potsdam conference, held in Cecilienhof, a palace of the Prussian military monarchy in a Berlin suburb, was the third and the last summit of the Big Three. It lasted from July 17 to August 2. The dynamics of Potsdam differed significantly from the previous two summits. Roosevelt was dead, replaced by Truman. Churchill was replaced on July 28 by Clement Attlee after the Labour Party was swept to power. Attlee, although deputy prime minister under Churchill, had not participated in Churchill's foreign negotiations. Consequently, he had little influence at Potsdam. Truman, convinced that the Soviets were not living up to their agreements regarding eastern Europe, wanted to deal with Stalin without Churchill's presence. He essentially got what he had hoped for.

Truman, known for his bluntness, lacked his predecessor's cosmopolitan charm. Soon after arriving at Potsdam he learned that the United States had a new weapon of awesome power, the atomic bomb. The first atomic explosion was on July 16, the eve of the conference's opening, and the success of the test was immediately reported to him. Truman's confidence was much improved by this time, leading some critics to charge that he tried to reverse the Yalta agreements through "atomic diplomacy." Truman casually informed Stalin, without being specific, about the new weapon. Stalin, who undoubtedly knew what Truman was referring to, said he hoped that he used it to end the war in Asia.

Much of the discussion at Potsdam among the Big Three dealt with refining decisions made at Yalta regarding Europe, especially those dealing with the boundary between Germany and Poland, the Oder-Neisse line. The German territory of East Prussia was partitioned between Russia (the largest member of the Soviet Union) and Poland, whereas the land between the Oder-Neisse Rivers and Poland's prewar western border went to Poland. This arrangement was for the purpose of administration pending a peace treaty to settle final boundaries.

Under the terms of German capitulation, all German state authority lay with the Allies. They now formalized the creation of four zones of military occupation (with a French zone carved from the previously arranged American zones). Berlin also was divided into four zones. The unity of the German economy was to be maintained. Similar arrangements were made for Austria. On issues such as denazification, democratization, and demilitarization of Germany, the Allies generally agreed, though in time how they thought these should be carried out varied greatly. The issue of reparations renewed tensions as the Western Allies became more interested in restoring the German economy, whereas the Soviets wanted to seize resources to restore their own destroyed industries. The Soviet zone was largely agricultural, but the industry the Soviets wanted was in the west. The western zones needed food supplies from the east to revive the economy of the western zones.

In addition to the Potsdam conference's associations with growing conflicts in Europe, it is also associated with the Potsdam Declaration, an ultimatum to Japan to surrender immediately and unconditionally, and threatened the complete destruction of Japanese forces and the Japanese homelands if resistance did not cease. The issue of the emperor was not mentioned. Truman knew through American intelligence that the Japanese were in contact with the Russians and trying to arrange a settlement with Moscow's help. Stalin did not inform the president of that fact, and Tokyo did not know that the Soviet Union was preparing to go to war against Japan in Manchuria on August 8.

Exactly when the Cold War began has been much debated. Wartime diplomacy has been examined and reexamined in great detail, especially the summit meetings. Advocates of "atomic diplomacy" have attempted to prove that Truman knew that Japan was near surrender and that an invasion would not be as costly as he later asserted. They claim that the real target was Stalin. Thus, Truman and American policy are primarily responsible for the Cold War. Their opponents find the evidence incomplete and unconvincing. This dispute may never be resolved. But what is clear is that although cooperation was strong at Tehran and weaker at Yalta, it was at Potsdam that the breakdown of the Alliance clearly emerged.

The Alliance had, however, achieved its purpose. It had been brought together by the aggressiveness of Hitler's Third Reich, not by the principles of the Atlantic Charter or the United Nations. That the Alliance failed to transcend its origin is unfortunate, but that does not make it any less of a Grand Alliance against the greatest threat the twentieth century has seen to peace and security.

3

World War II and the Changing Nature of Military Power

Although World War II lasted only six years, those years witnessed a dramatic evolution in military power and its geographic scale. The key factor was technology, though the number of belligerents, the global scale of the war, and the economies and social structures of the warring countries also played a part. Technology in and of itself does not produce change; otherwise, changing technologies would spread more rapidly from one society to another than they do. Thus, the history of technology during the war must be seen as a part of each society's culture and organization. Strategic planning, tactical practices, the structures of military command, and wartime economies are shaped by and in turn shape technologies.

World War II closed one age of military technology and brought on a new one. Every nation still had horse cavalry in 1939; by 1945 cavalry had disappeared from combat. Bombs in 1939 weighed a few hundred or a couple thousand pounds; the atomic bomb dropped on Hiroshima was equivalent to some 15,000 tons (3,000,000 pounds) of TNT. Jet planes and rockets, in the planning stages before 1939, emerged by 1944 as real weapons. Together, they laid much of the basis for postwar militaries.

These dramatic examples should not obscure the fact that much of the technology and weapons of the war stemmed from World War I, or earlier. Airplanes, tanks, radio, aircraft carriers, and much else preceded World War II by decades. Though informed observers of 1918 would have recognized their offspring in 1945, he or she would have also noted a colossal transformation in the years between 1939 and 1945.

More importantly, during the Great War, and even into the first years of World War II, there was uncertainty as to how these new technologies could be used. What was their strategic significance? Which had a practical chance of being developed? Which ones could be produced in the necessary quantities? The mobilization, the strategic planning, and the campaigns of World War II provided the tests that answered these questions.

In many respects, the Axis powers, especially Germany, but to some extent Japan and Italy, were ahead of their future opponents in their marriage of weapons development, economic mobilization, and strategy. This gave them an advantage in the early years of the war because their victims, with the exception of Russia, devoted less attention to rearmament and modernization of their military forces. On the other hand, because of the time lag between the development and the production of new weapons systems, the Axis powers began to fall behind when the Allies devoted their superior scientific, financial, and industrial resources to total war. The Germans, especially, were reaching the end of a cycle of development just as Britain and the United States were beginning to enter one. For reasons that had little to do with advanced planning and cycles, however, the Allies were more successful than the Germans in generating new or improved technologies with more-immediate, direct frontline application.

Among wartime technologies affecting strategy and the changing nature of mid-twentieth-century warfare were tanks, airplanes, aircraft carriers, radar and radio, signal intelligence, operations research, and the atomic bomb. Each had prewar precedents; each underwent dramatic change after 1939; each affected the outcome of the war; and each had a complex wartime history.

TANKS

To the newspaper reader in the summer of 1939 and to historians since, the tank (armored fighting vehicle, AFV) occupied first place in the changing face of war. The rapid defeat of Poland by Germany in September struck observers as the wave of the future. The previous month Soviet tanks had trounced the Japanese Army at Nomonhan (Russian Khalkhin-gol) in Manchuria, though very few in the West took notice.

So quick and startling was the German advance into Poland that an American journalist, it seems (the word was not used by the German army or Hitler), coined the German-sounding word *blitzkrieg*—lightning war—to describe it. The German strategy for the defeat of Poland called for a quick campaign, and blitzkrieg in the sense of coordinated tactics by tanks and dive bombers was part of the German campaign. But blitzkrieg as a strategy did not exist. Tanks made up only a part of the Wehrmacht, which still depended on careful planning, effective training and command, surprise, and mass to achieve its goals. Tanks were not central to the precampaign strategy, though their novelty and apparently key role in victory soon gained them that position.

Tanks were first used by the British in 1916. In the 1920s and 1930s, they became mechanically more reliable and developed along a broad range of sizes and characteristics. There was no agreement on exactly what tanks should be. Various countries produced tanks in 1939 ranging from under 10 tons each to 30–ton machines with heavier armor. Tacticians and strategists did not agree on how they should be employed. Should mobility be stressed at the cost of firepower? Major opinion held that tanks, if they had any future at all, should be a kind of mobile firepower unit in support of infantry. Their additional fire would enable infantry to sustain breakthroughs against World-War-I-type trench lines.

Others, such as J.F.C. Fuller and Basil Liddell Hart in Britain, Charles de Gaulle in France, and Heinz Guderian and Erich von Manstein in Germany, dissented from these views, believing that tanks should be formed into their own divisions and operated independently of infantry. Generally, they would have close tank formations, supported by coordinated tactical air strikes, penetrate enemy lines in depth. Through deep penetration, the tank forces would disrupt lines of communication and supply. In roving attacks, they would render helpless frontline soldiers deprived of orders, ammunition, and food. However used, tanks depended on radio communications for command and effective control.

Britain experimented with these ideas in the 1920s, but did not adopt them. Limited to a 100,000–man army, the German army took a keen interest in tanks as a way to enhance its offensive capabilities, but without making tanks central to overall strategy. Hitler authorized the establishment of tank divisions in 1935, but without allotting them the role their advocates wanted. France was in the process of forming tank divisions after 1939, though without rethinking its basically defensive strategy. The French, like the Soviets, favored mixed divisions of tanks and infantry. Soviet marshal Mikhail Tukhachevsky advocated developing independent tank divisions in the 1930s, but Stalin's purges ended in his execution and the breakup of tank units, except in eastern Manchuria.

Between the Polish campaign and the invasion of France in 1940, the Germans created more tank divisions. Initially, their plans called for spreading tanks out along the entire front in support of infantry divisions.

When this arrangement was compromised, General von Manstein convinced Hitler to concentrate tanks in the Ardennes and sweep west behind the Anglo-French forces. Their breakthrough to the English Channel and encirclement of the best of the Allied troops knocked France out of the war. Failing to foresee the tank's potential, the Allies had no defense. The Germans had no well-thought-out strategy; the High Command itself was surprised. But the strategic impact of the new technology caused every army to take note.

The French campaign became the classic instance of "blitzkrieg" and its last success in that form. It was tried against the Soviet Union in Operation Barbarossa, but failed. The reasons are still in dispute, but the size of the country made rapid, mobile operations less effective. Although the Germans surrounded masses of enemy troops, there were more to come. The terrain of the Ukraine and Belarus was also unsuitable to tank operations. Finally, the Soviets developed tactics—such as leaving a nest of antitank artillery guns behind the lines—to prevent tank forces from exploiting their advances. Nonetheless, without powerful tank divisions, the Germans would not have advanced as far into Soviet territory as they did in 1941 and 1942.

Even in 1941, the pattern of tank use began to change, as a race between heavier guns and more-elaborate, upgraded tanks. Between 1939 and 1945 the tanks of all the major belligerents, except Japan, went through rapid evolutions in variety, weight, thickness of armor, and gun size. In addition, assault guns were added to destroy armored enemy tanks.

Mobility, thick armor, and heavy firepower could not easily be combined in one machine. Tanks in 1945 were far more advanced than those of 1939 in capability and employment. As early as 1939 the Germans discovered, as did others later, that infantry fought more offensively when accompanied by tanks. Thus, though the spectacular tank triumphs of 1939–1940 were not repeated in the same form, tanks remained key offensive and defensive weapons in those campaigns with an open terrain, especially in eastern Europe, and in the Western Desert and North Africa.

By 1942, tank penetrations required reconnaissance and extensive antitank preparations with artillery, antitank guns, the clearing of minefields, and other defenses against their attacks. These became battles of attrition where surprise played little role and where a breakthrough came at the end of the battle. Also by 1942, when breakthrough was achieved, logistical restraints—for example, the lack of fuel and the need for repair of machines still susceptible to frequent breakdowns—and effective rear defenses thwarted the knockout examples of the first year of the war. This was the case after the second battle of El Alamein (November 1942), the battle of Kursk (July 1943), or the Anglo-American advances in France (summer 1944).

Even though counter measures against tanks were developed, tanks played a key role in land warfare. Whatever other technologies may have achieved, the decisive element in World War II was the conquest and occupation of land. Without tanks and infantry the Axis triumphs of 1939–1942 would have been impossible. And so would have the Allied victory in 1945.

AIR POWER AND STRATEGIC BOMBING

Airplanes were used extensively during World War I for reconnaissance, artillery observation, strafing, parachute drops, rescue, and transport. Aerial bombing of London by the Germans was more an indication of future developments than an effective instrument of war. Believing that there was no defense against a bombing offensive, the British created the Royal Air Force (RAF) in April 1918 to carry out their own air offensive. When the war ended, the RAF remained, but without the resources to make it into a strategic bombing force.

Hugh Trenchard, chief of air staff of the RAF throughout the 1920s, developed a doctrine of strategic bombing. Along with men like Giulio Douhet and Billy Mitchell, he was one of several advocates of an independent strategic role for air power. In 1936 Bomber Command was established and heavy bombers planned; they became operational in early 1942. In 1939 Germany had an independent air force, the Luftwaffe, but it lacked a strategic theory. The Luftwaffe's primary task was to support tank and other army operations. In 1939 there was still uncertainty about the role of airplanes. Technical advances were coming rapidly, but there had been little combat experience in European conditions.

Strategic air advocates generally ignored the importance of defense, but fortunately Hugh Dowding, commander in chief of the RAF's Fighter Command from 1936, built an air defense system that enabled the RAF to win the battle of Britain, history's first major campaign fought between air forces independently of ground action. Dowding was aided by German confusion over strategic goals, but the key element was a chain of radar stations, linked to central headquarters with effective radio communication with pilots. The Hurricane and Spitfire fighter planes, which entered service in 1939, were modern and fast. Bringing these diverse elements together gave Dowding control over the course of battle. No other example from World War II so clearly illustrates the value of integrating technological developments, industrial production, scientific management, and human resources.

The strategic bombing campaign against Germany was less successful, best shown in the continuing controversy regarding its effectiveness and morality. Those who think the campaigns of Bomber Command and the United States Army Air Force (USAAF) were effective admit that at least in the early stages of the war, theory outran technology. The Butt report, based on RAF attacks on German targets in June and July 1941, showed that only two thirds of all sorties attacked their targets and that of these, only one plane in three dropped its bombs within five miles of the target.

Arthur Harris, commander in chief of Bomber Command after February 1942, concluded that precision bombing would not work. Instead, area bombing with incendiary bombs would destroy German cities, dehouse their workers, and undermine civilian morale. To avoid being shot down, bombers flew at night. This limited accuracy, but the goal was to hit cities, not specific targets within cities. In May 1942 Harris dispatched the first of several thousand plane attacks and demolished Cologne.

Later that summer the Eighth USAAF began its own bombing campaign, using B-17 Fortresses. The B-17 first flew in 1935. Intended as a coastal defense plane, the B-17 required improvements after being used by the British in 1940 and 1941 for bombing missions over Europe. The USAAF intended to fly these planes in close formation so that they could defend one another. It was believed that this would enable them to fly at daytime and carry out precision bombing.

By July 1943, as the war continued and German morale seemed intact, Harris came under public criticism. "Pathfinder" planes were introduced in 1942 to guide bombers to their targets by dropping flares and incendiaries. Pathfinders and increasingly sophisticated radio navigational systems improved bombing accuracy, but Harris continued area bombing and ignored directives to target specific military and industrial targets, such as submarine construction sites and German fighter plane factories and airfields. The costs were high on both sides. Bomber Command lost more than 8,000 bombers and 55,000 crewmen; German losses were approximately 600,000 people, mostly due to area assaults.

At the January 1943 Casablanca conference, Churchill and Roosevelt accepted a plan for a combined bombing offensive (CBO) of the American and British bombing effort. The Americans would bomb by day, the British by night. General Ira Eaker believed that his B-17s and B-24s could carry out raids deep in Germany beyond fighter defense forces with minimal losses. Harris was skeptical and continued his own bombing campaign.

At the end of July 1943, Harris pounded Hamburg for four nights. To confuse German radar defenses, the RAF dropped small bits of metal foil, called WINDOW. On the second night, July 27, a combination of high explosives and incendiary bombs ignited the atmosphere, turning the downtown sections into a burning maelstrom suffocating and killing 45,000 men, women, and children. The USAAF bombed Hamburg port areas during two days.

In August and again in October 1943, the Eighth USAAF attacked ball-bearing factories at Schweinfurt. The intent was to justify pinpoint strategic bombing by destroying this vital part of German industry. The results were deeply disappointing. Of 376 bombers, 174 (46 percent) were lost. The second raid still suffered 60 planes destroyed out of 291 (21 percent loss). Losses of this magnitude could not be sustained.

More-intense bombing of Germany began in 1944. The Mustang P-51 fighter plane, and other fighters, became available, as did other improvements. The Eighth, Ninth, and Fifteenth USAAF were reorganized under General Carl Spaatz into a strategic air force in January 1944. During "Big Week," the last week of February 1944, more than 6,000 British and American bombers attacked German fighter plane factories. These continued into the following months, allowing the Anglo-Americans to gain air supremacy over Europe by June when the Normandy invasion took place.

By the end of 1944 the Allies had exhausted known targets over Germany. German rearmament after 1942 and the forced dispersal of industry rendered Allied knowledge of the economy near worthless. This is in part why the destruction of Dresden in mid-February 1945 has stirred controversy. Dresden, the elegant, baroque capital of Saxony, had no heavy industry and was not a military center.

The motives for the attack are unclear. The bombing was a part of Thunderclap, a campaign against several east German cities designed to spread chaos behind the German lines retreating from the Red Army's offensives. At Yalta the Soviets asked for such attacks. Bomber Command, as usual, bombed for three successive nights, with the USAAF attacking by day. The exact number killed is unknown, but probably was around 50,000. The historic parts of the city were leveled and much of its art work destroyed. The press soon labeled the raids terror bombing. Churchill briefly had second thoughts, but Harris defended the action.

Strategic bombing of Japan was more thoroughly thought-out, and the technology more clearly matched the doctrine than was the case in Europe. The B-29 Boeing Superfortress was rushed into production for the campaign. A monstrous plane weighing 50 tons when fully loaded, the B-29 had a range of 1,600 miles and could carry 10 tons of bombs.

It had many technical problems at first, most notably its engines' tendency to overheat and catch on fire. Its first use in bombing Japan came in June 1944 in raids from China, but they could only reach the southern island of Kyushu. They had no strategic effect. Continuous and ever-growing bombing began at the end of November when the Twentieth USAAF's 21st Bomber Command began daytime, high-altitude, precision bombing with 80 B-29s from bases in the Mariana Islands.

The campaign's effectiveness was undermined by difficulties with the plane and bad weather. Flying at such high levels, the planes encountered the as yet poorly understood jet stream. Japanese fighter resistance was strong. All this prevented an evaluation of the damage done. General Henry H. Arnold, Chief of the USAAF and champion of the B-29, was dissatisfied with the results and in January 1945 replaced Brigadier General Haywood Hansell with Major-General Curtis LeMay.

LeMay gradually substituted incendiary bombs. At the end of February 150 planes burned a square mile of Tokyo. LeMay switched entirely to nighttime, low-altitude bombing. On March 9, B-29s dropped 2,000 tons of incendiaries on Tokyo, creating a fire storm that destroyed one fourth of the city and killed more than 80,000 people, injuring 40,000, and leaving over a million homeless. During the next few months, Japanese cities were leveled. In June, the Japanese withdrew their fighters from defense, saving them for the expected invasion. By July, the 21st Bomber Command had run out of targets. Japan's economy was in shambles, transportation and communications networks were no longer functioning, and over 300,000 civilians were dead, thousands more wounded, and millions homeless.

The strategic air offensive against Japan had achieved all its goals except the defeat of the country. Although the emperor in April wanted to end the war and the advocates of peace were stronger, the military wanted to fight on, hoping to make the cost of an invasion so high that Japan could negotiate a surrender.

At that point, the atomic bombs dropped on Hiroshima and Nagasaki ended strategic bombing and Japanese resistance. From then on, the debate over strategic bombing was carried out in the books. Its advocates argued that the doctrine was sound; the technology needed to catch up. General Arnold, like his counterpart Harris, complained that the air forces never received the resources they needed. Critics believed that wars could not be won in the air, aside from the immorality of slaughtering so many civilians.

CARRIERS

Only three countries built fleet carriers during the war: Japan, Britain, and the United States. Of these, only Japan had prewar plans for carrier task forces operating independently of other fleet ships. During the 1930s the technologies advanced rapidly but ran up against the limitations of the Washington naval agreements of 1922. Carriers had their advocates, but the lack of combat experience left uncertainty as to exactly their role in future conflicts. Only Japanese and American experiments suggested their future importance.

The Washington treaty limited carrier tonnage for the United States Navy (USN) and Britain's Royal Navy (RN) at 121,500 metric tons, and 72,900 for the Imperial Japanese Navy (IJN), with any individual carrier limited to 24,300 tons. As aircraft became larger and faster, larger-sized carriers became more attractive, but that reduced the total number of carriers. Restrictions on construction ended at Pearl Harbor. Carriers were used in the Atlantic and the Mediterranean, but in the Pacific they were the key strategic offensive weapon.

The USN and IJN designed lighter craft carrying larger numbers of fighters than did the RN. The Japanese Zero had greater range than any American fighter planes throughout most of the war, giving the IJN an advantage in carrier-versus-carrier conflicts and in keeping USN reconnaissance planes at a distance from their capital ships. The Japanese torpedoes were far superior to the American torpedoes, which were plagued by problems until late 1943. Improvements in American aircraft, namely the F4U Vought Corsair and the F6F Grumman Hellcat, began to overcome USN weaknesses, as did the American lead in radar and its use in tactical fighter control.

The first demonstration of carrier fleet capabilities was the attack on Pearl Harbor on December 7, 1941, when the Japanese launched an attack from sea at great distance from their home ports. The dramatic Doolittle raid over Tokyo of April 1942 was not a true test. The carrier U.S.S. *Hornet* was loaded with 16 B-25s, which bombed several sites in Japan before flying on to China. Strategically insignificant, it caused the Japanese to strengthen their defenses and give the go ahead for the battle of Midway.

Before Midway, the USN and IJN clashed in the Coral Sea between May 4 and May 8, 1942. This was the first encounter between carriers in which the main ships never came within sight of one another. The battle was a tactical victory for Japan, but a strategic loss in that the United States thwarted a Japanese invasion of Port Moresby, New Guinea. Had that happened, Australia would have been cut off from American Pacific forces and brought within bomber range of Japanese forces. Although indecisive, the Battle of the Coral Sea clearly showed the strategic importance of carriers, and its results helped contribute to American victory at Midway the next month.

The Americans prevailed at Midway due to Isoruku Yamamoto's fatal decision to divide Japanese forces. He sent a main task force to invade Midway, but another force to the Aleutian Islands in hopes of diverting the Americans. Admiral Chester Nimitz, however, knew of Japanese intentions through signals intelligence and was able to lay in wait for the carrier fleet. Superior intelligence, superior tactics, determination, and some luck proved decisive.

Carrier battles such as Coral Sea and Midway were not typical of the strategic use of carriers for the remainder of the war. From late 1942 through the seizure of Okinawa, carriers were used to give air cover for amphibious operations and to attack enemy carriers.

Of all combatants, the Americans had more experience with amphibious warfare, though all combatants carried out some amphibious operations. The U.S. Marine Corps had the doctrine and the specialized equipment prepared to conduct amphibious operations. This began with Marine interventions in Central America in the 1920s. In the Pacific, it took time to integrate air, land, and sea forces into a smoothly running operation. The costly campaign on Guadalcanal, August 7 to February 9, 1943, showed that. But in combination with control of the air from carriers, the Marines spearheaded the phenomenal island-hopping across the central Pacific from Tarawa in November 1943 to the epic battle for Okinawa in April 1945. At Okinawa, 170,000 Marines and infantrymen fought the Japanese, and more than a thousand warships and another half million men lent support.

The equipment, training, and tactics perfected by the Marines became standard procedures for U.S. Army infantry in General Douglas MacArthur's Southwest Pacific Area, from New Guinea to the Philippine Islands and the Aleutian Islands. And, of course, the great amphibious operations of the war in Europe, Operation Torch and Operation Overlord, were critical to victory over the Axis powers. Admiral Ernest King and General Eisenhower both considered it the most difficult form of warfare. It necessitated complex planning and coordination, specific technologies, and men trained in their use. Amphibious warfare required complex industrial economies, highly educated populations, advanced technical accomplishments, and a political system organized to bring these together and mobilize them for national strategic purposes.

RADIO AND RADAR

Radio communications were used in World War I, but radio equipment and its reliability were much improved by 1939. The amount of radio (called wireless in Britain) broadcasting was much greater during World War II, and its security had also improved.

More important were the new uses to which radio was put. The vast array of naval and merchant marine ships were directed and coordinated by radio, as were their opponents, submarines. Radio traffic at sea was generally carried out with Morse code, because voice communication was too difficult for clarity. In addition, Morse code also could be encrypted and it could be broadcast in very short bursts, making it difficult to monitor.

During the battle of Britain, Fighter Command mobilized much more effectively than had any aerial defense force before. In this case, voice communication was essential because of the high demands on pilots and the need for near continuous contact between a plane and its base. Drawing on information provided by radar and the network to which it was connected, Fighter Command could centrally dispatch pilots to where they were most needed, or to help them avoid attacks by superior forces.

Ground forces also could be more effectively utilized due to radio. Some traditionalists scorned the use of radio, but in the 1930s radio began to be used to command tank forces, especially by the British and the Germans. France, Italy, and Japan gave radio a low priority. Communication among tanks preserved a united tactical attack and also maintained the essential link between men and their officers. The United States army developed portable radios weighing less than five pounds, the "walkie talkie," and provided them through Lend-Lease to its allies.

Aside from the problem of convincing commanders of radio's utility and devising methods for its effective use, radio still suffered from technical difficulties. In the 1940s, vacuum tubes were the heart of radio. Radio devices were fragile and unable to resist dampness and other vagaries of bad weather.

Radar, an acronym for *ra*dio *d*etecting *a*nd *r*anging, did not appear as a workable instrument until the mid-1930s. Inventors in several countries independently devised radar sets. The earliest successes were by the British and Germans. Radar's primary use was thought to be for air defense by giving early warning of approaching aircraft and to support better targeting by antiaircraft artillery.

Radar as isolated, individual units was important, but Robert Watson-Watts in Britain conceived the idea in 1935 of a network of radar sets along the coast that would feed their detections to a central place where planes in the air could be plotted for the entire country. The invention of a wide variety of radar systems followed. In 1940 the British shared their progress with the United States, which established a major research project at the Massachusetts Institute of Technology in Boston.

With radar placed in individual airplanes, bombing became more accurate. The extensive carrier fleet the United States built was also equipped with radar, as well as sonar, a development in which the Japanese were far behind.

By war's end, radar had become an integral part of military armament, especially for air and naval forces, and especially among the Western Allies.

SIGNALS INTELLIGENCE

Signals intelligence played a much greater role in World War II than previous conflicts. The term *signals intelligence* refers to the interception of all forms of signals, the decryption of signals (decoding), and the interpretation of their messages. Another field became important as well, that of analyzing the pattern of communications and signals without knowing their content. The level of radio activity (and its absence) can alert the listener to an impending attack.

American signals intelligence failed in the case of the attack on Pearl Harbor, as did the Soviet's service before Operation Barbarossa. Other examples could be cited: the invasion of Scandinavia by the Germans, the attack on France and the Benelux countries, and the Soviet attack on Japan at the end of the war.

By far the most successful intelligence was British ULTRA, which used new technologies, a form of the computer, to analyze millions of bits of data to decipher thousands of German messages. How these were used is still under investigation, but they gave the Allies a significant advantage in many of the military conflicts on land and in the air, and in assessing the military and economic strength of the Axis powers.

The American Operation Magic decoded primarily diplomatic messages among the Axis powers, but those messages also revealed details of both German and Japanese military strategic planning.

OPERATIONAL RESEARCH

Among the more interesting developments of the war was operational research. It is the scientific study of how procedures, practices, and organization work. As a field it preceded the war and is now generally known as industrial psychology, operations management, or organizational behavior.

Great Britain led in the use of operational research, though the United States soon followed. Mathematicians and other experts were brought into government in order to maximize the design of war equipment and to analyze how they could be used for maximum effectiveness. The range of human activities and machine operations that could be scientifically studied and improved extended throughout all aspects of the military and industry.

Operational research studies, for example, showed how best to repair aircraft, anticipating the breakdown of certain parts and replacing them before a malfunction. It showed how best to deploy aircraft throughout the Atlantic in order to optimize attacks on German submarines. It helped design instrument controls so that pilots and other operators of equipment could best avoid mistaking one control for another.

Operational research also was used to study the behavior of humans in relation to one another. The most famous of these was U.S. General S.L.A. Marshall's study of small group behavior to determine the effectiveness of combat. He demonstrated that soldiers in isolation fired their weapons less often than those in groups, and that groups of men in close communication with their commanders and other groups were the most effective combatants.

THE ATOMIC BOMB

Undoubtedly, the most important technical and scientific achievement of World War II was the atomic bomb.

The latent energy in splitting an atom had been known long before the war, but the experiment that proved that it could be done came in January 1938. The few informed physicists worldwide who understood the potential soon mobilized. In Germany, they were unable to get a full commitment from the government. They generally lacked the resources necessary to undertake the needed research and build the necessary manufacturing facilities. The Russians and the Japanese also set to work, but it was in the United Kingdom, and later the United States, where the government gave priority to determine the feasibility of a practical weapon and then to bring it into production.

Antifascist physicists, many of them refugees in France, Great Britain, and the United States, feared that Germany might be the first to create an atomic bomb. That would be disastrous for world civilization. They were important in stimulating the British into research, and later the United States.

In 1941 the United States began its own project, code-named the Manhattan Engineer District, to design and produce a nuclear weapon. During the next three and a half years, the American government expended over $2 billion and employed over 600,000 workers. By September 1944 the western Allies learned that Germany was not in an atomic arms race. Development continued, however, with the first atomic bomb, "Trinity," exploded on July 16, 1945, ten weeks after the end of the war in Europe.

The atomic bombs had no direct effect on Allied strategies to defeat the Axis powers until the first successful test. Strategic planners who knew of the project could not count on its success or that it would be ready in time. Planning continued for an invasion, code-named Olympic, on November 1, 1945, of Kyushu, Japan's southernmost main island.

Dropping the atomic bombs on the Japanese cities of Hiroshima on August 6, 1945, and on Nagasaki three days later has been and continues to remain controversial. The total number of people killed, including the aftereffects of radiation, has been variously estimated at between 120,000 and 240,000. The conventional strategic air offensive against Japan, which began in November 1944 cost approximately 300,000 dead in addition to half a million casualties and more than 8 million made homeless.

There was no decision to use the atomic bombs; their military use was always assumed. The question was how to use them to end the war quickly, and whether Japan was ready to surrender before their deployment. These issues were complicated by the Allied policy of unconditional surrender; the Japanese government did not want the emperor to be deposed and tried as a war criminal.

Once the war was over, American possession of atomic weapons made them part of the American diplomatic arsenal, especially against the Soviet Union. Immediately, observers knew that the nature of war and the issues of defense were forever changed. The technology could be reproduced by advanced industrial societies and, when linked to advanced rockets, would make it possible to deliver nuclear weapons anywhere on the earth.

Rocket technology rapidly developed during the war, especially in Germany. Hitler's plans for a speedy defeat of his European opponents led him to cancel work on rockets, but the German army continued the project, generally known as the V-2 (for Vergeltungswaffe, retaliation weapon). The V-1 was a pilotless jet missile with limited range. The V-2 was a true rocket, propelled by an alcohol and liquid oxygen fuel. It was capable of flight beyond the atmosphere and at higher speeds than the V-1. A little more than 1,000 landed in England, killing nearly 3,000 persons.

The rocket, like the jet engine, had no impact on the outcome of the war, but they were both significant harbingers of the postwar world. When developed to become powerful enough in the 1950s, rockets launched the world's first satellites and laid the basis for intercontinental ballistic missiles armed with nuclear warheads.

CONCLUSION

Technological innovations, development, and adaptations dramatically changed the nature of warfare during the early 1940s, both during the war and as the birthplace of post–World War II warfare. Technological advantage cannot be guaranteed by any nation, except through secrecy, but that also is difficult to maintain, especially if the weapon is employed. Enemy countries with the necessary resources can readily adapt and develop technologies invented by others.

World War II shows, however, that the United States and the United Kingdom were best able to mobilize science, technology in general, and information technologies specifically, for the purposes of victory. Their societies had a culture friendly to scientific investigation. They had the economic and productive requirements. Finally, their military services were flexible enough to adopt new technologies and apply them strategically and tactically for national political goals.

4

World War II on the Home Front

No war in human history affected as many civilians on the home fronts as did World War II. The war is sometimes depicted as a heroic age when patriotism, sacrifice, and common purposes transcended selfish individual and class interests. This romanticized, nostalgic view, though widely held, is a minor part of the wartime story. The war can also be portrayed as unrelieved death and horror—in combat, in concentration camps, from bombing, and in war-caused epidemics and famines. The war destroyed cultural and economic assets created by previous generations. It breached previous moral and psychological limits of violence in its genocide and nuclear bombings.

Home fronts also underwent permanent social and political change. Some see war as a catastrophic interruption requiring time for society to return to normalcy. In truth, domestically and internationally, World War II was a major force in shaping today's societies.

During the war the major belligerents recruited only a small part of the population as combatants. Although the total number of soldiers, some 50,000,000 worldwide, exceeded previous conflicts, as a percentage of population, they were fewer. A large population and access to raw materials were essential for successful production of the sinews of war. As what German and Japanese leaders hoped would be a short war turned into a protracted struggle, social and economic mobilization on a vast scale benefited the Allies. It also changed societies and the very nature of the conflict.

Prolonged industrialized warfare necessitated new factories, machines, and equipment. It demanded the reallocation of labor, capital, and raw materials. It involved new methods of planning and managing resources. A society's efficiency in doing this also rested on other factors such as the level of education, the willingness to embrace change, the acceptance of a work discipline, the availability of capital, the absence of social conflict, and the extent of identification with the state.

Marshaling the public in support of war absorbed more resources than before. Ideas, information, and opinions, like bullets and food, could be ordered, manufactured, and delivered according to centrally determined plans. The extent to which public opinion could be manipulated was remarkable, especially where advertising skills and totalitarian controls over media existed. Propaganda was pervasive and intimately tied to military strategies, political leadership, and economic mobilization, indeed to every phase of the war. Propaganda permeated sermons, feature articles in magazines, newsreels and animated cartoons preceding feature movies, as well as the comics, sports sections, even obituaries in newspapers. Images and attitudes generated by wartime propaganda continue to shape our very understanding of these years. Negative images of mutilated (or even bloodied) bodies found no place in domestic propaganda, except when the enemy's atrocities were reported. The idea of a highly mechanized, efficient, well-thought-out German blitzkrieg is one of the most enduring images.

Not all social classes, ethnic groups, geographic regions, or nations experienced the war in the same ways, but all felt the effects. Of the three major Allies, the United Kingdom had the least area and the least population, 48,000,000. It could draw on the vast resources of the Commonwealth and Empire, but those had to be mobilized in ways quite unlike those of the Soviet Union or the United States. The British fought longer—nearly six years—than did either the Soviets or the Americans. Soviet prewar population was 170,000,000 with at least 20,000,000, but more probably over 27,000,000 military and civilian deaths caused by the war, compared to 350,000 for Britain. The United States, with a population of 132,000,000, suffered only incidental bombing, and war-related deaths of 274,000. Germany's prewar population was 79,500,000 (with the annexations of Austria and western Czechoslovakia), Japan's 70,000,000, and Italy's 42,000,000 with war deaths of 6,500,000, 2,350,000, and 500,000 people respectively. These facts alone suggest the difference of homefront experiences.

GERMANY

Hitler created a Ministry of Public Enlightenment and Propaganda upon coming to power in 1933, with Joseph Goebbels at its head. Goebbels had a flair for public rhetoric and understood the value of controlling the news and ideas. In the Third Reich, as in the Soviet Union, publishing, radio, and film were totally directed by the government. Within Germany, Goebbels concentrated on themes such as the injustice of the Versailles Treaty, the oppression of German minorities in other countries, the restoration of German pride, the regime's economic successes, and its ambitious building programs. For foreign consumption, he emphasized German military preparedness and the inevitability of Nazi victory. His overblown depiction of German victories sometimes got him into trouble; public opinion was completely unprepared for the disaster at Stalingrad in 1943.

In 1933, depression and high unemployment pummeled Germany. By 1939 the Nazi regime had put people to work, and mobilized 6,000,000 into the military. Observers assumed that the economy was tuned for total war, a conclusion reinforced by propaganda and the quick, unexpected victories of 1939–1940. In 1939 most Germans dreaded a renewal of war, but the economy, though revived, was unprepared for a long war of attrition.

Hitler wanted a succession of short military campaigns; Poland's quick collapse was the ideal. The price in lost lives and expended material was low, while the political profits were high. Hitler believed that extended conflict in World War I had brought a revolution on the German home front and defeat in arms. Germany lacked the basic raw materials, except for coal, needed for 1940's warfare: petroleum, cotton and wool, iron, aluminum, copper, rubber, and so forth. Scarce resources required a short war.

Nazi ideology and administration thwarted full mobilization. The Nazis idealized the peasantry and a close connection between blood and soil. They encouraged women to give up their jobs and return to the home to raise children and serve in the kitchen. In this, they were only partly successful. The anarchy generated by competing Nazi satraps (subordinate officials) militated against rationalization and efficiency in war production. In addition, the Army, Navy, and Air Force each had its own procurement organization. Hermann Goering's Four Year Plan, established in 1936, only added to the layers of bureaucracy and confusion in economic planning. Finally, such organizations as the large private contracting and construction firm run by Fritz Todt and Heinrich Himmler's SS, through its business activities, escaped central control. These facts notwithstanding, Germany entered the war better prepared than its opponents.

In the early years Germany's lack of preparedness made little difference. The annexation of Austria brought in new financial reserves, labor, and raw materials. The absorption of Czechoslovakia added even more, especially in military equipment. The occupation of Poland and most of western

Europe further increased the supply of military hardware, labor, and manufacturing capacity. The Reich's population grew from 80,000,000 to
116,000,000 by the summer of 1941.

There had been skeptics in the German government, among businessmen, and in the army whether armament in breadth (a wide variety of weapons, but few in reserve) would be sufficient to establish German hegemony
in Europe. The events of 1939–1940 briefly dispelled their fears. But the
failure of Operation Barbarossa, the unexpected vitality of Soviet resistance, and then its counteroffensive of December 1941 demonstrated the
need for reorganizing production and building a total war economy.

Hitler already had made Fritz Todt Minister of Armaments and Munitions in 1940, but only the setback in the east led the Führer to give him
authority to introduce central planning and rationalize production. When
Todt was killed in a plane crash in February 1942, Hitler named his architect, Albert Speer, as successor. Speer continued Todt's schemes, but with
the advantage of Hitler's full support and the ability to bypass the myriad
other authorities. Production increased dramatically, by 50 percent between
January and July 1942 alone, and threefold by 1944. The production of
tanks grew by six times; airplane production quadrupled. Nonessential civilian production plummeted, the variety of weapons reduced in favor of
simplification and standardization, whereas raw materials were rationed
and centrally allocated with decisions based on strategic priorities. Some
6,000,000 and later 8,000,000 compulsory foreign laborers and prisoners of
war were brought to Germany to work in the arms industries.

From 1939 on, the SS and other organizations under Heinrich Himmler's
command grew in influence within the Reich and in occupied territories.
Euthanasia, genocide, concentration camps, arrests, and intimidation of domestic opponents became the Reich's hallmarks as those who did not agree
with the policies of the radical Nazis were driven from positions of authority. The abortive assassination of Hitler in July 1944 accelerated that process, leading to Himmler's usurpation of nearly all authority in
German-occupied Europe.

The impact of the war years on German civil society is hard to measure
due to the totalitarian nature of the regime. Security reports by the police,
court records, and even party files, however, give some insight into public
opinion. It appears that the "muddled majority" railed against the regime
and disbelieved its propaganda, but generally remained supportive, approving of the economic boom and social "tranquility."

The bombing offensive did not undermine morale as Allied planners had
hoped. The Nazi goal of removing women from the workforce was a failure.

In the long run, the most important social impact of the war was the destruction of the elitist military and bureaucratic aristocracy, due to battle deaths, the loss of the war, and Nazi reprisals for its involvement in the attempt on Hitler's life in July 1944.

Care was taken to shield Germans from the brunt of consumer shortages. Because of the economic exploitation of conquered territories, Germans only seriously began to experience the deprivations of war in 1942. By summer 1945 they were at point "zero." Twenty-five percent of males aged 35 to 50 years were casualties. Major cities were almost totally leveled by bombing. Occupied by the victorious powers in May 1945, German society was about to undergo dramatic changes.

THE UNITED KINGDOM

British society was unprepared for war in 1939. The desire for peace ran deep, unemployment was high, the economy was privately managed under the government's laissez-faire policies. Although Neville Chamberlain accelerated rearmament after the Munich conference of September 1938, especially of aircraft, the primary strategy in case of war was to deny Germany access to vital raw materials and force it into a negotiated settlement. The government did not want preparation for war to interfere with economic recovery. Only about a tenth of domestic product was spent on the military, much less than that of any Axis country or the Soviet Union. Universal military service was introduced in the spring of 1939, but the declaration of war brought little change in national policy.

The fear of things to come is seen in the blackouts at night and the evacuation of 3,500,000 mothers and children in September 1939. Authorities believed that an air war would mean catastrophic bombardment with thousands dead, more wounded, and the remainder of the population in panic or shock. The evacuees moved from the country's cities, especially London, to small towns and rural areas in the west. Mostly working class, their hosts were middle class, for they had the spare rooms for housing. The result was a massive, sometimes shocking, learning experience on both sides. Working class children's hygiene was not that of the middle classes. The undernourished, unkempt, and poorly educated children many well-to-do families met led them to see Britain's social problems in a different light. Whatever the impact of evacuation, when the bombs finally fell the next summer, the result was much less than forecast. Total deaths for the entire war in Britain from bombing were less than 60,000, not the predicted 60,000 each night.

Greater social change came from state planning for the expected medical crisis. With medical resources scarce and doctors needed in the armed forces, the government allocated doctors to where they were most needed, whether to undersupplied working class districts or the military. During the war health care was distributed less on the ability to pay than on need.

The shock of the fall of France, May 1940, showed the need for a total war mobilization. Parliament approved an Emergency Powers Act giving the state dictatorial power over all citizens and their property. The government adopted John Maynard Keynes's idea of a national budget based on all labor and material resources rather than a financial budget based on fiscal principles. This required a massive survey to establish what the gross national product was. When finished, this provided the state with the tools to eliminate nonessential consumption and direct the use of labor and raw materials to the war effort.

The Labour Party became part of the ruling coalition under Churchill, with Clement Attlee, its leader as deputy prime minister. Ernest Bevin, a trade union leader, was appointed Minister of Labour responsible for the employment, wages, and conditions of work of all working people. Men between the ages of 18 and 50 were conscripted into the military or into approved civilian work. Unmarried women between 20 and 30 (later in the war to age 50) had to register for an assignment. Three million British people (not including those from Commonwealth countries and the Empire) were recruited into the armed forces, and 2,800,000 more as workers, including 2,200,000 women. War-related output peaked in 1943 at nearly two thirds of the GDP, an extraordinary achievement given the country's low starting point in 1939.

Aircraft production had priority for defense and as the only means to inflict damage on Germany in the immediate future. Britain also manufactured other arms, but of special importance was the purchase of armaments from American and other foreign suppliers. After the passage of the Lend-Lease Act in March 1941, the rearmament problem was in meeting British needs while the Americans engaged in their own military buildup.

To save shipping space and monetary reserves, the government limited unnecessary imports and overconsumption with rationing. It rationed everything: clothing, food, household items, cigarettes, beverages. Each person could buy only that amount of food needed for his or her weight, age, and occupation. The sum of daily diets, minus the food produced in Britain, determined the quantity to be imported. As a result, the diets of society's poorest improved. The distribution of food and all other goods and services more or less according to need in a full-employment economy produced a degree of equality never achieved before in British history or any other democratic society. The impact transformed postwar Britain as many voters wanted the same principles applied in peacetime.

In 1944, British children were better fed than in 1939. Medical services reached more people than ever. Required to move from their parents' homes to work in war production plants, single women became socially and financially independent. They and women with husbands stationed abroad became more involved in the previously male, public world of offices, shop, and factory. On the other hand, women did not escape male domination. Their jobs were temporary; they did not get equal pay for equal work. After the war, women were told to return to their homes and have children. The war may have provoked women to assert their autonomy, but it did not get them equal rights.

By 1942 more than a million American soldiers (1,700,000 by May 1944), and many Commonwealth and other foreign soldiers as well, were stationed in Britain. GIs brought with them the trappings of American culture such as chewing gum and Coca Cola, more egalitarian social practices, a greater interest in American films, and more pay than British soldiers received. Among them were 130,000 African Americans, 10 times the number of blacks in British prewar society. Efforts to segregate and isolate African Americans (and nonwhites from the colonies) from British society failed, leading British citizens to face racial conflict in a way they had not done before. The British did not have to leave home to meet the world. It came to them.

British propaganda set new standards at home and abroad. Several government agencies were involved, and the publishing industry as well. Most important, however, was the British Broadcasting Corporation (BBC), which had a monopoly on radio broadcasting in Britain. It expanded its domestic service, giving it a more popular format. Abroad, it built a worldwide radio network, broadcasting in more than two dozen languages. Though the BBC depicted the war as a struggle between good and evil, democracy and human rights against perverted science and racism, its first charge was accuracy. This commitment gained it a large following in occupied Europe, including the German leadership. How important the BBC was in building consensus within Britain is hard to determine. Propaganda seems to be most effective when it reinforces popular perceptions and experiences.

After the victory at El Alamein in November 1942, the immediate threat of invasion was over and optimism began to rise. The semiofficial Beveridge report published the next month recommended a postwar extension of social security, with a guarantee of full employment, national health insurance, and other social benefits. The shared experiences of evacuation, near invasion, and the Blitz revolutionized the relationship between government and citizen. The Labour Party and Conservatives in the coalition government reached a broad consensus on the need for the state to provide for the population's health and well-being. In effect, the war paved the way for the landslide victory of the Labour Party in 1945 and the United Kingdom's welfare state.

THE SOVIET UNION

Of the major Allies, the Soviet Union suffered the most, not only because of calamities usually associated with invasion but because of the uninhibited exploitation and deliberate devastation wreaked by the German armies. The other effects of war are harder to assess. Soviet histories of the war reflected state policy more than past realities. Emphasis was on military operations and the people's heroic struggle under the leadership of the party. In the immediate postwar years, the role of comrade Stalin took center stage.

From 1941 on, carnage was everywhere. More than 1 in 10 Soviet citizens were killed: 27,000,000 soldiers or more and civilians, and not the 20,000,000 in earlier accounts. The dead were disproportionately young men. Nearly half of all males in the armed forces died, creating a gender imbalance of as much as 4 to 1 in some parts of the country. The Germans systematically looted, carrying off whatever could be moved, even destroying the livestock needed for future reproduction. The three-year siege of Leningrad caused over 600,000 deaths (and perhaps 1,000,000).

The economy reeled under the impact; 40 percent of the population was in occupied areas, though several millions were evacuated to the east. At first, industrial and agricultural production plummeted; the German advance was so rapid that much was lost. Nonetheless, the arms industries, many of which had been relocated east of the Ural Mountains, more than doubled their 1940 output by 1943 in spite of a 30 percent decrease in the number of workers. Labor mobilization was particularly difficult because of the large number of battle deaths and the dislocations caused by German occupation. Nonetheless, labor came under greater state control. There were no days off, and the work day lengthened. Labor mobilization spread different ethnic groups throughout the U.S.S.R., though whether it helped to integrate them into a more common citizenship is doubtful.

Women took up "male" jobs, even at the front. Several served as tank commanders, others as doctors and middle-level managers. The percent of women employed in industry rose from 38 percent to 53 percent. But no woman reached high levels in state or economic administration. The scarcity of males, Stalin's ruthless purges of the 1930s, and expanded wartime administration were significant in opening up or creating new party positions for younger men with fewer men to compete for them. The Soviet communist party after Stalin had little connection with the prewar era, but a lot of experience with the struggle against Germany.

Before the war, the economy was designed to maximize military production, while private consumption had low priority. This helped provide the necessary economic base for a war of attrition. From 1942 on, the Soviet economy produced more than Germany. The wartime production surged, with growing numbers of tanks, planes, and other arms, improved transportation, and larger stocks of fuel. Probably three fourths of Soviet national income was devoted to the war effort by the end of 1943.

Allied Lend-Lease aid was a minor part of the overall war effort but was more important in the critical year of 1942. Lend-Lease made up about 7 percent of total Soviet production (the exact amount is disputed). Its contribution to winning the war may have been greater than that percent suggests because the large number of American planes, trucks, and jeeps delivered to the Red Army gave it a mobility it otherwise would have lacked.

To win public support, Moscow soft-pedaled its communist message, toning down the rhetoric of class war and the fight against class enemies. During the war, the government spoke more often of Mother Russia; this was the Great Patriotic War, not a war in defense of Soviet communism. The party halted its attempt to suppress the Russian Orthodox Church, which now led the propaganda charge against the Nazis.

The Communist party monopolized all media after the 1917 revolution. Its propaganda extolled Soviet achievements but ignored the debilitating purges of the 1930s and attempted to justify Stalin's 1939 alliance with Hitler. The communists' internationalism and belief in human progress and their anticapitalism and anti-imperialism eased their task, especially during the depression. After 1941 the communists became supporters of bourgeois (i.e., capitalist) nationalism and stressed their solidarity with the Allied struggle against fascism. Unseemly propaganda, however, was no monopoly of either the Nazis or the Soviets. In 1943 when Stalin disbanded the Comintern (the international communist organization led by Moscow) as a sign of goodwill, Britain lauded communist accomplishments while Hollywood produced films showing Russian society as very similar to American democracy.

Ironically, the overall impact of the war on the Soviet Union may have been to reinforce the Communist party's central role and to reinforce the Soviet system.

THE UNITED STATES

In the six years after 1939, American society underwent dramatic changes as it mobilized for war. Unemployment ceased, wages rose, men and women moved from farms to centers of war production, and 12,000,000 Americans entered the armed forces. People prospered as never before. Except for sporadic rationing, especially of durable goods such as automobiles and refrigerators, Americans lived much better in 1945 than in 1941. A major industrial power even in depression, the United States became the world's leading economic powerhouse with a military establishment dwarfing all others.

The United States was woefully unready for war. In 1939 the government spent about 1.5 percent of the gross national product on the military, compared to 16 percent for Germany and 25 percent for Japan. After war broke out in Europe, the Roosevelt administration took the first steps to prepare for a national defense. It allowed the Reconstruction Finance Corporation to provide credit to businesses producing armaments. The next month, July 1940, Congress authorized a two-ocean navy and expanded tonnage 70 percent. By 1945 the U.S. Navy surpassed all others by far. The army also benefited from the government's largesse. In August 1940 the Selective Training and Service Act provided for the conscription of 900,000 men for service of 12 months. The next year, the draft was for the "duration" (of the war) plus 6 months. By 1945 service personnel numbered 12,000,000. During these same years, the defense budget swelled from $1.5 billion to more than $100 billion.

Far from bankrupting the country, mobilization on this scale catapulted the United States into global leadership while transforming the lives of average Americans, regardless of race, gender, class, or place of residence. Spared from invasion and more than minor bombing, American society had a "good war," with little of the suffering so common in Europe and East Asia. Americans had fewer than 300,000 dead from all causes, less than 1 percent of all killed in the war.

At first, American businesses reluctantly produced arms. The public had blamed arms manufacturers for dragging the country into World War I.

.he war might be of short duration and not repay the costs of investing ~ ~w plants and machines. To encourage arms production, Washington offered credits and tax write-offs; it relaxed antitrust suits and dropped New Deal programs businesses opposed. As the President said, "Dr. Win the War" replaced "Dr. New Deal."

Unlike other major belligerents, the United States government was a federal system; it developed no central authority to plan war production. Perhaps Roosevelt preferred it that way; certainly, his style of administration was to create divided, overlapping authorities with imprecise guidelines, a practice not unlike Hitler's. Thus, a host of agencies flourished in Washington as businesses pursued contracts and the military and other agencies had the authorized money to spend.

With a large reserve of skilled, but unemployed workers, a vast network of railroads and riverways, and an extraordinary panoply of mineral ores, energy, and agricultural produce, the American economy had few bottlenecks. Nonetheless, with expenditures high and demand brisk, the allocation of resources often needed to be managed. In the fall of 1942 Roosevelt named James Byrnes, a close friend and fellow Democratic politician, as chief of the Office of Economic Stabilization. His responsibility was to arbitrate disputes among the myriad federal agencies, rather than to create an orderly central administration.

The wartime economy generated a cornucopia of war matériel. Roosevelt called for 50,000 planes in 1940 to informed disbelief; the industry produced over 300,000 by 1945. Shipbuilders launched 60,000,000 tons of naval and merchant ships, a quantity nearly equal to the world's total tonnage in 1939. Before the war American workers were already twice as productive as their German counterparts. They improved this achievement. The Pentagon (a term referring to the United States military establishment, but taken from its newly constructed, purportedly temporary military headquarters for the war) absorbed millions of citizens into the armed forces. At the same time, the number of industrial workers grew from 45,700,000 to 52,800,000 in a population of 140,000,000. The American gross national product soared from $88.6 billion in 1939 constant dollars to $135 billion by the end of the war, an annual increase of 15 percent, the highest growth rate in American history. American workers had more to spend in 1945 than ever before. They had guns and butter.

Labor unions increased their memberships and gained greater recognition as a normal part of doing business. A National War Labor Board created in 1942 with representation from business, unions, and the public tried to mediate disputes before they erupted into strikes. Farmers benefited from the growing world demand for food even as one in five rural workers left the farm for industry.

With wage increases established by governmental formulas, unions sought "fringe benefits" for workers, and business grudgingly responded with offers of paid vacations, health insurance, and other benefits—all of which contributed to the "security" of labor and the growth of a leisure culture after the war. The GI Bill, which offered educational, health, and housing loan benefits to veterans, further assured patriotism during the war and postwar prosperity. Americans fought not only to defeat fascism, but to build a better America.

Women poured into war industries. In 1945, 36 percent of the workforce were women, up from 25 percent in 1939. "Rosie the Riveter" was largely propaganda, and not the usual experience for women workers who took up more menial, less-well-paying temporary jobs. Nevertheless, during the war, women made economic progress and became more independent of paternal or other male control. As in the United Kingdom, whether the war contributed in the long run to women's liberation and the postwar feminist movement is contested.

What is impressive is the variety and extent of women's war-related activities. In the long term, the war may have contributed to a new consciousness among women, but during the war they faced discrimination based on marital status and age, and especially on race. Women's wages never reached that of men's. Many joined the armed forces, but they were not generally well-regarded by the military establishment or the public. Perhaps the most important advance for women came for those moving from an agrarian life into urban settings, where they enjoyed improved wages and greater social freedom. The "baby boom" after the war, which returned women to more domestic ways, may have been an important factor in reducing wartime gains. But that depends on how the viewer interprets women's interests and ambitions in the war years.

African American leadership hoped to use the war effort to improve life for black Americans. In 1940 the labor leader A. Philip Randolph began organizing a march on Washington. He especially wanted a federal requirement that all companies with federal government contracts give equal consideration in hiring regardless of race and that the armed forces not be segregated. Roosevelt partially met Randolph's demands by creating a Fair Employment Practices Committee. Although it lacked effective means of enforcement, the committee brought together like-minded reformers and nudged the civil rights movement forward. In 1942 James Farmer organized the Committee (later Congress) on Racial Equality (CORE), which more aggressively pushed for equal rights in public facilities, housing, and employment.

The military remained segregated, with black servicemen struggling to prove their worth. In time, the determination of black soldiers and the experiences of combat led some whites to support a desegregated armed forces. For example, in the Air Force black airmen had to prove their value against overwhelming odds, as the history of the 99th Fighter Squadron shows. In the Pacific, American blacks joined in the battle for Iwo Jima, though their original assignments did not include combat. Examples could be multiplied. Some white officers changed their evaluation of the combat effectiveness of African Americans, causing the military leadership in time to advocate desegregation, which President Harry S Truman finally ordered in 1947.

The war years witnessed a massive African American migration from the South into northern and western defense industries. But black in-migration often was resented by whites who disliked the competition for jobs and housing. A shortage of housing and inadequate public facilities helped turn racism into overt violence. A race riot in Detroit in June 1943 ended with 25 African Americans and 9 whites dead. Similar riots occurred in other cities as well. Tensions greeted blacks almost everywhere they entered previously white-only work places. In Mobile, Alabama, for example, white shipworkers threatened to shut down the shipbuilding works when blacks entered the workforce, but government intervention forced a settlement.

Ethnic prejudice extended to other groups such as Italian Americans and Jews, but especially to Japanese Americans. Many Italian Americans were briefly interned in California when the United States entered the war. Public opinion began to change, however, as leaders such as Fiorello La Guardia, mayor of New York City, countered anti-Italian and anti-Catholic sentiments with their support for the war. Anti-Semitism was also prominent, even in urban areas such as New York with numerous Jews. Jews were routinely excluded from social clubs and public beaches. But the growing public awareness of the excesses of Nazi racism and anti-Semitism made overt anti-Semitism less acceptable in many circles.

Only Japanese Americans experienced prolonged loss of basic rights: 127,000 Japanese Americans, mostly Californians, were thrown into "relocation" centers without trial, deprived of their property, and all normal constitutional rights—all because of racial hysteria whipped up by superpatriots in the American West, who insisted that the Japanese Americans could not be trusted. At first, the Supreme Court refused to hear their case, but in 1944 it ruled that these Japanese Americans could not be detained without evidence of disloyalty. This finally brought the internment camps to a close, but without restitution of lost property or reparations for the period of internment. Anti-Japanese phobia even grew during the war. A 1944 Gallup poll showed that 13 percent of Americans believed that all Japanese should be exterminated. Japanese Canadians were treated much the same. In Hawaii, on the other hand, Japanese Americans, who made up a third of the population, escaped the worst of mainland racism. About 1 percent of them were "relocated." Eventually, the army permitted Japanese Americans to enter the 442nd Regimental Combat Team. It fought in Italy and was the war's most decorated unit.

Roosevelt approached propaganda differently than other world leaders. He used press conferences and fireside chats to get his message across. The 1940 presidential campaign, the fall of France, and the battle of Britain unleashed a great public debate over the United States' world role. The debate continued into 1941 when aid to Britain and Lend-Lease was the issue. In the end, Pearl Harbor did what propaganda could not do by galvanizing American support for the war.

In June 1942 Roosevelt took a more direct approach by establishing an Office of War Information (OWI) to promote propaganda (a word Americans studiously avoided), though Congress limited its domestic activities. Perhaps this explains why throughout the war, Gallup opinion polls showed that the American public was uninformed about the issues of the war. The OWI's activities were not coordinated with military propaganda and wartime strategies, making it less effective than British propaganda. Because it had responsibility for promoting Hollywood films abroad, its choices in films, and the guidelines it produced, greatly influenced wartime movie production. The United States military also produced films for "training" soldiers and educating them on the issues of the war. The most famous of these was Frank Capra's *Why We Fight* series, which covered a pro-Rooseveltian view of the origins of the war and of the contribution of the Allies in winning it.

Although much of the world in 1945 was devastated, filled with burned out cities, mourning millions of dead, and trying to care for millions of refugees, Americans had a different experience. There were the dead and wounded, but on the whole Americans felt this had been a "good war," good in its defeat of Nazism and aggression. The United States had made "progress" in raising its standard of living and sharing it more broadly, especially in benefits extended to veterans. It was secure and respected abroad. The publisher of *Time* and *Life* magazines, Henry Luce, greeted the new age as the American Century.

JAPAN

Although Japan joined the Axis in September 1940, it was not a totalitarian fascist state comparable to Germany or Italy. A few intellectuals were attracted to European fascist ideas, but Japan had no mass fascist party. There were no concentration camps, though prisoner of war camps rivaled those of Germany in their brutality. Political parties were banned after 1940, but in 1942 parliamentary elections, opposition candidates won a few seats.

On the other hand, a tradition of social discipline and respect for superiors when coupled with political suppression of dissent reduced opposition to a minimum and encouraged passivity and submissiveness. The government controlled the press, film, and radio and used them to cultivate public support of war after 1937. Indoctrination also came through the schools and the glorification of the military. It was primarily the spectacular victories of late 1941 and early 1942, however, that generated popular enthusiasm for the war.

The war years in Japan are often referred to as a "dark valley," not because of economic deprivation and American bombing, but because they were years of disgrace and failure. They were also years of transformation, and not simply because they ended in an American occupation with its own program of reforms.

The Japanese state had long played an active role in the economy, but it lacked the technical skills, capital, and time needed to mobilize the basic raw materials such as oil, bauxite, tin, rubber, and nickel as well as rice and other agricultural products found in conquered areas of Southeast Asia. By 1943, American submarines began to cut off all overseas trade. This coincided with more intense economic mobilization and state planning, especially after the string of military disasters at the end of 1942 and in early 1943. Arms production dramatically increased.

General Hideki Tojo, prime minister from October 1941 until July 1944, gained more control over industry than previous leaders, but he still had to work with the seven great industrial firms (zaibatsu); they did not always agree with the government's priorities. In an effort to increase the supply of labor, Tojo reversed previous policies by conscripting unmarried women under age 25 and encouraging other women to work outside the home. New employment patterns such as permanent job security and wages based on seniority were introduced as an enticement for the support of labor.

In the last year of the war, the Japanese people went through severe physical and psychological strains. At the front, the war intensified and the killing mounted; kamikaze missions were introduced in the fall of 1944. In

October, American bombing missions began pounding the islands. On March 9, 1945, 334 B-29s dropped 2,000 tons on Tokyo, killing 84,000 and injuring 41,000 more. Residents fled the cities. By summer, there were few targets left. The military prepared for resistance in Japan itself. Then the end came with the destruction of Hiroshima and Nagasaki.

CONCLUSION

Home-front experiences varied greatly from country to country. But there are some general conclusions. World War II does not support the notion that democracies are inferior to dictatorships in their war-making capacities. In 1941, Allied and Axis war production was nearly equal. By 1944 the Allied arms production was three times that of the Axis. In each country, regardless of when it entered the war and what its political system was, the war intensified state power. It brought about greater interaction among businessmen, managers, government, and labor. Democratic populations bore the cost of war as much as regimented ones.

Successful war mobilization was also a function of events. The United Kingdom and the United States shared many common social and political habits, but the Americans lacked the stimulus to an all-out effort for survival during the battle of Britain and the threat of invasion. Neither faced the long-term enslavement and eventual extermination of the Slavs. On the other hand, had Germany actually prepared for total war before 1939, the war might have concluded in 1941 before Pearl Harbor and American participation in the war.

Most importantly, the history of home fronts is the experiences of those who lived through those years. This history is in suffering the terrors of bombing, prisoners of war and death camps, in homelessness and statelessness, and in flight from compulsory labor and from genocide. It is in getting along and submitting to the decisions of governments. It is in relocating, in learning to deal with new social settings, and in working long hours in arms factories. And much more. There was no single "home front." It was the daily life of millions throughout the world.

5

Resistance Movements in Europe

Resistance to foreign occupation was stronger in World War II than in previous conflicts. This was in part because the war was an ideological struggle. Sometimes national survival was at stake. The war also saw more intensive war effort on all sides. Resistance had many faces. It could be a political movement, or an expression of individual outrage with little political content, or simply acts of sabotage and espionage. Resistance in World War II had all these meanings, and others as well.

Although widespread, resistance took place within national contexts and for that reason varied greatly from country to country. Each nation has seen its resistance to occupation as a unique aspect of its own history and often invested the resistance story with significance about the character of its own people. Resistance in World War II was, in most cases, against a common enemy, the Germans. The Nazis pursued different policies of war and occupation in eastern than western Europe, but everywhere the Germans infringed on national sovereignty and exploited labor and looted the national wealth and resources of occupied countries.

Resistance as a political movement often went beyond sabotage and harassment of the oppressor. Many resistance efforts sought to build a broad political and social consensus, linked with a fighting force, in order to restore national honor and sovereignty through national liberation. Domestic reform and fighting power were needed to establish legitimacy at home and with Allied governments. Thus, some resistance movements echoed Allied propaganda that the war aimed at a new world order of international cooperation without the scourge of war. At home, resistance leaders often advocated social reform, economic opportunities, and political unity in order to eliminate the causes of fascism.

The prominence of resistance movements, as opposed to Allied-sponsored sabotage or individual acts of violence against the enemy, is striking because organized resistance to occupation armies had no chance to achieve victory without massive external military invasion. Totalitarian police states and the nature of contemporary armaments eliminated civilians as decisive fighting forces. For this reason, the political and social significance of resistance surpassed its military importance.

RESISTANCE IN NORTHWESTERN EUROPE

In northwest Europe those countries whose legitimate governments escaped to London, Norway, the Netherlands, and later Belgium, provided the moral and legal basis for resistance. This made unnecessary the creation of anticollaborationist resistance movements looking forward to the establishment of new regimes after liberation.

In Norway, attacks on Germans came from an officially sponsored military group, Milorg. One of its most successful exploits was the sabotage of a heavy water plant in 1943 to disrupt the German atomic bomb project. Other resistance in Norway took the form of noncooperation, refusal to support the collaborationist government of Vidkun Quisling, and disobedience of Nazi instructions. The Lutheran church publicly condemned collaboration; the Norwegian Supreme Court discontinued its sessions so as not to have to submit to Nazi influence. Liberation brought few social or political changes as prewar patterns reemerged. Quisling and 23 others were executed, and 18,000 Norwegians received prison sentences for crimes committed under the occupation authorities. No other country purged itself of collaborators so thoroughly. King Haakon VII and his government returned from exile in the United Kingdom. With that, political life resumed its prewar patterns.

Denmark suffered less at German hands than any occupied country, as it had little military significance except as a gateway to Norway, and the German military government was sympathetic to the population. Only after 1942 did German demands become oppressive. Resistance was generally limited to relaying intelligence to the British or assisting the country's Jewish citizens to escape to Sweden. Resistance involved no demands for domestic political change, as the national elections of 1943 indicated.

Lacking mountains and remote countrysides, the Netherlands did not have terrain suitable for guerrilla activities. Widespread resistance, however, developed. An underground press published newspapers; over 150 appeared by 1943. The Dutch also met German occupation with strikes, work slowdowns, and noncompliance with rules. A quickly crushed trade union strike in 1941 against anti-Jewish regulations showed the difficulties of urban resistance. Some Dutch also risked their lives by hiding Jews. The roundup of Jews in the Netherlands was, however, more comprehensive than anywhere else in western Europe. Dutch espionage and sabotage efforts suffered a particular tragedy when the Germans penetrated the Dutch branch of the British SOE (Strategic Operations Executive in charge of underground activities) between March 1942 and November 1943. Known as *Englandspiel*, this German coup led to the arrest of 54 agents as well as Dutch civilians and RAF crewmen. As in Scandinavia, liberation restored the political structures of the 1930s. Queen Wilhelmina and the cabinet returned from Great Britain at the time of liberation. The government was reorganized to include representatives from resistance parties.

FRENCH RESISTANCE

France is often identified as the home of resistance. In fact, because the first year of German occupation was relatively mild and political fissures within France were deep, resistance developed slowly. Until June 1941 the French communists accepted Moscow's view that they should stand aside from the imperialist war between Britain and Germany. Many leading socialist and liberal politicians either fled to southern France or abroad, or withdrew from public life. On the right, many hated Britain as much as Germany. There was a plethora of fascist organizations; some of their leaders openly admired the Third Reich for its youthfulness and vigor. Significant organized resistance began only when Nazi exploitation stiffened after 1941 and the prospect of quick Axis victory faded.

Among the first resisters was Charles de Gaulle. Fleeing to England immediately after the fall of France, he asserted the illegitimacy of the Vichy government and formed the British-financed Free French, though at first he failed to attract many French supporters. London opened the BBC's airwaves for him, though it is doubtful that very many Frenchmen heard his famous message that "France has lost a battle, but France has not lost the war."

Resisters tended to come from among lower middle-class professionals such as teachers and lawyers, or from small property owners. Women were also very active, taking advantage of German stereotypes that they were harmless, passive females. Rural guerrillas, the *maquis*, were often young men escaping compulsory labor service in Germany, though others were trained by the SOE and joined regular military forces during the liberation. Urban working-class men, unless sought by the police, were less often part of the resistance, which is not surprising given the French 10-hour work day and the few resources workers had to fall back on.

To the politically organized and armed resistance must be added the individual deeds of sabotage, espionage, and anti-German actions. Banned national holidays were silently celebrated in public. Derailed trains or the assassination of Germans risked, however, brutal German retaliation, usually by shooting randomly seized hostages.

The value of sabotage and espionage to winning the war is hard to assess. The psychological impact of doing something, however, undoubtedly helped maintain a resistance morale, even if the contribution to winning the war was remote. Never was resistance popular, however. Most Frenchmen rarely saw German troops or the Gestapo. French police and administrators ran the country's administration, even after the Germans occupied the entire country in November 1942.

By 1943 General Charles de Gaulle gained the support of Free French military commanders and many French colonial subjects. To become recognized as a leader within France he accepted the program of reform of the united National Council of Resistance (Conseil National de la Résistance, CNR). The CNR wanted more than an expulsion of the Germans. Its economic and social program embodied many ideas from the ill-fated 1936 Popular Front government. These included a pension system for retired workers, a 40-hour work week, payments to families with children, paid vacations, and the benefits of education for the working and lower classes. It would nationalize large firms, especially those of collaborators such as the automobile manufacturer Renault. It would establish central government planning to modernize French industry and agriculture.

The resistance played an active role during the liberation of France. The *maquis*, engaged the Wehrmacht, though never decisively. In the Vercors in southeastern France, 3,500 fighters in June 1944 held off two German divisions for a month and a half before being annihilated. In western France 200,000 French Forces of the Interior (the combined armed resistance) attacked Germans behind the lines during the Allied invasion.

The resistance also advocated a united Europe in order to eliminate the threat of a postwar German military resurgence. Resistance leaders opined that an economically integrated Europe would be more prosperous, and one in which Germany would lack the ability to make war. For French colonies, the CNR promised greater self-determination.

During the liberation of France, de Gaulle managed to prevent a communist takeover of the country, as he placed men loyal to himself in key administrative positions. He proclaimed that the republic had never been abolished, though elections on October 21, 1945, in which women voted for the first time, resulted in a strong swing toward resistance parties—communist, socialist, and a new Catholic democratic party. Their fragile unity was soon eroded, and politics returned to prewar patterns.

A purge of collaborators took the lives of more than 10,000 men and women. The Vichy prime minister Pierre Laval was sentenced to death. The death sentence of Henri-Philippe Pétain, the head of state in the Vichy regime, was commuted to life imprisonment. These events did not, however, eliminate the sorry record of collaboration from French public life.

RESISTANCE IN ITALY BEFORE AND AFTER FASCISM

Resistance in Italy goes back to 1922 when Mussolini and his Fascist party entered the government. His dictatorship evolved more slowly than that of the Nazis in Germany, and the monarchy as well as the Catholic church always retained some independence. Opposition parties were banned, however, and the Italian secret police, OVRA, infiltrated their memberships and wiped out organized resistance. Because Mussolini's government was internationally recognized, antifascists received no foreign support, except from the Soviet Union. In addition, the fascists portrayed opposition as unpatriotic.

Mussolini's military ambitions, especially after his entry into the war in June 1940, changed that. The war in Africa was costly in lives and treasure, contributing to increased discontent with the regime.

Even so, resistance remained insignificant until Allied military advances fueled hope for success. A group of communists, socialists, and liberals formed a Committee of Action in France around a program of getting out of the war and restoring of political freedoms. As the Allies advanced in Africa, resistance spread, with strikes in 1942 and 1943. In 1943 a coalition of resistance groups formed within Italy and the Christian Democratic party was reconstituted.

The Allied invasion of Sicily in July 1943 led to Mussolini's arrest and Italy's withdrawal from the war. Mussolini's successor, Pietro Badoglio, had to accept unconditional surrender and an Anglo-American military occupation. Anticipating the surrender, the Germans quickly occupied much of the country and reinstalled Mussolini in a puppet government. Discredited, the fascist regime had, however, lost its legitimacy. In this transformed political environment, resistance, armed and otherwise, sprang up throughout the country. In the north, Committees of National Liberation formed clandestine governments uniting various social classes in the struggle against German labor quotas and arrests. By 1944 they fielded more than 100,000 partisans and received Allied military supplies.

When the Allied campaign in Italy stalled in the winter of 1943–1944, partisan guerrilla attacks on Germans grew steadily. In the south some resistance groups continued to cooperate with the ex-fascist Badoglio, but in the north leftists and communists dominated. They wanted deep social and economic reforms, including the redistribution of land, the nationalization of large businesses, and the purging of fascists from government. The Christian Democrats also advocated similar radical measures. When the war ended, the Allies, including the Soviet Union, disregarded the resistance program. Factionalism and a punitive peace condemned it to postwar ineffectiveness.

RESISTANCE IN EASTERN EUROPE

Throughout occupied eastern Europe, the Germans' ultimate goal was to expunge the state and people. There were few opportunities to collaborate. There was only resistance or submission, if not enslavement or death. This was in contrast to western Europe where German occupation and repression was less severe.

Czechoslovakia

The first resistance to occupation came in Czechoslovakia, which became a German protectorate in March 1939. Led by Eduard Benes, the president until his resignation after the Munich Agreement, former soldiers and political leaders tried to maintain a semblance of national identity. The intensity of German control allowed them to do little beyond circulating newspapers and gathering intelligence for the Allies. In May 1942, the Czech underground did manage to assassinate Reinhard Heydrich, the "protector" of Bohemia and Moravia who had reached prominence within the SS and was one of the principal organizers of the genocide of Jews. In retaliation, the Germans obliterated the village of Lidice, murdering 198 men, sending its women to concentration camps, and carrying the children off to Germany. The Czech resistance never dared another such attack on Germans. It became weak, limiting its activities for the most part in providing intelligence information to the Allies. An uprising in Prague helped the Soviet army drive the Germans from the country, but otherwise, the resistance within the country had little impact on its liberation.

Slovakia, the eastern part of Czechoslovakia, became a nominally independent state, but one very much under German domination. Slovak dissatisfaction with these conditions led many to fight on the side of the Red Army after 1941, and briefly toward the end of the war Slovaks attempted to gain recognition from Stalin for an independent Slovakia. An uprising in late 1944 and early 1945 illustrates disgust with the collaborationist government of Josef Tiso, but also marks the end of the dream of independence when the Red Army restored Slovakia to the prewar Czechoslovakian state.

Poland

Poland had the most active resistance in the east. A government-in-exile was led by Wladsylaw Sikorski, a retired general and moderate liberal. A Polish Home Army formed from among soldiers who had managed to escape German capture. It fought throughout the war. After June 1941, many resistance movements in Europe included communists, but the division of Poland between Germany and the Soviet Union in 1939 precluded such an alliance. After June 1941, Moscow extended recognition to the exiled Polish government, but that made little difference in Poland, all of which fell under German domination. For a while, Sikorski had hopes of forming a Polish army in Russia to fight the Germans. Many roadblocks arose in the negotiation, recruitment, and arming of Polish troops. Above all, Stalin was unwilling to promise a restoration of Poland's prewar boundaries. Some of the troops raised in the Soviet Union were eventually evacuated to British-held Persia and fought in Italy along with other Polish units.

Relations between Moscow and the London Polish government-in-exile took a sharp turn for the worse in April 1943 with the discovery of the mass grave of 4,400 Polish officers murdered in the Katyn forest near Smolensk, a Russian city. When Sikorski asked for an investigation, Moscow broke off diplomatic relations. For the remainder of the war Russo-Polish relations festered as one of the most difficult sores in the grand alliance. Only in 1990 did the Russian government accept responsibility for the crime.

Inside their occupied country, the Poles fell back on their own limited resources. In spite of unparalleled difficulties, they established a secret state under the very nose of the German authorities. Underground policemen arrested Polish citizens guilty of Polish crimes, who were then tried by underground courts and, if found guilty, sentenced to serve time in underground prisons. The Germans set about to destroy Poland's educated classes by abolishing all but elementary education for Poles, closing universities, seminaries, and all other institutions of higher education. Underground schools soon opened, however, and the University of Warsaw secretly graduated students.

The Poles' most impressive accomplishment was the training and maintaining of an underground army, the Home Army, under the command of Tadeusz Komorowski. Between 1940 and 1944, they prepared for a general uprising against the Germans. As the war drew to an end and the Russians advanced into Poland, the Polish government reasoned that the Home Army should launch its own operations, joining with other Allied forces to free their own country. Their contribution to Germany's defeat would help secure a place at the peace settlement as an independent state.

On August 1, 1944, as Soviet troops approached Warsaw, the Home Army rose up against the Germans, liberating most of the city with 50,000 armed fighters. Once victory was in their grasp, the Soviets wanted the Polish resistance crushed to make way for Soviet dominance in postwar Poland. The Russians, whose propaganda had encouraged open resistance, halted on the east bank of the Vistula opposite the Polish capital, isolating the newly risen Polish army to stand alone against the Germans. The German Waffen SS counterattacked, completely destroying the Home Army in two months of fighting. It then systematically demolished what remained of the city. With that, the Polish resistance ceased to exist, as did any major anticommunist forces in Poland. The Polish population did not forget the Soviet role in the suppression of resistance, a bitter legacy that seethed below the surface during the Cold War and contributed to anticommunist and anti-Russian movement of the 1980s

The Soviet Union

Resistance behind the German military frontier in the Soviet Union began soon after the invasion, fed by the harsh, racist occupation. Soviet partisans, often regulars as well as members of the Communist party, differed from other resistance fighters in that they were backed and coordinated by the state. Still, the anti-Soviet local population often treated them little better than the Germans. Beginning in 1942, the Soviet government trained and equipped partisans and directed them, especially in disrupting German communications. Their total number may have exceeded 200,000, but probably not 700,000 or 1,000,000 as sometimes claimed. Certainly their impact was not as great as their numbers, largely due to popular hostility. Jewish partisans also organized and fought against the Germans.

Yugoslavia

As in Poland, the Axis takeover of Yugoslavia in April 1941 threatened the existence of the state and much of its population. The country was partitioned among several Axis states, with Germany and Italy annexing or administering the largest portions. An independent state of Croatia was created, whose Ustasa party in 1941 murdered some 2,000,000 Serbs and other ethnic "undesirables."

Yugoslav, or rather Serb, resistance began immediately. Colonel Draza Mihailovic, a Serb officer in the Royal Yugoslav Army, organized former soldiers into armed bands (Chetniks). Ethnic tensions had always been high; they now led to the breakup of the Yugoslav army. The government-in-exile, headed by the teenaged Peter II, tried to turn Mihailovic into an anti-German force, but lacking communications and direct contact with the Chetniks, no one among the Allies could direct their activities or even determine their effectiveness.

Mihailovic's nemesis, the communist Croat Josip Broz, returned to Yugoslavia in the spring of 1941 from fighting in the Spanish Civil War and a sojourn in Moscow. Relations between Broz, who had the nom de guerre of Tito, and Mihailovic were never good. Tito may have offered to join a national, that is, Yugoslav front against the Axis. If so, the Serbian Chetniks did not welcome the communists with their internationalism and revolutionary program. Whatever, Tito's partisans and Mihailovic's men fought separate battles against the Germans. Sometimes they fought each other.

In late 1941 the British discovered through their agents in Yugoslavia that the Chetniks were not effectively taking on the Germans. Meanwhile, the previously unknown partisans of Tito were found to be harassing the Germans and growing in numbers. Because of the partisans' strength, the German Wehrmacht kept fifteen or more divisions in the country throughout the war. It waged four campaigns in a fruitless effort to destroy them. No other armed resistance achieved that level of success.

Because of Tito's record, the British and American governments in 1943 withdrew support from the Chetniks and began sending military aid to the partisans. Italy's surrender in September 1943 ended their struggle with the Italian Army and brought the partisans into direct contact with the Allies. Though they had to endure yet one more campaign by the Germans, by the next year they could field a force of 250,000 men and women.

King Peter's government in London and Tito, under British pressure, formed a coalition government in June 1944. But Tito had no intentions of allowing a few Serbian monarchists to thwart his revolutionary program. When the war ended, Tito's forces had not only been the primary force in driving the Germans out—and averting a Soviet occupation—Tito was premier and the partisans held over three fourths of the seats in the government's cabinet. No other resistance movement in Europe did so much to liberate itself and become the basis of the postwar state. Tito's prestige at home and abroad assured him of unrivaled power for decades to come. Mihailovic was tried and executed as a collaborator with the Germans.

Greece

Resistance in Greece paralleled that in Yugoslavia. Two main rival groups, the National Liberation Front (EAM) under communist leadership and the National Democratic Greek Union (EDES) led by Napoleon Zervas, contended for control over the country in what amounted to a civil war after 1943. The British favored the reestablishment of the monarchy and intervened militarily to drive out the Germans and to prop up the monarchy. When the Germans evacuated the country in September 1944, fighting among the Greeks quickened. A cease-fire was arranged in early 1945, but civil war broke out again the next year. Thus, unlike Yugoslavia, the Greek resistance led to greater disunity and protracted conflict over the country's political future that continued into the late 1940s. Indeed, it was the prospect of communist success in Greece and Turkey after the war that led the United States to announce the Truman Doctrine and pledge to fight communist invasion or insurgency in Europe. Romania and Bulgaria, allies of Germany, experienced no significant internal resistance.

THE GERMAN OPPOSITION TO HITLER

The importance of German resistance to the National Socialist regime remains controversial. Some prefer to call it opposition, because many opposed the regime's policies, especially the continuation of the war, rather than the regime itself. Others would limit the word resistance to the struggle against an occupying force. Such restrictions seem unwarranted. There were Germans deeply committed out of moral outrage, religious conviction, and simple human decency to removing the scourge of Nazism from Germany and Europe. They came from all walks of life. Because of the Gestapo's tight control and a developed infrastructure of concentration camps and official terror, any kind of opposition was difficult. Armed resistance was not a realistic option. Attempts to assassinate Hitler would have to come from persons with access to him, and that was difficult, given the security surrounding him.

Initially, anti-Nazi opposition continued the political struggle begun during the 1933 Nazi takeover when the Communist party and later the Social Democratic party and their organizations were outlawed. That opposition soon faded under intense police suppression. The Nazi leadership also successfully wrapped its early successes in foreign affairs and an apparent economic recovery in the patriotic guise of national rebirth. Many sectors of German society, big business, other former political parties, the peasantry, the urban middle classes, and the main elements of the churches either endorsed, or at least accepted the changes. When they did not, they withdrew into private life. Inner migration, it was called. Resistance posed no serious threat to the Third Reich.

Protests and expression of opposition existed. There were occasional industrial actions in working-class districts of major cities. But only rarely did they involve strikes or sabotage. Occasionally, groups like the White Rose, a Christian student group at the University of Munich, attempted to publicize the regime's crimes. In 1942 its leaders, Sophie and Hans Scholl, and nearly a hundred associates were arrested. Many were beheaded. Such heroic and admirable acts of protest as the White Rose made no impact on society or on the course of the war. Other forms of protest had some effect, perhaps none more so than disaffected army officers such as Friedrich Paulus, who surrendered the German Sixth Army at Stalingrad and joined the Soviet-sponsored National Committee for Free Germany. It broadcast anti-Hitler propaganda and encouraged soldiers to desert.

The state Lutheran Church and the German Catholic Church at times spoke out against some National Socialist policies. In 1934 when the Nazis tried to force the Lutherans to remove all non-Aryans from the church, a group of clergy and laymen formed the dissenting Confessing Church. Many of these were harassed by the Gestapo or thrown into concentration camps. Some were executed. World War I U-boat captain and pastor Martin Niemöller railed against the regime and on one occasion personally confronted Hitler. The theologian Dietrich Bonhoeffer was involved in the conspiracy against Hitler and was killed in the last days of the war.

German Catholics were a minority in Germany with a history of political opposition to the Reich's government. But they, too, provided little resistance, aside from occasional rebukes by some bishops and the bravery of isolated priests. As did the Protestants, they generally accepted the authoritarian nature of the government, even appreciating its anticommunism. It is true that Pope Pius XI condemned the Nazi glorification of race, but nothing was done for Jews, unless they were in the churches. Some church leaders condemned the euthanasia campaign of 1939, but not the genocide after 1941.

Effective resistance in Germany required the assassination of Hitler and a coup d'état. Only military leaders or high civil officials with access to the Führer could do that. Early right-wing opponents of Nazism included notables such as Carl Goerdeler and Ludwig Beck. Goerdeler, onetime economic advisor to Hitler, had resigned as mayor of Leipzig in 1937 in protest of Nazi policies. He had contacts in England and tried in vain to warn the British of Hitler's true intentions. General Beck, Chief of the German General Staff, resigned to protest Hitler's plans for war against Czechoslovakia in 1938. Afterwards, he led the Black Orchestra (Schwarze Kapelle), the nickname given to the group of conspirators by the Gestapo. The popularity of the unexpected, spectacular German military victories of 1939 and 1940 initially undercut their efforts, but the failure of Operation Barbarossa and the growing ferocity of racial war in the east after 1941 renewed opposition to Hitler's policies.

Many of the ideas of this elite opposition were unrealistic, and its conspiracy was amateurish. For example, it was thought that a negotiated peace could leave Germany united with Austria, or that the Western Allies could be played off against the Soviet Union. Even the announcement of unconditional surrender in January 1943 did not end such fantasies, though the determination to act deepened as genocide got into high gear, the bombing of Germany intensified, and the Red Army approached the Reich. These facts support the opposition's critics that it talked of resistance only when the country's defeat was assured.

There were attempts at assassination. General Henning von Treschkow placed a bomb in Hitler's airplane in March 1943, but it failed to go off. In 1944 the conspirators arranged a detailed plan for a coup by a number of officers and devised a shadow government. Claus von Stauffenberg, a staff officer with access to Hitler, smuggled a bomb into the Führer's headquarters. This bomb exploded but failed to kill the dictator. News of Hitler's survival caused the carefully laid scheme to unravel. Overwhelmingly, German officers backed Hitler. Those who did not support Hitler either committed suicide or were executed. About 5,000 died as the Gestapo took its revenge after the failed 1944 assassination attempt.

JEWISH RESISTANCE

Contrary to some popular beliefs, there was a Jewish resistance to Nazi genocide, and there was active Jewish participation in national resistance

movements. Jews faced many difficulties in resistance. No one was prepared for the ferocity and ruthlessness of Hitler's "Final Solution." There
was no precedent for genocide (indeed, the word itself first appeared in
1943). Jews had long suffered segregation into ghettos, civil disabilities, ex-
pulsions, and pogroms (massacres). But in one way or another, the community had survived, often by securing friends in high places and strictly
adhering to gentile authorities. In the more secularized, liberal environment
of early twentieth-century Germany, many Jews assimilated into German
culture and society. None of these traditional methods worked against the
radical, Nazi anti-Semites whose goal was a Germany "cleansed" of Jews
and a world with no Jews. Never before had Jews faced such a determined
enemy, now in control of an industrialized, bureaucratic state.

Under the Nazi regime in occupied Europe, Jews were identified and, in
the east, forced into ghettos. Few non-Jews offered help; many in fact either
stood aside or supported the removal of Jews from society (if not their murder). Jewish refugees were "stateless," with no national government to represent them. At one time or another, most European nation-states either
volunteered to send, willingly sent, or acquiesced in sending their Jewish
citizens to their almost certain deaths. Unlike occupied countries, Jews
could not prepare to fight the undeclared war of annihilation. They lacked
armies and received no support from the Allies.

Organized, officially sponsored genocide, what the Nazis called the "Final Solution," began in 1941. Jews were transported to "resettlement"
camps and later slaughtered in mass executions. In the east, where most
Jews lived, they lacked resources beyond the walls of their own ghetto.
News of the killings in the death camps spread slowly and was often not believed.

Nonetheless, Jews resisted. Some reaffirmed religious traditions and
kept records as witnesses. Some sabotaged war production and occasionally organized strikes. In western Europe, they joined national movements
of resistance in numbers greater than their proportion of the population. In
eastern Europe, they battled as guerrillas to protect themselves and harass
the Germans and their confederates. As prisoners in death camps, they re-
belled, as in Treblinka in August 1943 and at Sobibor later that October.
They resisted in their ghettos, most notably in Warsaw, but also in Vilna,
Cracow, Lodz and in more than 100 uprisings elsewhere as well.

When the Warsaw ghetto population was reduced to fewer than 70,000
from an original 400,000, the Jewish Fighting Organization (ZOB) killed
about 50 German soldiers in January 1943. Without Allied support or aid
from the Polish resistance, the ZOB, under the youthful leadership of Mor-

dechai Anielewicz, prepared for the final German assault. It came on April 19 when 2,000 SS men, many of whom were not Germans, assaulted the ghetto with a tank, armored cars, and flamethrowers. The ZOB drove them back. The SS regrouped and counterattacked with more force. After three weeks of resistance, the ghetto was crushed, though several ZOB fighters escaped through the sewers.Their heroism wiped out the lie that Jews accepted their fate passively.

THE VATICAN AND RESISTANCE

The absence of overt resistance from the Vatican has been much criticized, by Catholics as well as others. Pius XII, elected pope in March 1939, was a trained diplomat who had spent his earlier career in Germany. He had worked to avoid war, but favored Germany's campaign against Bolshevism, which Hitler claimed to be fighting. The pope was also compromised by his support of fascist regimes, especially that in Croatia, where the Catholic hierarchy, with the pope's knowledge, backed the Ustasa genocide against Serbian Orthodox Christians.

Throughout the war, however, the Vatican retained a measure of independence through its newspaper and radio. Belligerent diplomats could meet one another in the Vatican and through its links to all European countries benefit from its flow of information. This, however, has suggested to the critics that had the Vatican denounced genocide (which it knew about) and the bestial German occupation, it might have ameliorated the crimes of the Nazi regime. On the other hand, the Dutch Catholic hierarchy's condemnation of Jewish deportations in 1943 led to the immediate arrest of Jewish Catholics.

Perhaps neutral, behind-the-scenes diplomacy achieved more than ostentatious denunciations. On occasion, the Vatican condemned aggression, the sufferings caused by war, and the persecutions of ethnic groups, but only in general terms. Genocide of Jews was never publicly decried. The Church helped many victims of the Nazis, but it also aided Nazis after the war and never excommunicated prominent fascist Catholics, such as Hitler and Mussolini, or those who collaborated with them.

Of course, individual Catholics, priests, and lay persons alike, as well as many non-Catholics, showed great personal courage in resisting fascism. But these were individual acts of conscience rather than organized Christian resistance.

CONCLUSION

Historians are not agreed on the importance of resistance movements. Their military role was not decisive, though in the case of Yugoslavia, the resistance played a significant role in military operations. Sabotage and intelligence gathering, however, often provided the Allies considerable assistance, as during the Normandy invasion of France.

In some cases, the potential postwar political role of resistance was great. Because resisters tended to be on the political left in western Europe and anti-Soviet in the east, as in Poland for instance, the Allies had little reason to support their goals. Nonetheless, resistance movements in western Europe, especially France and Italy where coalitions of resistance parties won elections, nudged reforms forward as in the case of social welfare and the rights of women.

In the postwar world, the fact of resistance helped to legitimize a greater degree of democracy and improved social welfare. That resisters were a minority is true, but a determined minority can redirect a society's political culture. In countries such as France and Norway, one's ties to the resistance, or to collaboration, defined political categories for years after the war. Also, open resistance and the defeat of the fascist governments helped discredit the authoritarian, chauvinist, and racist elements in European societies. Although the European resistance movements failed to link up across national lines, they left a heritage that Europe must never again permit a catastrophe on the scale of World War II.

6

The Continuing Significance of World War II

During the six years between Germany's invasion of Poland on September 1, 1939, and the Japanese surrender aboard the U.S.S. *Missouri* on September 2, 1945, the world experienced unprecedented revolutions. Prewar harbingers were evident, and the transformations that took place may have occurred regardless, yet many characteristics of the world after 1945 are an outcome of the war. The decline of Europe as the focus of the globe's military and economic power was predicted, but it was not inevitable had Europe not exhausted itself in a binge of destruction. Military and commercial competition among European nations was the engine that drove the continent to global dominion during the nineteenth century. During World War II, it did the reverse. Changing that pattern to cooperation would not be easy.

That an American military presence would extend from Berlin around the earth to China and into the Indian Ocean was something even American leaders had not yet absorbed in 1945. That the world was on the verge of its greatest economic expansion would have struck 1945 observers as utopian in the extreme. That European colonial empires in Africa and Asia would implode and virtually disappear within a generation seemed unlikely.

There were prewar visions of atomic weapons and atomic-generated energy; jet planes, rockets, and other technological marvels of 1945 were on the design boards, but others realized by war's end, such as computers, had seemed fantasy before, relegated to comic books.

Atrocities and cruelties abound in human history, but deliberate, organized, industrialized, methodical killing of millions of fellow citizens, with wide support, in the heart of "civilization," was new. That experience—compounded by more than 55,000,000 dead, ancient cities leveled, and environments damaged—pierced and undermined the core foundations of Western civilization's culture and power.

In some respects, from the distance of more than half a century, the impact of World War II has receded. The world, or at least the "West," has adjusted to the end of directly ruled imperial colonies. The Cold War is over; fascist, communist, and other forms of authoritarian rule are discredited. International cooperation has strengthened, even if the level of violence has not subsided. Much of the wartime technological accomplishments have been turned to better-than-expected purposes, whether it is rapid flight across the oceans, women and men in space stations, global communications open to all, or myriad daily domestic conveniences, such as microwave ovens or antibiotics. On the other hand, nuclear weapons exist in surfeit. Genocide, with its perpetrators and bystanders, continues as a daily fact, as do napalm and land mines. Biological and chemical weapons, although not used in World War II, loom over our future.

Some of the deepest fears the war aroused have not been realized. Yet, World War II remains *the* war in the popular consciousness of much of the world. There were wars before, there were many after, but even for those born long after 1945 who have been torn by other conflicts, the phrase "the war" still means World War II. Why this is true is not easy to explain. Perhaps it is a human fascination with death and violence on an unprecedented scale. Or perhaps it is that this war breeched previous limits of moral restraint.

World War II greatly strengthened the power of the state. The state pervades social life—in both democracies and dictatorships—more intensely than before the war. It continues to grow. The war generated unprecedented, massive migrations, most often involuntarily. It accelerated the homogenization of cultures, symbolized in part by the globalization of Coca Cola and chewing gum.

THE NEW INTERNATIONAL ORDER

In the late nineteenth century, Europeans attempted to moderate the horrors of war. Provisions for more humane treatment of wounded soldiers and prisoners of war preceded prohibitions on the use of certain kinds of especially cruel weapons. World War I led to attempts to punish perpetrators of war crimes, but they failed. During World War II the Allies declared their intention to hold war crimes trials, and they did. The Nuremberg Trials are the most famous, but trials were also held in East Asia. In addition, there were thousands of trials throughout Europe, including Germany, with thousands of convictions. International and national war crimes tribunals have not lived up to their advocates' hopes, but an important precedent was set. War crimes flourish and few are punished, but the basis for prosecution was established by the war. In time this may be the war's most important outcome for the abolition of war and securing human rights.

Before the war, great power politics were largely played out in Europe, although not with its traditional dynamics, given the revisionist ambitions of Germany and Italy, and the frequently self-imposed isolation of the Soviet Union. The United States and Japan were involved, but in secondary roles. By 1945 everything was changed. The fall of France in 1940 removed it from great power status, except in the mind of de Gaulle and some other French nationalists. The United Kingdom ended the war victorious, but near bankruptcy. It had to adjust to a postimperial role, a process begun during the war but lasting decades beyond. The return of Hong Kong to China in 1997 conveniently marked the final curtain call, with only fragments of empire surviving. France, Belgium, the Netherlands, Italy, and Portugal also had to yield their colonies to indigenous nationalist forces, however grudging and bloody the process.

Germany as a sovereign state no longer existed; it was occupied, divided, and discredited. Its neighbors intended to keep it that way or to integrate the country into a federated Europe where it would be rendered harmless. German society was transformed by infusions of refugees (12,000,000—15 percent of its prewar population) from the east and by the physical reminders of the destruction of war—over 3,000,000 dead and a landscape in ruins. The so-called reunification of Germany in 1990 did not restore the nation to its previous role. Its borders have shrunk; Russia and Poland divided East Prussia, and Poland annexed territory to its west. Although its population is Europe's greatest west of the Russian Federation, Germany is now contained within the European Union and NATO.

Japan's experience was similar, although it had the advantage of only one occupying power, the United States. The Americans retained the emperor, and he renounced his divinity. General Douglas MacArthur, head of the American military government, introduced reforms. They were not as extensive as some would have liked, but they included the introduction of a more effective parliamentary, constitutional regime, the reform of the big industrial combines, and the recognition of labor unions, and moved toward integrating the country into the world economy. Japan, however, because of its wartime treatment of conquered peoples and widespread unrepentant attitude, remains an outcast for much of East and Southeast Asia.

Thanks to Hitler, Soviet power extended further west than the Russian empire under the czars. Stalin's takeover of the Baltic states of Estonia, Lithuania, and Latvia was confirmed by the Allies, as were other 1940 annexations. Throughout the rest of eastern Europe from Poland to Romania, Soviet authorities, backed by the Red Army, imposed Soviet-style governments, a process completed in February 1948 in Czechoslovakia. Only Turkey, aloof from the war, and Greece escaped the Soviet orbit, although Yugoslavia extricated itself from Moscow in 1948. Soviet communism's appeal for many, tarnished by Stalin's collaboration with the Nazis between 1939 and 1941, was restored, with wider support in Europe, including the West, and in Africa and Asia than before the war.

Similarly, by starting the war and declaring war on the United States, Hitler brought a sleeping military giant to central Europe. Previously eager to remain at a distance from European affairs, the United States assumed a pivotal role on the continent. As the world's richest power, with its most advanced technologies, its strongest industrial base, and an occupying army in Europe, the United States became a global power. It held sway over the western half of the European continent, but predominated in the world's oceans and economically penetrated former European colonies.

American power rested not only on its military and its domestic economic strength, but also in its founding role in promoting international economic recovery and growth. Through the Bretton Woods agreements of 1944, which included provisions for the International Monetary Fund (IMF) and the World Bank (originally the International Bank for Reconstruction and Development), the United States helped lay the financial foundation for rebuilding a war-ravaged world. The IMF began operations in 1945 in Washington, where its headquarters still are located. Its purpose was to solve the prewar problem of anarchic exchange rates, one factor preventing the restoration of international trade, by managing them in order to achieve predictable, stable currency markets. This was a prerequisite for the expansion of trade and necessary to encourage international investment. At war's end, the United States dollar, with the largest reserves by far, played a crucial role.

These changes decreased national sovereignty over fiscal and monetary matters, hampering the introduction of social reforms advocated in many countries by resistance leaders. Conservatives, especially those with colonies, also disliked the IMF, with its thrust to create a worldwide, open market trading system. The Soviet Union, and consequently its client states, did not participate in the IMF, as their currencies were not convertible under their centralized, state-planned, nonmarket economies. In spite of this, the IMF and its companion World Bank became basic institutions of the post-war world economic order.

CHANGES WITHIN WEST EUROPEAN SOCIETIES

In the United Kingdom and Western Europe, the war produced a move toward the left. In countries occupied by the Germans, resistance parties wanted more-equitable societies with reduced class conflict and greater opportunities for all. Some advocated a united Europe.

In France the collaborationist Vichy government undermined the right's electoral support. General de Gaulle and his resistance associates quickly took control over the day-to-day administration of French government after the liberation in June 1944. Several thousand alleged collaborators were executed without trial. In October 1945 elections, the first in which French women could vote, three resistance parties gained three fourths of the vote—the Communists, the Socialists, and a liberal, democratic Catholic party, the Mouvement Républicain Populaire (MRP). They immediately set about to introduce collective bargaining for trade unions, wider educational opportunities, state control of major financial and industrial institutions, paid vacations, child support, and other welfare measures. The relation of state to citizen permanently changed.

British elections were postponed in 1940 to the end of the war. When held in July 1945, the Labour Party overwhelmingly defeated the Conservatives. Voters agreed to Labour's advocacy of extensive social and economic changes. Wartime mobilization showed that the state could be an effective force in improving medical service and education. Wartime measures also indicated that the state could manage major industries in order to provide for full employment and secure social welfare. As in France, an extensive welfare state emerged and remained largely unchallenged for the next 30 years.

CHANGES BEYOND EUROPE

British Commonwealth countries experienced a weakening of ties with Britain, as trade with the United States and elsewhere replaced that with the mother country. This was especially true for Canada, Australia, and New Zealand, but applied to South Africa as well. American investments and trade expanded as Britain's declined throughout much of Latin America, Africa, and the Middle East.

The most dramatic changes in the British Empire came in the colony of India. The United States funneled in $2 billion of Lend-Lease aid to India during the war. Indian trade with the mother country amounted to only one fourth of all trade by 1945, while the latter owed India £1.3 billion. To gain Indian support during the war, London offered postwar self-government in early 1942 as the Japanese advanced into Burma, but the Congress Party under Mohandas Gandhi and Jawaharlal Nehru rejected the offer. The Muslim League, on the other hand, cooperated with the British, reaping the political benefits after the war with the division of the subcontinent in 1947 into a Muslim state of Pakistan and a secular India, although with a Hindu majority. Burma became independent the same year also.

The goals of the Atlantic Charter also inspired other nationalists throughout Asia and Africa, while the Soviets and Americans pressured European empires to grant independence. The rapid collapse of Japanese military power in Southeast Asia and the inability of the Europeans to reoccupy the area doomed quick reconquest. The Dutch in the Netherlands East Indies fought Indonesian nationalists trained by the Japanese, but they were forced to extend independence in 1949. In those same years the French waged a losing war in Indochina, which gained its fragile independence in 1954 as three separate countries, Cambodia, Laos, and a divided Vietnam. Britain's Malaysia became independent in 1957.

The war weakened European claims in China. In 1943 Western countries, as well as the Japanese, renounced their rights of extraterritoriality that exempted their citizens from Chinese law. The communist victory in 1949 over the Nationalists closed China to Westerners, except for Macao and Hong Kong. The war was not decisive, as the 15-year struggle of the Chinese against Japan is part of a longer and deeper story of Chinese recovery and self-strengthening since the early nineteenth century. But without it, the communists may never have triumphed over their opponents.

Latin America remained more aloof from the global conflict than any other region. Only Brazil and Mexico dispatched troops abroad. Chile remained neutral until February 1945, and Argentina until the next month. The impact of the war, however, continued to reorient Latin countries from British, French, and German influence to the United States. Nearly half a billion dollars worth of Lend-Lease reached Latin American countries, three fourths of it to Brazil.

The war stirred economic activity, increasing American investments in mining, metallurgy, manufacturing, and oil production throughout Latin America. These changes widened the gap between the Europeanized elites and the working classes and peasants. The war stimulated nationalism, but also further polarized societies between prosperous upper classes and the poorer masses.

For the Arab and Muslim societies of North Africa and the Middle East, World War II is part of a larger and longer struggle against West European domination, especially Britain and France. Imperial retreat, which lasted for nearly two decades after the war, was the precondition for realizing the aims of Arabs for unity and national independence and of Muslims for restoration of Islamic civilization.

The most important Arab state, Egypt, was a British protectorate ruled by a pro-German King Farouk in 1939. Egypt and its Suez Canal linked the British economic and military domination of the Mediterranean with its control of the Indian Ocean, the Strait of Malacca, and the waters of the southwest Pacific. Thus, Arab national resistance, a growing problem for London in the 1930s, had to be appeased to build support for the war against Italy and Germany and keep the region British. Concessions were self-defeating. The investments in installations and logistics further stimulated economic development and the formation of nationalist classes among merchants and within the Egyptian army.

In 1944 the Egyptian government demanded a renegotiation of treaties with Britain. It actively supported the newly founded Arab League, an organization of several Arab states dedicated to Arab cooperation. Their unity was largely negative: opposition to British hegemony and resistance to Jewish influence in Palestine, a British protectorate. As Anglo-French influence waned, that of the United States grew; American planners thought that American oil reserves would not support the American economy and its new military power and wanted access to Middle Eastern reserves. Roosevelt, for example, extended Lend-Lease to Saudi Arabia and expressed American desires for Arab independence to King Ibn Saud. The oil-rich states of the Arabian peninsula, as well as Iraq and Iran, needed the markets of the increasingly oil-hungry industrialized West. This gave them interests very different from resource-poor Syria, Lebanon, Egypt, and the North African states. As often happened, the war transformed the landscape without producing a unity of purpose among former European colonies.

The war reversed developments in Palestine. In the Balfour Declaration of 1917 Britain recognized the Jewish right to a homeland in Palestine. By 1939 there were a million Arabs and nearly a half million Jews. To pacify Arab opposition to the growing number of Jewish communities, London in 1939 limited further Jewish settlers to 75,000, with all immigration to cease in 1945. It also announced the intention of creating a single independent state to include both Arabs and Jews.

During the war Zionists pressured Britain and the United States to recognize their goal of a separate Jewish nation. They recruited more than 26,000 Jews into the British Army but were unable to change Britain's policy. The genocide of Jews in Europe and a quarter of a million postwar Jewish refugees reinforced arguments for creating a Jewish state.

By 1945 Britain was in an impossible dilemma. It wanted stability in the Middle East with Palestine as a last military strong point because independence for Egypt and Iraq seemed inevitable. It could not simultaneously satisfy Arab and Jewish demands. The British attempted to prevent Jewish migration, but faced with Jewish persistence and changing world opinion they were unsuccessful. Armed Jewish resistance and terrorism weakened London's desire to keep Palestine British.

In 1947 the United Nations, with Soviet and American backing, created a special commission that recommended the partitioning of Palestine into a Jewish and an Arab state. The Jews accepted the plan; the Arabs rejected it. When the British finished withdrawing on May 14, 1948, David Ben-Gurion proclaimed a provisional government of Israel in Tel Aviv and several Arab countries attacked the newborn state. World War II and the Holocaust had paved the way for the establishment of an independent Jewish state.

In 1939 non-Arab Iran and its oil was under British domination. In 1941 the Soviet Union and Britain jointly occupied the country militarily after ousting its pro-Axis shah. Washington backed the Iranians, but for the price of breaking the Anglo-Iranian Oil Company's monopoly and opening up oil fields to the American Standard Oil Company.

The eclipse of French power among its Arab colonies came even faster. The defeat of France spurred greater nationalist demands. Although de Gaulle intended to restore the colonies to future liberated France, in the struggle for Arab backing in Syria and Lebanon (and faced with U.S. and British opposition) he had to abandon direct rule. In Morocco, Algeria, and Tunisia, Arab nationalists rejected Free French leadership and offers of assimilation into France. An influential French population in Morocco and Algeria persuaded postwar France to join the colonies to metropolitan France. This, however, only postponed the conflict between the two populations. Eventually the French, unwilling to pay the bloody costs of continued domination, bowed out of Morocco and Tunisia in 1956 and Algeria in 1962.

In Sub-Saharan Africa the war was as much a watershed as in Asia, although no Axis power occupied any colonies there. The need of the British to mobilize agriculture and manufacturing for the war effort necessitated concessions to colonial elites, while the French hopes of regaining control also required conferring greater rights. Wartime propaganda, especially the Atlantic Charter, and Soviet and American proclamations of anti-imperialism popularized the belief that the war was indeed a struggle for national freedom.

In white settler colonies such as Kenya, Southern and Northern Rhodesia (now Zimbabwe), and the Union of South Africa (now the Republic of South Africa), the war strengthened the economic and political power of the settlers as the United Kingdom increased its purchases and the world shortage of raw materials drove up prices. In South Africa, for example, the United Party split over whether to back Britain in the war. Parliament narrowly agreed to do so, but limited military participation to Africa and the Mediterranean. Even so, many left the party to form the Afrikaner Nationalist Party, which ruled South Africa after the war and introduced apartheid, providing for strict racial separation and privileging whites. The war economically and politically benefited the white nationalist bourgeoisie, who owned the mines and the best agricultural land.

The war was also a turning point for South Africa's African National Congress. Its leaders appealed to the principles of the Atlantic Charter but met a deaf ear, which convinced some of its membership to abandon racial cooperation in favor of violent opposition. The main outlines of the next 40-year struggle lay before the country.

In British colonies with few Europeans, African nationalists appealed to the principles of the Atlantic Charter and called for self-government or independence. The need for labor, raw materials, recruits for the army (over 400,000 throughout Africa), or construction crews in war zones necessitated extending rights. Army experience and working outside their home country also sensitized Africans to their political conditions and the unity of African opposition to imperial rule. Pan-Africanists attended the founding of the United Nations in San Francisco in April 1945 to press their demands. Later that year, the Fifth Pan-African Congress opened in England, the first in which Africans, rather than African Americans and sympathetic whites, dominated the proceedings. They were determined to unite all black Africans.

Indicative of international changes was Wendell Willkie's global trek in 1942. Roosevelt's Republican opponent in the 1940 presidential election, he was the highest-ranking American to that date to visit Britain's west African colonies of Ghana and Nigeria. He publicly backed African independence. His account of the trip, *One World* (1943), became a best-seller. Independence came in 1957. The handwriting was on the wall; others soon followed. The British colony of Nigeria became independent in 1960. Though the details differed, in part because of France's 1940 defeat and the struggle between Vichy France and the Free French, the move toward independence for French colonies also became irresistible. Thirteen French colonies also became independent in 1960, along with the Belgian colony of the Congo.

Establishing a United Nations organization was one of Roosevelt's most important projects. The Big Three tried to retain control over its structure by planning the organization, its charter, and its membership in advance of its founding conference. At the Yalta conference they reached general agreement. At the San Francisco Conference, attended by delegates from all countries that signed the United Nations Declaration, the Big Three did not entirely get their way. Nine north African and Asian nations were present, along with 2 black African states (Liberia and Ethiopia) and 20 Latin American countries. In addition, New Zealand and Australia supported changes to the proposed organization.

The Conference expanded the role of the General Assembly. It changed the League of Nations' mandate system (for colonies taken over from the Central Powers after World War I), replacing it with trusteeships that gave UN authorities the right to supervise the administration of the trustees. It gave inhabitants of the trusteeships the right to petition the UN. The United States, which had supported independence for mandates while Roosevelt lived, now opposed them. The American Joint Chiefs of Staff wanted to preserve many of them for air and naval bases.

CONCLUSION

Like tectonic plates around the globe, changes throughout world societies move slowly at times, but at others reconfigure the landscape in dramatic ways. Such was true of World War II. Most prominent of those was the emergence of a bipolar world, a world split between the United States and the Soviet Union. In 1945 the world war between Axis and Allies became a global Cold War between the West and the communist East.

Although the Soviet Union suffered greatly during the war, with extraordinary loss of life and property, it emerged with the world's largest army in 1945. Whether Stalin had aggressive designs after 1945 or basically wanted only a buffer in eastern Europe against a potentially renewed German state is unclear. In fact, for the four decades of the postwar world, Soviet land-based military power was limited to areas it acquired through the defeat of

Germany. Its influence, however, grew throughout the world as it offered an alternative to the American system and could support forces opposing it.

The United States abandoned political and military isolationism during the war. Its global system of open trade and currency stability began to reshape the global economy in ways that continue and deepen year by year. American entrepreneurial and technological innovation maintained its march, borrowing generously from the achievements of Europeans. Instead of collapsing into a troubling depression as many feared, the United States led the world's longest period of sustained economic growth, ushering in new wonders in communications, data processing, and medicine. Ironically, and unanticipated, it also opened up an age of overpopulation, planetary pollution, and resource depletion. There are twice as many people today as in 1945.

American hopes for the world in 1941 were clear: Roosevelt's four freedoms: "freedom of speech and expression—everywhere in the world," freedom of religion, freedom from want, and freedom from fear. Nostalgia for the years of World War II stems in part from the wartime belief that these could be reached and from knowing now that those freedoms have yet to be achieved. The legacy of the war is, thus, ambiguous.

The Women's Land Army in Britain was recruited to replace male workers in agriculture to do what was considered to be traditional men's work. Office of War Information. Courtesy of the Franklin D. Roosevelt Library

Soviet T-34 tanks in action against the German Army in 1942. Sovfoto. Courtesy of the Franklin D. Roosevelt Library

Marshal Stalin, President Roosevelt, and Prime Minister Churchill are seated on the portico of the Russian embassy in Tehran, Iran, on December 1, 1943. The photograph gave no indication of the differences they had over the conduct of the war and the postwar settlement. Courtesy of the Franklin D. Roosevelt Library

American Military Police (MPs) show German civilians from Weimar the corpses of Nazi victims at Buchenwald concentration camp. Signal Corps Photo. Courtesy of the Franklin D. Roosevelt Library

An Essex class carrier and two light carriers in the background in the western Pacific Ocean, March 1945. Essex carriers formed the core of American naval operations against the Japanese Imperial Navy. U.S. Navy Photograph. Courtesy of the Franklin D. Roosevelt Library

A beach on Iwo Jima strewn with American dead and equipment. Courtesy of the Franklin D. Roosevelt Library

U.S. Marines on Iwo Jima eagerly inspect a B-29, which weighed more than 50 tons when loaded. Its wingspan was 141 feet with a length of 99 feet. Courtesy of the Franklin D. Roosevelt Library

Hiroshima after the atomic bombing of August 6, 1945. The bomb destroyed all wooden structures and killed half of all people within one mile of the point of explosion. U.S. Army Photo. Courtesy of the Franklin D. Roosevelt Library

Biographies: The Personalities Behind the War

Dietrich Bonhoeffer (1906–1945)

Dietrich Bonhoeffer was one of the most noted German Christian theologians involved in resistance to the Nazis. He was born on February 4, 1906, in Breslau. He studied at Berlin University where his father was a psychiatrist. He early gained international experience as a pastor in Barcelona, Spain, and as a student at Union Theological Seminary in New York in 1930. He was also a pastor to a German congregation in London where he lectured and preached from 1933 to 1935. Life abroad brought him into contact with the international ecumenical movement.

Bonhoeffer deliberately chose to return to Germany and take up the struggle within the Confessing Church against National Socialism and the so-called German Christians who supported the Third Reich. He was deeply influenced by the neo-Orthodox Swiss theologian Karl Barth, who emphasized themes of Christ the suffering servant and the need of believers to serve others. Bonhoeffer taught at an underground seminary until the Gestapo intervened and banned him. During these years he wrote *The Cost of Discipleship* (1937 in German; 1949 in English) and *Life Together* (1939 in German; 1954 in English) as a part of the Church struggle against Nazism. He abandoned his earlier pacifism and became more involved in the resistance associated with General Ludwig Beck, Admiral Wilhelm Canaris, and the Kreisau circle around Helmut von Moltke.

After returning from a lecture tour in the United States in 1939, he gained employment as a courier in the military's Abwehr, the counterintelligence agency headed by Canaris. This enabled him to travel more freely. In May 1942 he met with George Bell, English bishop of Chichester, in Stockholm to present proposals for negotiating an end to the war. Bell, however, was out of favor with the Churchill government because of his criticism of the strategic bombing campaign. Nothing came of the mission.

Arrested in April 1943 for his role in the conspiracy against Hitler, Bonhoeffer further developed his ideas on Christianity in a post-Christian, religionless age in essays, poems, and letters he wrote to his parents and friends. These were published after the war first as *Prisoner for God* (1951 in German; 1953 in English), and later as *Letters and Papers from Prison*. Implicated in the July 1944 plot against Hitler, Bonhoeffer was executed in Flossenbürg concentration camp on April 8, 1945.

Arthur Neville Chamberlain (1869–1940)

Born into a distinguished business and political family in Birmingham on March 18, 1869, Arthur Neville Chamberlain started as a businessman in industrial Birmingham, rising to become the city's lord mayor, a position his father had held. He entered Parliament in 1918. He held several cabinet positions as a Conservative, before becoming prime minister in 1937.

Chamberlain's name will continue to be associated with appeasement and showing weakness when confronted with aggressive dictators. In fact, his foreign policies were much more complicated and principled than often thought. He was acutely aware of the great cost in lives and treasure of World War I. He also was prime minister during the Great Depression, when orthodox fiscal policy was to cut government expenditures in order to revive the economy.

British overseas military commitments had expanded, not contracted, after 1918. Former German and Ottoman colonies were acquired. More importantly, the rise of Arab nationalism, the growing strength of the Congress Party in India, and unrest in other colonial areas in Africa and southeast Asia increased British military costs. In addition, the assertion of Japanese naval power in the western Pacific and Mussolini's ambitions of making the British-dominated Mediterranean into an Italian sea, not to speak of the American challenge, complicated the defense of the British Empire and resistance to a revisionist Germany.

Although appeasement is generally associated with Chamberlain's dealings with Hitler, the policy included a broad attempt worldwide to match the Empire and Commonwealth's defense needs to its financial abilities. A resurgent Germany was only one part of the problem.

Chamberlain had great confidence in his ability to negotiate settlements. Like many contemporaries, he misjudged Hitler, taking at face value the dictator's claim that he sought a revision of the punitive features of the Versailles Treaty and a rectification of European boundaries to satisfy the unjust suppression of German self-determination. What Chamberlain, and no one else, knew was that Hitler was determined on war and world domination. For Hitler, German grievances were excuses for war, not negotiable points to be settled peacefully.

In the spring and summer of 1938, Hitler intended to provoke a war with Czechoslovakia, but by posing the issues in terms of bringing ethnic Germans into the Third Reich, he presented Chamberlain with an opportunity to settle the dispute by agreement. Chamberlain took the unprecedented step of flying to Germany to negotiate directly with Hitler. Although the Führer raised the ante, Chamberlain was able to persuade the French and force the Czech government into accepting the Munich agreement. It legitimized the German seizure of territories in the Sudeten mountains around the western peripheries of the Czechoslovak state.

Hitler considered Munich his greatest failure, because it deprived him of his much desired war. It also gave Britain time to improve its military strength, especially in air power and air defense. The turning point came with Hitler's blatant violation of the Munich agreement in March 1939 when he occupied the remainder of western Czechoslovakia and recognized the pseudo-independence of Slovakia. This demonstrated before British and world opinion that Hitler's interests were not in redressing injustices against a German minority. Whereas in 1938 the public strongly opposed war, most now supported the need to stop German expansion. Whether Chamberlain understood these benefits of appeasement is not clear, but he did lead Britain into war in September 1939 ready to fight and better prepared to do so.

Although this ameliorated criticism of appeasement, Chamberlain's political base was eroding. It collapsed with the failure of the Norwegian campaign in April 1940. He resigned on May 10, the day the Germans invaded western Europe. He continued as leader of the Conservative party and served in Churchill's cabinet, but died of cancer on November 9, 1941.

Chiang Kai-shek (Jiang Jieshi in Pinyin Spelling) (1887–1975)

Born of obscure parentage on October 31, 1887, Chiang Kai-shek served in the Japanese Army for two years, 1909–1911, returning to China in time to help overthrow the Manchu Qing dynasty. He became a military aide to Sun Yatsen and was sent to the Soviet Union to study. He returned as commandant of the new Whampoa Military Academy, where many Chinese revolutionaries of all political persuasions were trained in modern warfare.

After Sun's death in 1925, Chiang became leader of the Chinese Nationalist Party (Guomindang) and commander in chief of the Chinese army, positions he held until his death. Chiang sought military assistance from Germany in the mid-1930s to build up his army in preparation for what he saw as a coming conflict with Japan. Politically, he had to try to unite the country while holding together a coalition of diverse agrarian warlords, military leaders, and noncommunist reformers.

The Japanese campaign, beginning with the Marco Polo Bridge incident in 1937, forced Chiang and the Nationalists into the fight. Chiang's only hope was to win international support for his cause. During the next four years, he traded land for survival, retreating into the less urbanized and less industrialized western China while the Japanese seized China's coasts and major cities. He established his capital at Chongqing, on the upper Yangtze River. The fragile united front with the communists arranged in 1936 broke down in early 1941. His critics charged him with more enthusiastically fighting fellow Chinese in the communist party than the Japanese.

After American entry into the war, the defeat of Japan seemed secured. Chiang now devoted his resources, including American aid, to preparing for victory over his domestic opponents. Acclaimed as the leader of China during the war, he was recognized as president in 1943 and was appointed Allied Supreme Commander of the China Theater of Operations, though his command never came under general Allied control.

During those same years, the Americans wanted China's assistance in driving the Japanese, whose main military forces were in China, from the continent. Roosevelt appointed General Joseph Stilwell as his Chief of Staff and supervisor of Lend-Lease. The two did not get along. "Vinegar Joe," as Stilwell was known, referred to Chiang as "Peanut." Stilwell attempted to improve the efficiency of Chinese troops and stem the flow of graft and greed surrounding Chiang, but to no avail. He was not a diplomat, and Chiang had little interest in, or knowledge of, American or Allied strategic priorities.

When the war ended, the Chinese communists were in the north, Manchuria, which gave them access to Soviet military aid and to the supplies of the collapsing Japanese armies. Attempts to bring the Nationalists and communists together failed. A civil war broke out, which culminated in 1949 with the establishment of two Chinas, one on the mainland and the other under Chiang on the island of Taiwan. Chiang's wartime regime came to be viewed as desultory and corrupt.

On Taiwan, Chiang set up a dictatorship dedicated to the recovery of the mainland. He lost his claim to represent China in the United Nations in 1972. He died on April 5, 1975.

Winston Churchill (1874-1965)

Winston Churchill was British prime minister and one of the "Big Three" of the Allied leaders during World War II. A most public man politically and in his writings, he shared very little of the lives of ordinary people. He remains enigmatic and controversial. His oratory was brilliant. A master of the English language, he won the Nobel prize for literature.

Born into an aristocratic family as son of Lord Randolph Churchill and an American, Jennie Jerome, on November 30, 1874, Churchill was educated at the elite schools of Harrow and Sandhurst. He entered the army in 1894, but soon returned to civilian life.

Decades before the war, he attained celebrity as a journalist, author, and politician. A political maverick, he was elected a Conservative in 1900, but switched to the Liberal party, then became a Conservative in the late 1920s. He firmly believed in the British Empire, Anglo-Saxon superiority, and his own importance. Prime Minister Stanley Baldwin said Churchill had written an autobiography, calling it *The World Crisis* (1923–1929). No one else wrote their memoirs (in his case in six volumes) of the war with the overall title of *The Second World War* (1948–1953).

Steeped in the study of history and intensely interested in naval and military matters, Churchill traveled widely. Well-informed and acquainted with leaders worldwide, he was a superb strategist and took direct control over managing the military side of the war, though he was sometimes disastrously wrong. He worked hard, and also worked his assistants hard. He regularly smoked cigars and drank excessively, though apparently was never drunk. When a candidate for a military assignment said he never smoked or drank and was 100 percent fit, Churchill replied that he did both and was 200 percent fit.

Head of the Admiralty before World War I, Churchill was forced to resign in 1915 when the Gallipoli invasion of the Ottoman Empire in 1915, which he supported, failed to gain control of the Dardanelles and Bosporus straits. He held several cabinet posts later in the war and in the 1920s. He became Chancellor of the Exchequer in Baldwin's 1920s Conservative government, but resigned over the government's concessions to Gandhi and the

Congress Party in India. He took the unpopular position of supporting Edward VIII during the abdication crisis of 1936.

Chamberlain brought Churchill back to head the Admiralty when war broke out. He immediately initiated an extensive correspondence with President Roosevelt, which continued until the latter's death. He revamped the navy and burst forth with a host of schemes to attack the Germans, some of which disregarded the rights of neutrals or were strategically unsound. He championed the ill-fated Norwegian campaign that, ironically, led to Chamberlain's resignation and his appointment as prime minister.

In his first speech before Parliament as prime minister, he stated "I have nothing to offer but blood, toil, tears and sweat." During the next frantic six weeks he worked to avoid defeat in France, even offering the French joint citizenship to encourage them to continue the fight. By mid-June, however, the United Kingdom and the British Commonwealth stood alone in what he saw as a cosmic clash between the forces of good and evil.

As prime minister, Churchill set about to reorganize the government. He brought the Labour Party into a coalition with the Conservatives, with its leader Clement Attlee as deputy prime minister. He appointed himself minister of defense, garnering military and foreign policy for himself and leaving domestic affairs to others. He made changes in the military staffs, but then and throughout the war, he kept close tabs on each branch of the armed forces, meddling in their affairs at will. His strategy to defeat Germany was to intensify the bombing campaign, blockade Germany, support subversion in occupied countries, and begin commando raids along Europe's coasts to wear the Germans down. He realized, however, that Britain and the empire could not defeat the Germans alone.

Churchill's first foreign policy mission was to bring the United States into the war as a belligerent. Between 1940 and 1941, the British launched an extensive propaganda campaign in the United States, made easier by their control over the transatlantic cables and news from Europe. Live radio broadcasts and the terror attacks of the German blitz aided Churchill's cause. His memorandum of December 1940 to Roosevelt warning of imminent British collapse if they did not receive American aid led the president to introduce the Lend-Lease bill into Congress, which passed in March 1941.

The Italian attack on Egypt in September 1940 and the invasion of Greece the next month embroiled Churchill in a protracted struggle in North Africa and the Balkans for the next two years. The decision to split British forces and aid Greece proved a disaster, with Crete falling in May to the Germans, who appeared set to threaten the Suez Canal. The sinking of the *Bismarck* the same month was the only relief from the continuing setbacks in the battle of the Atlantic.

From January 1941 to December of that year, increasing cooperation between the British and American governments in intelligence, science, and the economy laid the basis for the Grand Alliance. Churchill willingly granted the Americans leases on important naval bases in the western Atlantic and Caribbean, and ceded the western Pacific in return for vital supplies and naval assistance in the Atlantic.

Though Churchill also tried to woo the Soviets, ironically it was Hitler who expanded the Allied alliance when he invaded the U.S.S.R. in June 1941. Churchill quickly yielded his notorious anticommunism to seek a treaty of alliance with Stalin, even recognizing the 1941 western boundaries of the Soviet Union. At the Placentia Bay Conference two months later with Roosevelt, their first meeting, they took up matters of military strategy against Germany as well as Japan. The Atlantic Charter they issued strengthened mutual ties and laid the ideological basis for further cooperation. In the following months the U.S. Navy stepped up its support for the British naval war against German submarines, though neither Roosevelt nor Hitler was inclined to allow this to lead directly to war.

The Japanese attack on Pearl Harbor was the moment Churchill had waited for—it made the end certain, he said. He immediately left with his advisors for Washington, for a three-week stay at the White House. They agreed with the Americans to establish a Combined Chiefs of Staff and integrate their arms production. They reaffirmed an earlier decision to defeat Germany first and issued the United Nations declaration, among other key decisions. The American chiefs of staff disliked the British proposals to carry the war into the Mediterranean before crossing the English Channel. For the next year and a half, Churchill, with two years of planning behind him and his military staff, argued successfully against the American position. Only in mid-1943, when American military strength began rapidly to overtake that of Britain, did policymaking pass to Roosevelt.

At the Tehran Conference (late 1943), Churchill's suspicions of Stalin reemerged. With the United States vetoing further operations in the Mediterranean area and the Red Army moving into eastern Europe, he decided to strike a deal with Stalin. In October 1944 he met with the dictator in Moscow and agreed to a percentage deal, whereby they assigned relative postwar influence to one another throughout eastern Europe and the Balkans—for example, Romania, 90 percent Soviet influence; Greece, 90 percent United Kingdom; Yugoslavia, 50 percent to each of them.

Churchill's differences with American policy over the Soviet threat deepened. He opposed Eisenhower's broad front strategy as too slow to beat the Red Army into central Europe. He objected to the Supreme Commander's decision to let the Soviets take Berlin as agreed at Yalta. He also differed with Washington over British participation in the Pacific war. Roosevelt wanted to keep the British at arm's length. He did not even inform Churchill of the details of Stalin's agreement to enter the war against Japan. Churchill had no greater luck with Truman, who wanted to exercise an independent American role in world affairs, one not attached to British imperial interests.

Victory in Europe came on May 7, 1945. Churchill announced elections for July (the previous ones had been held in 1935). He returned to Britain during the Potsdam conference to campaign, but endured a stunning defeat in favor of Labour. The last election had been in 1935. Labour's role in domestic affairs made it more attuned to public opinion than the part of a war leader with little sympathy for social reform. Churchill retired to write his six-volume "memoirs," using memoranda he had written and other papers not available to historians. He downplayed his differences with Roosevelt, elaborating the idea of a "special relationship" in which the two great English-speaking nations had worked as coequals.

In 1951 Churchill again became prime minister when the Conservatives won the election, but had to retire for health reasons in 1955. He wrote a four-volume *History of the English Speaking Peoples* (1956–1958) before he died on January 24, 1965.

Dwight David Eisenhower (1890–1969)

Supreme commander of the Allied forces, Eisenhower was born in Denison, Texas, on October 14, 1890. He grew up in Abilene, Kansas, and graduated from West Point in 1915, where he already had the nickname of Ike. He commanded a training camp for the new U.S. Army tank corps from 1916 to 1918. He was later stationed in the Panama Canal Zone and attended the Command and General Staff School before serving in the Philippine Islands under Douglas MacArthur.

George Marshall, then Chief of Staff, brought him to Washington immediately after the American entry into the war to head the War Plans Division, later called the Operations Division. Eisenhower advocated a direct invasion of the European continent in 1942, Operation Bolero, instead of a worldwide buildup of American military power. His rise was rapid. In June 1942 he became commander of American forces in the European theater, and then commander of U.S. troops in Operation Torch (North Africa) the following November. He attempted to keep military considerations out of politics, though the ill-fated Darlan deal led to charges that he was tolerating fascists and collaborators in arranging surrenders. His strength was his effective cooperation with Allied staff officers from different countries, whom he carefully integrated into close working relationships.

In February 1943, he assumed command of all Allied operations in North Africa. His responsibilities included the invasion of Sicily in July and the Italian mainland in September as well as the Italian surrender.

After the Tehran conference, Roosevelt, who had originally wanted Marshall as Supreme Commander, Allied Expeditionary Force, decided to appoint Eisenhower to the position in January 1944. Although often called an unpolitical general, Eisenhower showed extraordinary political skills as Allied commander. He persuaded Arthur Harris and Carl Spaatz to divert strategic air raids from Germany to communications lines in France in preparation of D-Day. During the Normandy campaign, he had to contend with divided opinion from Bernard Law Montgomery, Omar Bradley, and George Patton. Montgomery and Patton, in particular, were stars seeking publicity and pursuing their own campaign strategies.

Eisenhower resisted demands for independent forays by individual commanders and their armies, insisting instead on a broad-front strategy. Eisenhower moved to the continent and took command of the Expeditionary Force on September 1, 1943, but yielded to Montgomery's demand for an attack across the Rhine at Arnhem later that month. Montgomery's operation Market-Garden proved a mistake, for which Eisenhower shares some responsibility.

Though undoubtedly correct in his broad-front strategy—there was no need to risk lives in favor of uncertain operations for a quicker defeat of Germany—Eisenhower failed to anticipate the Battle of the Bulge (Ardennes campaign) of December 1944. In a final wartime controversy, Eisenhower decided not to advance beyond the boundaries of the assigned military occupation zones in the spring of 1945. That would have needlessly risked lives and challenged political decisions already made at Yalta. He also has been criticized, unfairly, for the unpublicized way he took the German surrender on May 7, 1945, at Rheims, France.

Promoted to five-star general in December 1944, Eisenhower served after the war as U.S. Army chief of staff. From 1948 to 1950 he was president of Columbia University in New York City. He commanded NATO forces from 1950 to 1952 before being elected the 34th President of the United

States in 1952. At the end of his presidency in 1961, he warned the nation of the danger of the military-industrial complex.

He retired to his farm adjacent to Gettysburg battlefield, Pennsylvania, and to his favorite sport, golf. He died March 28, 1969.

Charles de Gaulle (1890–1970)

In June 1940, after the fall of France, Charles de Gaulle, with the rank of brigadier general, fled to England. He denounced the request of Henri Pétain, the new head of state of France, for an armistice with Germany. Backed by a strong sense of history and his country's greatness, de Gaulle claimed to speak for France and urged his countrymen to resist. Four years later, he returned home, the leader of the Free French and head of a newly formed government composed of resistance parties.

Born in Lille, France, on November 22, 1890, the son of a career officer, de Gaulle entered the infantry before World War I in Henri Pétain's regiment. He achieved some notoriety through his 1934 advocacy in *Vers l'Armée de Métier* (*Towards a Professional Army*) of a mobile armored military, rather than the mass conscription army with its defensive strategy and stress on firepower preferred at the time.

During the summer of 1940, the British government recognized de Gaulle's leadership of the Free French movement and agreed to finance all who fought for it. There was little response to de Gaulle among French leaders, however, and the French Empire remained loyal to Pétain's Vichy government. In late 1940 and 1941, the Free French movement's appeal began to rise with the expulsion of Vichy troops from Libreville, the capital of Gabon, the first step toward liberation. De Gaulle also laid the basis for his legitimacy as the leader of the French government in the Brazzaville declarations of October 1940 stating that the Vichy French government was illegitimate and under German control. With this, de Gaulle began to garner support from leaders throughout the French empire.

At the same time, however, his quarrels with the British increased. The 1941 Allied campaign against the Vichy forces in Lebanon and Syria resulted in these two colonies coming under British control, rather than that of the Free French as de Gaulle insisted. A compromise was worked out, but de Gaulle intended to restore the French empire in the face of an Arab nationalism that the British were attempting to appease. Conflicts over the British occupation of Madagascar and the support some British officials gave to de Gaulle's opponents within the Free French exacerbated relations.

Although President Franklin D. Roosevelt opened up Lend-Lease to the Free French, Roosevelt personally disliked de Gaulle, being possibly influenced by anti–de Gaullist French émigrés. He also wanted to maintain good relations with Vichy, which the Americans continued to recognize as the legitimate government of France, believing that it would welcome an American liberation of North Africa.

The Free French military engagements at Bir Hakeim (June 1942) in North Africa reinforced de Gaulle's claim to leadership. The Anglo-Americans, however, still disregarded him. He was not informed of Operation Torch, nor was he party to the Darlan deal of December 1942 whereby Vichy troops in North Africa surrendered to the Allies. Instead, the Allies supported their own candidate, General Henri-Honoré Giraud. De Gaulle's alliance with the resistance within France and his own political acumen, however, enabled him to outmaneuver Giraud and abort the American and British plans. De Gaulle's sense of isolation from Anglo-American councils bred resentments on his part that would emerge after the war in his insistence on an independent French policy during the Cold War.

Resistance within occupied France developed with little regard to the Free French. Until 1942 de Gaulle had only limited contacts with the continent, and few resistance leaders were able to go abroad. The coalition of socialists, communists, reformist democrats, nationalists, and trade unionists not only struggled against the Germans, it also developed a program to change postliberation France. To strengthen his role in relation to the Allies and within France, de Gaulle accepted much of the resistance movement's goals: a secure democracy and social reform.

In this, Jean Moulin, a former provincial administrator, played a key role. Escaping to Britain in 1941, he returned to France as a representative of de Gaulle. By early 1943 he skillfully welded the various resistance forces together into a unified group, the National Council for Resistance. He also strengthened links with the British SOE (Strategic Operations Executive), an organization set up to promote sabotage and resistance in occupied Europe. Arrested by the Gestapo in June of that year, Moulin was tortured so badly that he died en route to Germany. His work, however, set de Gaulle on the road to recognition as leader of the resistance at home and among the Allies abroad.

Uniting the Fighting French and the former Vichy armed forces into one organization proved a difficult task for de Gaulle, given his previous total rejection of Vichy collaborators. In achieving this, however, he formed a much larger French army able to participate in major military operations in Italy and southern France.

Although still rebuffed by Britain and the United States, de Gaulle proceeded to prepare for governing France. Early in 1944 he appointed administrators for areas to be liberated who would be representatives of the French—that is, his—government. On June 4, two days before the Normandy invasion (de Gaulle was not informed of the date), the French Committee for National Liberation (CNFL) took the title of provisional government and was recognized as such by several governments over the protests of Britain and the United States.

The Allies planned a military administration of France, similar to that arranged for Italy. But during the invasion, Eisenhower's armies, engaged in a deadly battle against the Germans, happily let de Gaulle's provisional government take over. It soon struck popular roots. The enthusiasm for him during his appearance at the liberation of Paris in August gave him the opportunity to outflank those on the left in the resistance who called for revolution. By October the United States and Britain recognized the CNFL as the French government.

This by no means ended de Gaulle's difficulties. The resistance parties bickered over the future French constitution. The Allies did not consider France a great power, and de Gaulle was not invited to the Yalta conference. Indochina declared its independence, whereupon de Gaulle started a war to reverse the claim. The resistance parties' inability to agree on a program for France led de Gaulle to resign the presidency in January 1946 and retire.

In 1958 de Gaulle was recalled to lead the country and form the Fifth French Republic. He negotiated an end to the Algerian war. Otherwise, he pursued controversial policies with the United States, Britain, and the Common Market. He resigned in 1969 when a referendum on constitutional reforms he supported failed. He died November 9, 1970.

Hermann Goering (1893–1946)

Hermann Goering occupied some of the highest positions in the Third Reich, including head of the Four Year Plan responsible for rearming Germany after 1936 and the newly established Luftwaffe. Goering was born in Bavaria on January 12, 1893, son of a minor German diplomatic official. His mother was mistress of a partly Jewish doctor, in one of whose castles the young Goering spent much of his teenage years.

Goering served as a pilot in the German Army Air Force during World War I and became a celebrated ace. In 1918 he took command of the famous Richthofen squadron. He joined the Nazi party in 1922 and was wounded in the Beer Hall Putsch of November 1923. He became addicted to a morphine treatment to ease the pain from this wound and was periodically hospitalized in later years.

When the Nazis became the largest party in the Reichstag in 1932, Goering became its president. Upon Hitler's appointment as Reichschancellor in January 1933, Goering headed the Ministry of the Interior of Prussia, Germany's largest state. In this position, he established himself as a key figure in the Third Reich, initially in control of concentration camps and the Gestapo, the German secret police. He was Hitler's chief troubleshooter, ruthless, and known as the "iron man."

As chief of the newly created Luftwaffe after 1935 he built an independent organization. Goering was interested in building a strategic air force, but the Luftwaffe's main responsibility remained, as always, tactical support for the German army.

Hitler appointed Goering field marshal in 1938, and bestowed the unique title of *Reichsmarschall* on him in 1940. The high point of his career came during the Polish and French campaigns of 1939 and 1940. His command of the Luftwaffe during the battle of Britain showed that the Luftwaffe lacked a strategy to defeat the RAF. Although the Luftwaffe played a significant role in the invasion of the Soviet Union in 1941, it was unable to relieve the Sixth Army at the battle of Stalingrad or to meet the expanding Allied strategic air offensive. A staunch proponent of the Third Reich's anti-Jewish policies, Goering signed the 1941 order authorizing Reinhard Heydrich to take steps to solve the "Jewish problem."

Within Nazi and government circles, Goering's influence rapidly deteriorated after 1940, in part due to his drug addiction and inability to manage the war economy effectively. He spent much of his last years furnishing various mansions with stolen art. Throughout, he was obsessed with elaborate uniforms. As one of his powerful cronies, Hitler stuck by Goering throughout most of the war, having named him as his successor in 1939. Toward the end of April 1945 Goering took steps to assume power, whereupon Hitler expelled him from the party and had him arrested.

Goering surrendered to the Americans at the war's end and at the Nuremberg war crime trials became the Nazis' star witness, vigorously and knowledgeably defending himself. He escaped the hangman by taking his own life with cyanide on October 15, 1946.

Arthur Harris (1892–1984)

One of the war's most controversial commanders, Arthur Harris was born on April 13, 1892, in Cheltenham, Kent, England, and spent his childhood in Rhodesia. During World War I he joined the Royal Air Corps, renamed the Royal Air Force (RAF) in 1919. He became a prominent airman, serving in the Middle East during most of the interwar period. When the war started, he returned to Britain to command No. 5 Bomber Group, then headed a RAF mission to Washington. In February 1942 he was promoted to commander in chief, Bomber Command (BC), a position he held until September 1945, with the title of Air Chief Marshal from 1942.

Harris's authority lay in great part in his detailed knowledge of all aspects of air power. He concluded early in the war that incendiary bombs and area bombing, rather than precision bombing with high explosives, were key to effective strategic bombing. Above all, Harris, like many other British commanders, wanted to avoid the bloodletting of World War I. He firmly believed that area bombing would be less costly than ground battles and could, if applied in sufficient quantity, knock Germany out of the war.

Harris's appointment as Bomber Command's head coincided with a rapid increase in the number of bombers, allowing him in May 1942 to launch the first thousand-bomber attack. Carried out at night to thwart German defenses, the raid greatly restored the reputation of BC. The target was Cologne in western Germany. The city center was leveled at a cost of forty bombers. Later similar large-scale raids did less damage and none brought Germany to its knees, though there may have been some benefit in building morale in Britain.

Improved German air defenses and fighter forces deprived BC of air supremacy into 1943, though the beginning of American daytime bombing in late 1942 added to the overall effect of the bombing campaign. Harris shared with the American commanders, from General of the Army Henry Arnold down, the same belief that strategic air attacks could win the war, although they differed over the tactics for achieving that goal.

Harris's critics during the war argued that air power could be better used in search-and-destroy operations against submarines in the battle of the Atlantic, in the bombing of specific production targets (what Harris derided as "panacea" bombing), or in tactical support for ground operations after the invasion of France. At the Casablanca conference in January 1943, the Combined Bomber Offensive of British and American air forces was created and charged with coordinated attacks against specific targets, but Harris and the American General Ira Eaker remained free to choose their own targets. The introduction of Pathfinder techniques to help bombers identify targets improved BC's record from 1943 on, but its success was largely due to drying up the German supply of pilots, forcing the Germans to disperse their factories, and keeping over a million Germans occupied with civilian defense.

Harris was vigorously criticized for the bombing of civilians on moral grounds by a few during the war and by many afterwards. The extent of the damage to German and other European cities shocked contemporaries, and the inconclusive assessment of strategic bombing's impact combined to raise both moral and military questions. The more than 57,000 British airmen killed, an extraordinarily high number, also raised doubts. During the war Churchill and the war cabinet supported Harris, but in the postwar striking of medals, Bomber Command was passed over and Harris was not given a title until 1953. Harris resigned in 1946, living the next four decades in public disgrace. The erection of a statue in his honor in London in 1992 renewed the controversy. He died in Paris on April 5, 1984.

Heinrich Himmler (1900–1945)

Born October 7, 1900, the son of a Catholic school teacher in Munich, Bavaria, Heinrich Himmler built an unrivaled empire within the Nazi state. Too young to serve in World War I, he studied agriculture and became a chicken farmer for a short time before joining the Nazi party in 1925 and becoming head of the SS (Schutzstaffel, protective squad) in 1929 at the age of 29. Initially a bodyguard organization wearing sharp, black uniforms, the SS under Himmler evolved into a party police force, before taking on a host of activities such as concentration camps, state security, an intelligence service (SD, Sicherheitsdienst), the implementation of Nazi racial policies, an armed force (Waffen-SS), and the death camps to carry out National Socialist genocide.

No one in the Third Reich did more to carry out Nazi ideology. Himmler had little concern for personal advantage. He worked hard and lived a frugal, spartan life, shunning publicity in favor of building his beloved SS. As Nazis went, Himmler was an idealist, making every effort to transform German society into his image of a racially pure community, restoring it in accord with his ideas of the pre-Christian, Germanic past. The men of SS, who were supposed to be pure Nordic blonds, were the core of a future agrarian people devoted to working the soil and subjecting other races to the service of the master Aryans.

Shortly after the Nazi takeover in January 1933, Himmler established the concentration camp Dachau, the model for other camps. He then took over the police forces of the various German states. Goering gave him control of the Gestapo in 1934. He helped to emasculate the rival Nazi paramilitary organization, the SA (Sturmabteilung, storm troops), in June of that year.

The war gave Himmler the real opportunity to expand his realm. At the same time, his health deteriorated under the strain of his ceaseless administration. Armed units of the SS were organized in November 1939 as the Waffen-SS (Armed SS) with three divisions. Under operational control of the army, the Waffen-SS was otherwise under Himmler, though conflicts between him and the army soon surfaced. Because SS recruitment within Germany was limited, the SS began eliciting recruits from Germans outside the Reich (Volksdeutsche) and foreign volunteers from throughout Europe. By 1943 half of the Waffen-SS soldiers were non-Germans, though they were not recognized as full SS members.

During the war years the concentration camp system expanded from some 20,000 inmates to more than 667,000 by 1945. It no longer aimed to destroy domestic opposition; it now became a part of an SS-directed economy and extermination program.

The 1939 campaign resulted in Himmler's takeover of German occupied Poland. He also became the Reich Commissioner for the Strengthening of Germandom with the goal of moving several hundred thousand ethnic Germans, often against their wishes, into the Reich and clearing conquered territories of Slavs. Himmler also promoted *Lebensborn* (fountain of life) to increase the stock of racially pure Germans. It provided care for women and their babies born of liaisons with SS men. It also searched for "Aryans" among conquered peoples. A minor program in the Third Reich, it is indicative of Himmler's seriousness in advancing his racial utopia.

Himmler's most important role in the Third Reich was preparing for and orchestrating genocide. Although no specific, written order from Hitler to exterminate all of Europe's Jews exists, Himmler undoubtedly believed that he was carrying out the Führer's will in this as in all his other projects. The "Final Solution" was decided upon in late spring or early summer 1941 in association with Operation Barbarossa. Death camps were constructed and "resettlement" began. Himmler supervised genocide and the rest of his burgeoning state within a state from a specially constructed railroad car. He spoke of the genocide of Jews to Nazi leaders as one of the glorious pages of German history. The death camps consumed 6,000,000 Jews and another 4,000,000 victims from across Europe, including Sinta and Roma (gypsies), homosexuals, opponents of Nazi rule, and other undesirables.

Enjoying extraordinary power by the end of 1943, Himmler, though no intimate of Hitler, worried over the Führer's health. He desired to stand next in line in case of Hitler's death so that he could complete the task of racial reformation. After the attempted assassination of Hitler, he was appointed as head of a "Replacement Army." Early in 1945, he realized that the war was lost, ordered the "Final Solution" to halt, and prepared to negotiate with the Allies. Upon learning this, Hitler ordered his arrest, but Himmler escaped and surrendered to the British in disguise. When his identity was discovered, he committed suicide on May 22, 1945.

Hirohito (1901–1989)

Born on April 29, 1901, into the world's oldest continuing imperial family, and reputed descendent of the sun goddess, Hirohito became the 124th emperor of Japan in 1926 and reigned for the next 63 years. Under traditional Shinto practices, the emperor was a divine figure and symbol of the Japanese national community. Theoretically, all power flowed from his will, though Japan had a constitution and a representative assembly from the end of the nineteenth century. In fact, the emperor presided at Imperial Conferences made up of top civil and military officials that primarily confirmed decisions already made. Indeed, before the war and during it, Hirohito expressed his reservations about the wisdom of Japan's decision for war.

Hirohito's role in World War II remains controversial. During the war, he was often depicted along with Hitler and Mussolini as one of the leaders of Axis aggression. He appeared in public, urging the nation to carry out its duties to win. Hirohito was pleased with Japan's early victories and as commander in chief closely followed Japan's military campaigns.

The emperor's exalted position became a barrier to ending the war in 1945. The Allied policy of unconditional surrender and the demand of many that Hirohito be tried as a war criminal was anathema to the Japanese government, even to the advocates of peace in Tokyo. In the event, Hirohito was permitted to retain his position as emperor, though he renounced claims to divinity. Desacralized, Hirohito was depicted after the war as a silent, constitutional ruler who did not intervene into policymaking, except on a few occasions to warn against war and, more dramatically, in August 1945, to decree acceptance of Allied terms of surrender. The truth lies somewhere between these two views.

Although the war was clearly being lost by 1944, Tokyo's militarists continued to fight, hoping to make the cost of complete victory so great that the United States would accept a negotiated settlement. In April 1945, Hirohito had in the appointment of Admiral Suzuki Kantaro as prime minister, a respected statesman who supported his desire for peace. The naval blockade and the accelerated bombing left the country with no alternative. Unknown to Hirohito or Suzuki, time was running out. Attempts to initiate negotiations led nowhere. Hirohito advised acceptance of unconditional surrender, but the government, pressured by the military, chose to ignore the Potsdam ultimatum, a last-minute warning to Japan to surrender or suffer the full Allied military vengeance. The two atomic bombs were the Americans' answer.

On August 9, 1945, Hirohito insisted that Japan surrender. Facing continued military resistance, Hirohito repeated his will at a second Imperial Conference on August 14. The next day, he took the unprecedented step of broadcasting his decision to the people of Japan.

After the surrender, Hirohito offered to accept responsibility for the war, but General Douglas MacArthur, as Supreme Commander, Allied Powers, rejected the idea. MacArthur intended to reform Japan during the occupation by using the prestige and authority of the emperor. Hirohito returned to his research interests in marine biology, and devoted the next 44 years to implementing a constitutional monarchy modeled on that of Great Britain. He died January 7, 1989.

Adolf Hitler (1889–1945)

Born on April 29, 1889, in Braunau on Inn, Austria, the future dictator of the Third Reich spent his first three decades in obscurity, except for the Iron Cross (First Class) awarded to him as a lance corporal during World War I. By the time Adolf Hitler headed the small National Socialist German Workers Party in 1921, he was a convinced racist, blaming the Jews for Germany's defeat. After the Beer Hall Putsch, a failed coup in November 1923, Hitler was briefly imprisoned under comfortable conditions. He dictated *Mein Kampf* (*My Struggle*, 1925), a rambling diatribe against liberalism, socialism, Jews, internationalism, and much else in favor of assertive leadership. In 1925 Hitler refounded the party, making himself unchallenged Führer (Leader), charismatically inspired, and surrounded by unquestioning followers.

Benefiting from the depression and the stalemated Weimar parliamentary system, the Nazi party flourished, becoming the largest political party in the German Parliament by 1932. In January 1933, Hitler risked all in joining a coalition dominated by conservatives. Within a year, however, he abolished all other political parties, ended constitutional government, subverted the judiciary, and removed his conservative allies from their posts. When the president, Paul von Hindenburg, died in 1934, Hitler made him-

self president. He also eliminated the last opposition to his unfettered dictatorship within the Nazi party. In domestic and foreign policy, Hitler's will
alone determined policy. In February 1938, he took over the supreme command of the armed forces, bringing the last independent German state institution under his control.

In steady succession, Hitler withdrew from the League of Nations, renounced the disarmament clauses of the Versailles Treaty, created the Luftwaffe under Goering's leadership, remilitarized the Rhineland, and
annexed Austria. While Germany's and Hitler's power grew, Europeans
watched in dismay or courted his friendship. Rearmament brought full employment. Most Germans applauded; too few took seriously the regime's
violence and illegalities. They failed to see that these were endemic in the
Führer's policies.

In the summer of 1938 Hitler hoped to provoke a war with Czechoslovakia, but instead accepted Chamberlain's negotiated settlement. Ever more
convinced of his willpower, and tenacity to fulfill his mission as Germany's
savior, Hitler willingly took the risk of war in September 1939. The Polish
campaign enabled him to pursue the goal of Lebensraum, territory in eastern Europe for settling Germans, and the extermination of Jews. What Hitler did not anticipate was that France and Britain would honor their pledges
to declare war on Germany in case of an attack on Poland.

The rapid collapse of Poland and the brilliant 1940 campaigns in Scandinavia and in western Europe against the Netherlands, Belgium, and France
confirmed Hitler's power. In quick operations with little loss of life, Germany became Europe's premier power. Hitler had opposed expert military
advice; he now reaped the benefits of victory, though in letting the British
and French escape at Dunkirk, he failed to consolidate German military supremacy. Nonetheless, from this time on, he became fully absorbed in the
war effort. He was rarely away from his various command posts for the next
five years.

Hitler had no clearly thought-out grand strategy. Instead, he relied on instinct and hunches, and in taking great risks. When Britain refused to ca-
pitulate, he launched the battle of Britain. The Luftwaffe was not prepared
for the task; it had neither strategic theory nor the aircraft to carry one out.
And Germany did not have the naval means to launch an invasion with the
Royal Air Force and the Royal Navy still intact.

Thwarted by Britain, Hitler ordered preparations for a massive invasion
of the Soviet Union. The army was to be expanded; increased armaments
were ordered. Operation Barbarossa, however, was overly complex with no

clear strategic focus. During the opening months of the campaign, Hitler interfered with the command and the conduct of operations.

By December 1941, the German army was bogged down in the vast wastes of the Soviet Union, exhausted, and facing new Soviet troops and a Red Army counteroffensive. In a rage against his commanders, Hitler dismissed 35 generals, 4 field marshals, and all army group commanders, including the head of the army, Field Marshal Walter von Brauchitsch. Hitler replaced the deposed commander with himself. At the same time, Germany's international situation worsened. Japan brought the United States into the war with Hitler unnecessarily declaring war on America. Germany experienced its first defeats and faced a combination of enemies with economic and material resources greatly exceeding that of German-occupied Europe.

Unalterably convinced of his genius, Hitler brooked no opposition or criticism. He had an incredible ability to master details of geography and military equipment, thus further intimidating subordinates who differed from his judgments. He began to eat alone, became obsessed with his health, and imagined conspiracy all around him.

The renewed German offensives of 1942 did not bring the expected benefits, even though the Third Reich was ever more strained to meet the new requirements. German troops were overextended in southern Russia and the Caucasus. The Allied invasion of North Africa began the steady roll back of German forces there. British victory at El Alamein and the fall of Stalingrad showed that Germany could not win the war. Meanwhile, the "Final Solution" went into high gear, often taking priority over strategic military interests.

Hitler blamed failure on the lack of morale and on cowardice. Sacking officers became common. He refused permission to effect tactical withdrawals. He interfered in the chain of command. Although he had earlier ordered rocket research cancelled when it did not promise immediate results, he turned to rockets and jets in 1943 as the wonder weapons that would win the war.

Opposition within a segment of Germany's conservative elite led to the attempt on Hitler's life in July 1944. When it failed, Hitler retaliated with extraordinary brutality. Some 5,000 former ministers, mayors, and political leaders were arrested. Spared assassination, Hitler identified himself as the only person assigned by providence with the will to see Germany to victory. He unleashed the SS within Germany, and organized one last, futile offensive in the Ardennes in December 1944 against the Western Allies. Not until the last days of the war did he accept that it was lost; the German people, he said in his last will, were not worthy of him. On April 30, 1945, he committed suicide immediately after marrying his mistress, Eva Braun.

Tadeusz Komorowski (1895–1966)

When Germany invaded Poland in 1939, the tall, slender Colonel Tadeusz Komorowski was well-known within the Polish army as an accomplished horseman. Like many fellow officers and Polish soldiers, he remained behind to organize armed resistance to German and, until 1941, Soviet occupation. Komoroski was born in 1895 in Trembowla, Upper Galicia, into the lower Polish nobility. He served as an officer in the Austro-Hungarian army in World War I, and in the Polish Army after the war.

In January 1940 Wladyslaw Sikorski, General and head of the Polish government-in-exile, named Komorowski commander of the Union for Armed Struggle in the region around Cracow. He took on the underground name of Bor (forest) and is subsequently often called Bor-Komorowski. The armed resistance in Poland was able to draw on officers and soldiers from the prewar armed forces, thus making it one of Europe's most effective military resistances to the Germans. The members of the Home Army (Armia Krajowa, or AK), as the combined Polish armed forces were called after February 1942, were reorganized under Stefan Rowecki. It did not need to be trained in arms, the use of explosives, or military discipline. In order to avoid harsh German reprisals against civilians, the Home Army pursued restraint, reserving its strength for the moment of a decisive uprising.

The Polish guerrillas benefited from a tradition of resistance, as Poland had not existed as an independent state from the end of the eighteenth century until 1919. The extraordinary harshness of German rule also encouraged underground war as the only alternative to enslavement.

In 1943 Rowecki was captured by the Gestapo and later murdered in Sachsenhausen concentration camp. The London Polish government appointed Komorowski his successor. The Home Army now included remnants of the prewar army as well as partisans and Soviet soldiers left behind the advancing German lines.

Komorowski, like most Poles, was suspicious of the Soviets both as Russians and as communists. News of the massacre at Katyn, where 4,400 Polish officers' graves were found, was announced by the Germans in April 1943. It led to a break in diplomatic relations between Moscow and the London Poles. Although widely suspected, Soviet responsibility was not proven until 1990. In spite of these tensions, Komorowski's warfare against

Germany gave substantial aid to the Red Army. Komorowski also tried to work with the small Polish Communist party and its military branch, the People's Guard, later named the People's Army. The People's Army carried out a more aggressive war against the Germans than Komorowski, but at great costs to civilians. In late 1943 it launched its own uprising, claiming to speak for the general population.

Contact for Komorowski and Home Army commanders with the London government was difficult. Radio signals could be tracked by the Germans. The border crossings were closely watched, and when all of eastern Europe came under German control, communications with the outside world were limited to Stockholm and Istanbul. Komorowski had to make many decisions on his own. He was captured once but luckily escaped before being identified.

In January 1944 Komorowski launched Tempest, the code name for the long-awaited Polish uprising against the German occupation. The purpose was to establish Poland's claims for self-liberation and to strengthen its bargaining position among the Allies, especially against Stalin. The AK's military training enabled it to inflict significant damage on the Wehrmacht. The Home Army liberated several cities and captured German arms. Military success did not have the desired political effect.

Plans for Tempest provided for the distribution of arms throughout the Polish countryside, rather than attempt uprisings in cities. In July, however, Komorowski ordered an uprising in Warsaw as the Red Army approached from the east. Poorly armed, the 37,000 guerrillas struggled for over two months. Stalin belittled the uprising as foolhardy. The Red Army, for reasons still unclear, did not advance to aid the rebels, though eventually some supplies were dropped by planes. Efforts to supply the Home Army from the west failed. The German counteroffensive was devastating, killing 250,000.

On October 1 Bor-Komorowski decided to surrender. He survived the war but went into exile in London where he lived the rest of his life, writing his memoirs, *The Secret Army* (1948, 1984 repr.). He died in England on August 25, 1966.

Douglas MacArthur (1880–1964)

Commander of U.S. Army forces in the Far East, Douglas MacArthur was born on January 26, 1880, in Little Rock, Arkansas, into a military family. He attended a military school and graduated first in his class at West Point in 1903. He was an aide to President Theodore Roosevelt, and served

in the 42nd Rainbow Division during World War I, being promoted to brigadier general in 1918, the youngest divisional commander in the American
army. He already was known for his flamboyant character and dress.

MacArthur subsequently was superintendent of West Point and chief of
staff in the Army in 1930. In that position he courted controversy by sup-
pressing in 1932 the "Bonus Army" of unemployed World War I veterans
who wanted immediate payment of their wartime bonuses. In 1935 he accepted the title of field marshal and advisor to the Filipino government. In
1937 he retired from the army. In Manila, MacArthur lived a lavish life-
style, with a generous government salary. He did, however, train a Filipino
army. In the summer of 1941, Roosevelt named him commander of U.S.
Army Forces in the Far East, a ploy intended to warn the Japanese. At the
same time, the Army decided that the Philippine Islands, which had been
promised independence in 1946, could not be defended. This policy was
reversed in late 1941, too late to reinforce the islands for an adequate defense.

MacArthur failed to attack Japanese air bases on Taiwan after the Japanese raid on Pearl Harbor. Ten hours later Japan struck air bases under his
command, destroying aircraft on the ground. MacArthur retreated to
Bataan. In March 1942 Roosevelt ordered him to leave for Australia where
he was appointed commander of the Southwest Pacific Area. He resolved,
"I shall return."

MacArthur distrusted the Australians, an attitude they reciprocated. By
1943 he had enough American troops under his command that he could
largely ignore the Australians and carry out his march toward the Philippines. MacArthur gained a reputation for self-promotion, surrounding himself with sympathetic officers and controlling news releases to celebrate his
own successes. He took credit for leapfrogging over Japanese islands, leaving them to wither from lack of supplies, even though he originally opposed
the strategy. He refused to let the intelligence officers of the Office of Strategic Services (OSS, the Joint Chiefs of Staff's intelligence organization)
work under his command. He often ignored intelligence if it did not suit his
purposes. Throughout the war, he disagreed with the JCS and the navy command over the proper Pacific strategy. Indeed, he opposed the Germany-
first policy to defeat the Third Reich before defeating Japan.

A right-wing Republican with popular support among important segments of the American electorate, MacArthur openly expressed his disdain
for Roosevelt's liberalism. The president, not wishing to antagonize
MacArthur's supporters, approved, in the face of navy opposition, his plans
to retake the Philippines in 1944, a presidential election year. MacArthur

continued the fight in the Philippines after the main thrust against Japan had moved north and the liberated islands had no strategic value in winning the war.

Given a fifth star as General of the Army in December 1944, MacArthur was named to the command of all U.S. Army forces in the Pacific the following spring. This gave him responsibility for the planned invasion of Japan's home islands. After Tokyo's capitulation, MacArthur formally accepted surrender aboard the U.S.S. *Missouri* in an elaborate display of American military power and in full view of the cameras.

MacArthur was appointed Supreme Commander, Allied Powers (SCAP), in charge of the administration of military government, though the occupation was an exclusively American affair. As an American proconsul, MacArthur kept Hirohito as emperor and through him introduced reforms modernizing Japan's economy and political system. This was undoubtedly one of his greatest achievements.

In 1950 MacArthur became commander in chief of United Nations forces in the Korean War. He quarreled with Truman over the conduct of the war and was relieved of command in 1951. More popular than ever, he appeared before Congress bidding farewell with the words "Old soldiers never die, they just fade away." In fact, he spent the last decade of his life in obscurity, dying on April 5, 1964.

Erich von Manstein (1887–1973)

Erich von Manstein was a master strategist, aggressive field commander, and talented general in all major German campaigns in Europe. The son of an aristocrat and artillery officer, Erich von Manstein took the name of his uncle who adopted him. Born in Berlin, November 24, 1997, he early served as a staff officer, becoming deputy to General Ludwig Beck, chief of the General Staff, in 1936. Manstein admired Beck, who resigned in protest of Hitler's policies after the Munich conference. While chief of the General Staff, Beck backed Manstein's idea of establishing armored divisions within the German army. Hitler's purge of the army in February 1938 had led to his demotion, but he soon returned to a staff position and participated in the occupation of the Sudetenland later that year.

In the Polish campaign of September 1939, Manstein was chief of staff to Gerd von Rundstedt, and accompanied the latter the next month on the western front as they prepared for the invasion of France. Rundstedt's Army Group A had only a secondary role in the plans. Manstein believed that the operational plans under consideration erred in emphasizing the northern flank. Instead, he thought concentrated tank forces in the Ardennes in the south could make a breakthrough behind the French armies and the British Expeditionary Force, drawing them into Belgium where they would be cut off and encircled.

The repeated postponement of the campaign originally set for fall 1939 gave Manstein the opportunity to present his ideas to Hitler, who already had some of the same thoughts. When the Führer seconded his scheme, the German High Command reworked its strategy. It succeeded beyond all expectations. Although neither Manstein nor the Wehrmacht labeled the strategy blitzkrieg, that is how it soon became known.

Manstein showed himself to be not only an excellent strategist and staff planner, but as field commander of the 38th Corps in France he proved an aggressive and able leader. During Operation Barbarossa, he demonstrated the same skills, receiving rapid promotions. His 1942 campaign in the Crimea and capture of Sevastapol that July led to his promotion to field marshal.

Manstein's Army Group Don attempted the rescue of the German Sixth Army at Stalingrad, but failed. After the Stalingrad defeat in early 1943, Manstein continued to execute brilliant offensives in mobile warfare, but dwindling German strength and Hitler's unreasoned policy of a rigid, inflexible defense could not prevent the slow German retreat.

Possibly one of Hitler's most talented generals, Manstein was one of the few generals to oppose Hitler in person, and, consequently, did not escape the dictator's wrath. Dismissed in March 1944, he did not serve again. In 1949 Manstein was sentenced by a British military tribunal for crimes in the Soviet Union; he served only 4 of 18 years. He died on June 12, 1973.

George Catlett Marshall (1880–1959)

Although relatively unknown today as a soldier even among Americans, George C. Marshall was the United States' most influential strategist and military administrator during World War II. In neither world war did he have a field command. Born in Pennsylvania on December 31, 1880, he attended Virginia Military Institute rather than West Point. Although young, his reputation began to grow through his graduation at the top of the class at the Army Staff College at Fort Leavenworth and his performance on assignment in the Philippines. He served in France during World War I, and was chief aide to General John Pershing, Army Chief of Staff, from 1921 until Pershing's retirement in 1924. A tour of China followed this, as did a stint as instructor at the Army War College and the Fort Benning infantry school. In these positions, he came to know all the future major general officers of World War II. Marshall was also an advisor to the White House. As a consequence Roosevelt passed over others with seniority to make him Chief of Staff on September 1, 1939, a position he held until the autumn of 1945.

Marshall's responsibilities included turning the small 174,000–man U.S. Army, including its Army Air Forces, into the 1944 colossus of 8,000,000. He pushed preparedness with skill and determination. He understood the need for public acceptance of his program and adherence to the principles of democratic, representative government. Consequently, he worked well with members of Congress in gaining the financial and organizational authority needed to win the war. As an advocate of air power, he gave the Air Force the independence to develop its own strategic strengths. He was effective with Roosevelt, willing and able to present his differences without losing the president's trust. The same was true of his relations with the secretary of war, Henry Stimson, and his counterpart in the U.S. Navy, Admiral Ernest King, and among the British members of the Combined Chiefs of Staff.

Marshall strongly defended the Germany-first strategy of defeating the Third Reich before Japan and the need for a direct assault on Germany from Britain across the English Channel. This brought him into conflict with American notables such as General MacArthur, and with Prime Minister Churchill. He vigorously advised against Operation Torch, the 1942 landing in North Africa, but accepted Roosevelt's orders to plan and execute the invasion.

It was anticipated, including by Roosevelt, that Marshall would be Supreme Commander for Operation Overlord. Roosevelt expressed such views at the Tehran Conference, but soon decided to keep Marshall in Washington—so that he (Roosevelt) could sleep at ease, he said. He gave Eisenhower the job instead.

After Marshall's resignation as Chief of Staff in 1945, President Truman appointed him head of a mission to China to bring the Nationalists and the communists together. The mission failed. In February 1947 Truman named him Secretary of State. In that role he proposed the Marshall Plan of June 1947 for the reconstruction of western Europe. He resigned that post in January 1949, but was recalled as Secretary of Defense in September 1950, a post he held for one year. He was given the Nobel Peace Prize in 1953.

Although a reserved person (no one outside his family and a small circle of friends called him by his first name), Marshall had a reputation for fairness and for listening to all sides before making a decision. He believed politics should be left to elected officials. He was an exemplary civilian and officer.

When Congress authorized a fifth star for generals in 1944, Marshall received his with the title General of the Army. His importance to the war effort is summarized by Churchill's epithet "organizer of victory" and Truman's statement that whereas millions of Americans had rendered the nation service, Marshall had given it victory. Marshall died October 16, 1959.

Bernard Montgomery of Alamein, Bernard Law Montgomery, 1st Viscount (1887–1976)

The leading British commander in North Africa and Western Europe, Bernard Montgomery was born on November 17, 1887, in London. A graduate of the Royal Military Academy at Sandhurst, he served in the army in India before being wounded early in World War I. After that he was a staff officer. Based on those experiences, he chose to live a spartan, even austere life, avoiding tobacco and alcohol, and devoted himself to the study of war and command. He married at age 39 in 1927; his wife, Betty Carver Montgomery, died ten years later. During the interwar years he again served in India as well as Egypt and Palestine. His promotion during these years was hampered by his curt and frank treatment of others.

In 1939 Montgomery received command of the British 3rd Division, part of the Expeditionary Force in France. He also led his troops during the Dunkirk evacuation in May 1940, earning a reputation for leadership that led to higher appointments in the next two years.

In August 1942 Churchill picked Lieutenant-General William Gott to head the as yet unsuccessful Eighth Army in the Western Desert in Egypt. Gott, however, was killed when his plane was shot down on his way to take command. Montgomery replaced him. Monty, as he was popularly known, inspired confidence in the Eighth Army, turned it around and achieved victory over Field Marshal Erwin Rommel in the second battle of El Alamein in early November 1942. Montgomery had worked out a meticulous plan of attack, though he also was aided by ULTRA's intelligence on Rommel's defenses and the Afrika Korps' lack of fuel. Montgomery's reputation among his troops and the public soared. He reinforced El Alamein as a turning point in the war by pursuing Rommel across North Africa. During 1943 his achievements in Sicily and Italy were less outstanding; he was accused of excessive caution and lack of maneuver.

With his confirmation as Supreme Commander of the Allied invasion of Normandy in 1944 and in accordance with his commitment to shared commands, Eisenhower asked Montgomery to take the task of leading the Allied land operations during the first months of Overlord. Montgomery made an important contribution to planning the assault, but the failure of his 21st Army Group to capture Caen on D-Day led to rumors of his replacement. After the breakout in August, a dispute over the so-called broad-front versus a narrow thrust strategy emerged. Eisenhower, and most American generals, stuck to the broad-front approach, arguing that Allied victory was inevitable because of the growing numbers of men and supplies on their side. Therefore, any risky operations to break through German lines might cost more lives and prolong the war. Montgomery argued the opposite, that Eisenhower's sticking to pre-invasion plans prevented taking advantage of the tenuous German hold along the front in late August. Eisenhower arrived in France on September 1 and assumed command of land forces, while Montgomery was promoted to Field Marshal.

This did not resolve the conflict of personalities. Montgomery became increasingly divisive, even publicly challenging Eisenhower's conduct of the campaign. Although he failed to advance beyond Antwerp, a key port on the North Sea, and cut off German troops, he advocated Market-Garden, an airborne and tank drive across the Rhine at Arnhem to outflank the German defenses. Eisenhower reluctantly approved, as the operation required diverting supplies away from other sectors of the front. Nonetheless, he approved the plan, which in its implementation was a disaster.

This did not end the dispute, as Montgomery became more arrogant and insistent that his strategies had won the invasion thus far and would win it. Eisenhower, determined to maintain consensus among his lieutenants, kept his peace and Montgomery survived. In a January 1945 press conference, Montgomery unwisely suggested that he was responsible for the defeat of the German offensive at Ardennes the previous December. He apologized, but only after Churchill reproached him. Regardless, at war's end he was Britain's best known, most famous, and for some, most notorious general.

Certainly a singularly outstanding commander of the war, he was also one of its most controversial. He believed that effective military leaders had to make themselves visible to and well-known by their troops. He stressed training and discipline and was generally loved by his subordinates. He also was convinced of his strategic and command prowess, and the need to keep the British army, as well as his name, in the headlines, especially after American military strength overshadowed that of the Empire and Commonwealth after 1943.

Made Viscount Montgomery of Alamein in 1946, he was commander in chief of the British zone of occupation in Germany. He was Chief of the Imperial General Staff for two years and Deputy Supreme Allied Commander of Europe in NATO from 1951 to 1958. He died March 25, 1976.

Benito Mussolini (1883–1945)

Il Duce (Leader) of the Italian Fascist party and premier Benito Mussolini was born on July 29, 1883. The son of an anticlerical, socialist blacksmith father and a schoolteacher mother in the province of Flori, Mussolini traversed the entire span of politics during his lifetime. His first name was in honor of Benito Juárez, the Mexican revolutionary. He was well-educated and became fluent in German. He began a career as a schoolteacher at age 18 but gave it up for that of a revolutionary and journalist.

He joined the staff of *Avanti*, the Italian Socialist party's newspaper, becoming its editor and spokesman for the revolutionary left. A draft-dodger and pacifist before 1914, Mussolini turned nationalist when World War I broke out. Expelled from the Socialist party, he founded his own newspaper, *Il Popolo d'Italia*. He joined the army in 1915 and after the war founded the *Fasci di combattimento* (fasci referred to an ancient Roman symbol of authority, strength, and union), from which the word fascism derives.

The Fascists, originally mostly veterans, advocated radical nationalism, anticommunism, the restoration of domestic order, and a revision of the Paris peace treaties in Italy's favor. Mussolini organized paramilitary groups dressed in black shirts who pursued their goals through terror and violence as well as electoral politics. Mussolini invented much of the practice and trappings of fascism: the authoritarian leadership principle (he was Il Duce); continual marches and parading; monumental architecture; the glorification of violence, war, and the state; and the total submission of the individual in the national community. Mussolini coined the word totalitarian.

Elected to parliament, Mussolini convinced the Italian nationalists, the propertied right, and the army to support his bid for the premiership, which he gained in October 1922. Mussolini's secret police eliminated much opposition while he pursued a bellicose foreign policy. He instigated a war against Ethiopia in 1935 to avenge a humiliating defeat by the Ethiopians of 1896 and to launch a new Roman empire around the Mediterranean—*mare nostrum*, he called it. The war generated friction with Britain and France and led to cooperation between Mussolini and Hitler. An extravagant propaganda gesture, the Ethiopian war brought Italy no economic benefit, only additional expenditures.

Winning great power acquiesence to his aggression in Ethiopia, Mussolini intervened in the Spanish Civil War on the side of Franco and the Nationalists, against the Republic and its left and liberal supporters. This proved costly and brought Italy no advantage. It also further strained relations with Britain and France, though both wanted to avoid driving Mussolini into German arms.

From 1933 to 1943, Mussolini held the post of prime minister, as well as that of minister of the air force, of the army, and of the navy, along with other ministries. He did not, however, acquaint himself in detail with military issues, nor did he develop a staff to assist in that process. He did this to strengthen his role as Il Duce. The result was a lack of coordination and planning as each service pursued its own interests.

Mussolini partly feared and partly admired Hitler. Hitler used his personal charm and displays of militarism to bring Italy in March 1939 into a military alliance, the Pact of Steel, the basis of the Axis. Mussolini was cool toward German expansion, but when the Western powers stood by while Hitler violated the Munich agreement by occupying the rump Czech state in March 1939, Mussolini ordered the invasion of Albania. As later in the war, Mussolini wanted to share in the glory of imperial conquest.

Italy, however, was in no condition economically for war. Mussolini's jingoistic speeches and militant swaggering were no substitutes for the requirements of mid-century warfare. Mussolini did not join in the war in September 1939, but when Germany's quick victory over France hinted at an early peace settlement dictated by Hitler, he attacked France on June 10, 1940, without prior consultation with his cabinet or his generals. The invasion into the French Alps failed, and brought Italy only minor concessions at the armistice.

The declaration of war greatly overextended the Italian armed forces in the Mediterranean and East Africa. Anticipating German victory over Britain, Mussolini, however, ordered an advance into Egypt from the Italian colony of Libya in September so that he could claim Egypt at the peace table. The next month Italy opened a campaign against Greece. Neither succeeded. In November the torpedoes dropped by planes from the British carrier *Illustrious* sank much of the Italian navy at Taranto. The next month the British drove the Italians back into Libya, and the Greek campaign was halted by Greek resistance. The British attacked Italian forces in East Africa in January 1941. Only the German intervention in the Balkans and North Africa that spring saved the Italians from a complete rout. In exchange for military aid, Italy provided the Germans with food and labor. Mussolini's support at home, already weakened after 1939, fell precipitously.

What Mussolini called Italy's "parallel war" lasted one year. In 1941 and after, his role, never that of an equal with Hitler, became completely subordinate to the Führer. It was his decision to send troops to participate in Operation Barbarossa, but he had no influence over Rommel, nominally under Italian command. The collapse of Axis power in North Africa at the end of 1942 and the invasion of Sicily the next July led to Mussolini's downfall. On July 23, King Victor Emmanuel III, backed by the army and several leading Fascists, dismissed Mussolini from his offices. He was arrested and sequestered in a mountain sanitarium from which Hitler had him snatched by gliders.

In the 1920s Hitler idolized Mussolini, modeling much of his Nazi party activities after that of the Fascists. After Mussolini's rescue in September 1943, Hitler set him up with a pathetic Italian Social Republic with the Germans in control. On April 27, 1945, partisans arrested him and his mistress. The next day they were shot and their bodies displayed upside down from a gas station.

Chester William Nimitz (1885–1966)

Commander of the Pacific Fleet, Admiral Nimitz was born in Fredericksburg, Texas, on February 24, 1885, son of German immigrants. He wanted to attend West Point, but entered Annapolis Naval Academy instead at the age of 15, graduating in 1905. He developed an interest in submarines and in 1913 went to Germany to study diesel engines, which he helped make standard for the U.S. Navy. In 1939 he headed the Bureau of Navigation, which introduced him to President Roosevelt, who was keenly interested in naval affairs. The president regarded him favorably. In 1940 Nimitz and Admiral Husband Kimmel were the top candidates for command of the Pacific Fleet. When Kimmel was cashiered (dishonorably dismissed) after the Pearl Harbor disaster, Nimitz reluctantly took over his post; he preferred to be at sea.

Unlike most contemporaries, Nimitz did not see Pearl Harbor as a crippling blow to the U.S. Navy. The base survived, with its depots and fuel supplies; the all-important aircraft carriers were untouched. Nimitz unexpectedly did not purge Kimmel's staff in Hawaii. Instead, he built upon them to assemble a superb group to work directly with him, and William

Halsey, Raymond Spruance, Marc Mitscher, Richmond Turner, and Alexander Vandegrift.

Determined to take the offensive, Nimitz supported the Doolittle raid on Japan of April 1942. It was primarily of psychological importance to American public opinion, though it also caused the Japanese to expend scarce resources beefing up their air defenses. That same month he was named commander in chief, Pacific (CINCPAC). In the battle of Midway of June 1942 Nimitz used naval intelligence to position American forces so as to surprise and thwart the Japanese attack. Four Japanese carriers plus other ships were sunk, marking a turning point in the Pacific conflict.

Nimitz strongly advocated an aircraft-carrier-based campaign of amphibious assaults across the central Pacific to Japan. Beginning in the Marianas with the capture of Tarawa in November 1943, each assault grew in size and in numbers of casualties until they culminated in the battle of Okinawa in April 1945. Each phase of the central Pacific campaign was planned and organized by a staff in Hawaii under either Spruance or Halsey, as the two admirals and their officers alternated with one another in conducting each new operation. While this strategy was carried out, Nimitz's submarine forces devastated Japanese merchant shipping, bringing the importation of food and raw materials to half its prewar volume in early 1945. By the summer of 1945 Nimitz commanded over 6,000 ships, nearly 15,000 aircraft, and 2,000,000 men and women.

Nimitz differed with MacArthur over the strategy for the defeat of Japan. In July 1944 Roosevelt met with the two and their staffs in Hawaii. He decided to support both a liberation of the Philippines as MacArthur wanted and the island-hopping approach to Japan that Nimitz backed.

Although MacArthur planned the ceremonies aboard the U.S.S. *Missouri* ending the war, Nimitz signed the surrender document. He was promoted to fleet admiral in December 1944 and in November 1945 was appointed chief of naval operations. He retired from the Navy in 1947. In retirement he undertook several public services until his death on February 20, 1966.

Friedrich Paulus (1890–1957)

Although not one of Germany's greatest general officers, Friedrich Paulus experienced acutely the vagaries of being a career officer in the German army. He was born in Hesse on September 23, 1890, son of a reform school administrator, and thus neither Prussian nor of aristocratic birth (though he is sometimes mistakenly given a "von" in his name). Both were distinct disadvantages throughout most of his life. He compensated in part by marrying into the Romanian royal family. His wife, Elena Constance, however, disliked Hitler and his policies, though Paulus greatly admired both until 1943.

A law student, Paulus had wanted to join the navy, but was rejected. He joined the army in 1910 and served as a staff officer during World War I. At the rank of colonel, he became a chief of staff in the newly established Armored Troops Command. He was later chief of staff to Walther von Reichenau, who commanded the Tenth Army during the Polish campaign and the invasion of France. In September 1940 Paulus followed Franz Halder as chief of operations in the Army High Command, a position that brought him into close contact with Hitler. He helped plan Operation Barbarossa and in January 1942 assumed command of the Sixth Army. In this position, he took part in the renewed 1942 German offensive, this time into the Ukraine and the Caucasus. Critics questioned his appointment, because he lacked combat experience. His leadership proved satisfactory, however, at least until the Battle of Stalingrad.

In the summer of 1942 the Sixth Army's mission was to take Stalingrad, a target of questionable military value and a vast urban complex difficult to seize. In mid-September the Sixth Army and the Fourth Panzer Army under Hermann Hoth entered the city, conquering most of it by the end of the month. The next two months were decisive on the eastern front as Stalin poured troops into the city to prevent Hitler from making good his promise to take his namesake.

The Russians launched a counteroffensive in November against a sector held by Romanian armies. The Germans were surrounded by the end of the month. Paulus asked permission for a breakout, which Hitler refused. He put the prestige of the Third Reich and massive resources into the effort to hold the city. Goering promised that the Luftwaffe could supply the 250,000 troops by an airlift, but under the conditions of winter, that proved impossible. Hitler also created a new Army Group Don under Erich von Manstein.

Manstein could not relieve Paulus and advised Hitler that he should be allowed to break out while he could. Paulus remained loyal to Hitler, refusing to join with other officers who wanted to disobey the Führer. The Russians tightened the ring, leading Paulus to ask for authority to surrender on January 22, 1943. Furious, Hitler refused and promoted Paulus on January 31 to field marshal—no German field marshal had ever surrendered. That same day, Paulus surrendered. The Red Army crushed all resistance three days later.

Stalingrad cost Germany some 200,000 men, plus 30,000 wounded evacuees. Perhaps a more decisive commander willing to stand up to Hitler might have saved German lives and the country from this catastrophic defeat. The experiences of those few German generals who tried suggest that was not probable.

After the July 1944 assassination attempt on Hitler, Paulus joined the League of German Officers, formed in 1943 by officers from his Sixth Army taken prisoner by the Russians. In that role, he broadcast against the Nazi regime. Freed by the Soviets in 1953, he lived in the German Democratic Republic until his death on February 1, 1957.

Franklin Delano Roosevelt (1882–1945)

President Franklin Roosevelt was born in Hyde Park, New York, on January 3, 1882, into an upper-class family. He had a privileged childhood, with an education at Groton and at Harvard and Columbia Universities. In 1905 he married his distant cousin, Eleanor Roosevelt, the niece of President Theodore Roosevelt. From 1913 to 1920, he was Assistant Secretary of the Navy. A vice presidential candidate in 1920 with James Cox, he was defeated. The next year he suffered a debilitating attack of polio. He was never able to walk again without the assistance of braces or other support.

Eleanor helped keep him in the public eye, and in 1928 he successfully stood for governor of New York. His administration proved him a capable politician and leader. A skillful radio speaker able to instill confidence, he swept the presidential election of 1932 to begin an unprecedented thirteen years in the White House. Immediately after taking office, he used his presidential powers to begin efforts to restore the economy and put people back to work. He began the Social Security system and a host of government-sponsored programs known as the New Deal.

To some, Roosevelt was a dictator, "that man in the White House," whose measures undermined traditional American economic principles and smacked of fascism. Others praised him for steering American society away from revolution into cooperation among government, business, and labor.

Roosevelt's method of government does not permit an easy judgment about what his principles were. In foreign affairs, he seems early to have realized the challenges presented by the revisionist Axis powers, especially Germany. If so, he also understood the need to have firm public support for national policies, especially in matters of war and peace. He accepted, and signed into law, the Neutrality Acts that prohibited Americans from supplying arms or loans to nations at war. He also, however, in September 1939 suggested that Americans need not be neutral in "thought as well as in action" and succeeded in persuading Congress to modify the Neutrality Acts to permit sales of arms on a cash-and-carry basis—that is, that purchases be paid in full and carried in non-American vessels. To broaden his political support, he named the prominent Republicans Henry Stimson as Secretary of War and Franklin Knox as Secretary of the Navy.

In running for an unprecedented third term in 1940, Roosevelt irritated his opponents, but also oversaw one of the greatest debates of the American republic, that of the American role in world affairs and the heated conflict in Europe. During the summer of 1940, he agreed to supply destroyers and other arms to Britain in return for 99-year leases on western Atlantic bases. He also persuaded Congress to introduce a selective service system, the first peacetime draft in American history.

With the 1940 presidential campaign over, Roosevelt responded positively to Churchill's request for an extension of American aid, promising in December to make America the "arsenal of democracy." The resulting Lend-Lease Act of March 1941 authorized the president to extend aid to any country whose defense he saw as vital to the security of the United States. That one piece of legislation vastly extended presidential power and sped the process of rearmament in the United States. Under Roosevelt the United States emerged from its third-rate military standing to become the world's premier military power.

Simultaneously with the passing of Lend-Lease, Roosevelt entered into secret negotiations with the British over joint strategies for the defeat of Germany, and of Japan, in case of American entry into war. During the summer of 1941, this cooperation expanded into intelligence operations and scientific and technological research. Roosevelt also met with Churchill off the coast of Newfoundland in August, at Placentia Bay. Together, they issued the Atlantic Charter, a statement of democratic principles, national self-determination, and open trade.

Simultaneously, negotiations with Japan over its war in China and aggression against Indochina continued. Roosevelt responded with embargoes, but he believed that war with Japan would divert resources from the European theater at a time when the United States was rearming. Limiting the war to Europe was not to be when Tokyo decided on war.

The Japanese attack on Pearl Harbor on December 7 led to a full-fledged economic and military coordination with the British Empire and Commonwealth. Hitler and Mussolini made this acceptable to Congress by declaring war on the United States three days later.

Roosevelt moved quickly to consolidate the Grand Alliance. A United Nations Declaration came on January 1, 1942. A Combined Chiefs of Staff, including the top British and American staff officers, was created. Joint economic planning assured the continued supplying of British forces. When it became clear that the Soviet Union would survive the German onslaught, the president provided Lend-Lease aid to Moscow.

Compared to other major wartime leaders, Roosevelt intervened less often in military decisions. After realizing that the United States was unprepared for an invasion of the European continent in 1942, Roosevelt supported the Doolittle raid against Japan in April and the invasion of Guadalcanal in the Solomon Islands in August. He ordered a reluctant Chief of Staff George Marshall to prepare an invasion for November of North Africa, Operation Torch, a plan that Marshall strenuously opposed. Roosevelt felt compelled to take that action to satisfy the Russian demand for a so-called second front and to maintain American support for the Europe-first policy.

The issue of the second front plagued the alliance until June 1944. At the Casablanca conference in January 1943, the British persuaded Roosevelt that it was premature to attempt a cross-channel invasion in 1943 and that the seizure of Sicily and removal of Italy from the war was desirable and attainable. American military leaders demurred and Stalin protested, but the Italian campaign was duly opened in July during the Battle of Kursk, which drew German troops away from Russia.

At Casablanca, Roosevelt also issued an unconditional surrender declaration, designed in part to assure Stalin that the United States and the United Kingdom would not seek a separate peace. Unconditional surrender has been criticized for prolonging the war by the uncertainty as to what was meant and by eliminating the possibility of a negotiated settlement. Hitler, however, would not have negotiated and there was no opposition to his regime strong enough to overthrow it. On the other hand, the policy of unconditional surrender made an end to the Pacific war more difficult.

Roosevelt also had difficulties with Charles de Gaulle because of American recognition of the Vichy regime. Roosevelt's motives were to prevent Vichy France from allying with Germany and bringing the French colonial empire into Germany's orbit. Roosevelt also felt that France's defeat had undermined its claim to great power status, while de Gaulle's wartime activities were devoted precisely to restoring France to that status. The two men were never reconciled.

In domestic affairs, Roosevelt gave a free hand to myriad competing agencies, while he intervened to resolve conflicts. His approval of the detention of Japanese-Americans and his limited efforts to rescue Jews in Europe have overshadowed his other achievements.

Roosevelt had great interest in international affairs, but was frustrated during his first two terms as president by American isolationism. The war, its transformation of the United States into the major military power, and the domestic political support it provided gave him the opportunity to realize some of his goals. Aside from maintaining the anti-Axis coalition, Roosevelt devoted his efforts to building support in the United States Senate for an international organization. He wanted to avoid the mistakes in founding the League of Nations by bringing as many countries at the start into the United Nations as possible. The core of the United Nations would be his "four policemen": the United Kingdom, China, the Soviet Union, and the United States. Roosevelt realized the corrupt nature of Chiang Kai-shek's regime and that China was not yet a great power. He also believed, however, that China's interests conflicted less with American goals and that it would be a dependent power. Neither Churchill nor Stalin accepted that assessment, though they did agree to make China a permanent member of the UN Security Council.

Roosevelt first met Stalin at the Tehran Conference, where he stayed in the Soviet embassy and tried to mediate between Stalin and Churchill. The conference outlined future strategy for the war and began planning the postwar world order. Stalin gave a commitment to enter the East Asian war three months after the defeat of Germany. Roosevelt reluctantly agreed to the great powers staking out spheres of influence, but also realized the impossibility of winning the war without Soviet cooperation and preventing the expansion of Soviet territory.

The Yalta conference of February 1945 has been much criticized, though it largely advanced decisions agreed at Tehran. Roosevelt contributed to these criticisms by failing to inform Congress or the public about his real views on issues dealing with Poland, China, or the Soviet Union. He was determined to keep Americans in the alliance and to build an international system able to ameliorate conditions for all nations. While at Yalta, he sponsored the Declaration on Liberated Europe, which promised freely elected governments. It bound Stalin to nothing; instead, it misled Americans and laid the basis for charges that the president was ill or naive or both in dealing with Moscow.

In the weeks before he died, Roosevelt understood the real course of Soviet domination in eastern Europe. He pressed Stalin to understand American reactions and what he must do to maintain international cooperation. At the same time, Roosevelt was willing to extend American power by approving plans to establish American military bases in Africa, in the western Pacific, and elsewhere under the guise of UN trusteeships.

The president died on April 12, 1945, at Warm Springs, Georgia, while preparing to attend the founding meeting of the United Nations in San Francisco. Victory in Europe was near at hand, and the struggle against Japan was soon to be terminated, not by invasion as Roosevelt had feared, but by two atomic bombs, whose development he had endorsed even before the United States got involved in the war. Widely mourned, he is remembered largely for his New Deal administration and wartime leadership.

Albert Speer (1905–1981)

The official architect of Nazi Germany and responsible for the German arms buildup after 1942, Albert Speer was born the son of an architect in Mannheim, March 19, 1905. He came to the attention of Hitler through his work for the Nazi party. Hitler's charismatic, personal appeal made a deep impression on him. He became a close confidant of the Führer, though his social background and interests were quite different from that of other Nazi leaders. In the 1930s he organized the spectacular annual Nuremberg rallies, and designed grandiose buildings in the Nazi neoclassic style. Hitler considered him a fellow artist. They spent many hours together planning the rebuilding of postwar Berlin and the city of Linz, Austria, near Hitler's birthplace.

Speer entered the center of the National Socialist government in 1942 when he succeeded the contractor Fritz Todt as Minister of Armaments and Munitions. Todt was killed in a plane crash in February. In that position, Speer assumed control of the German war economy, though he never succeeded in subordinating the SS and other Nazi organizations to centralized direction. At no point did he control the National Socialist labor force. He also advocated a shorter work week and more-humane conditions for forced laborers, but was overruled.

With his plans, based in large part on Todt's work, Speer managed to triple Germany's arms production. He replaced Goering's unsuccessful four-year plan and an inefficient system of military procurement with a rationalized system for the allocation of resources for more clearly defined strategic objectives. He was able to do this because of his close relationship with Hitler, who gave him full support. Speer also had a talent for improvisation and getting diverse administrators in and out of government to work together. He wanted, for example, to keep labor and production in occupied countries rather than move both into the Reich.

After mid-1944, Speer lost Hitler's backing as the Allies' strategic air war took an increased toll on German war production and Himmler and the SS gained a greater voice in the war effort following the attempted assassination of the Führer in June. By the end of 1944, Speer became completely disillusioned with Hitler and countermanded his orders to leave Germany in rubble. He did, however, continue to work during the last days of the war for Hitler's successor, Admiral Karl Dönitz.

Speer was tried at Nuremberg and found guilty of war crimes and crimes against humanity. He was sentenced to 20 years in Spandau prison in Berlin. His role in the Third Reich remains controversial, in part because of the memoirs he wrote while in prison and afterwards in which he claimed not to have known about the worst aspects of the regime. He shared little of the radical racism of Hitler, but his self-depiction as an apolitical, naïve technocrat is wide of the mark. He was released from prison in 1966 and died on September 1, 1981.

Joseph Stalin (1879–1953)

The future dictator of the Soviet Union, known during the war as Marshal Stalin, was born Josif Vissarionovich Dzhugashvili on December 21, 1879, in Gori, Georgia, then part of Russia and later one of the minor republics of the Soviet Union. He studied theology, but became a Marxist and follower of Lenin's Bolshevik faction. He took the pseudonym of Stalin, man of steel, in 1913. After Lenin's death in 1924, he consolidated his control over the Communist party, and remained a dictator until his death in 1953.

Although Stalin never served as a soldier, he took an intense interest in military matters. His "Five Year Plans" stressed military preparedness. Ironically, he also conducted purges of officers in the late 1930s, which decimated the leadership of the Soviet army. Although the Soviet Union's primary threats were Japan and Germany, Stalin believed that any future military conflicts would be between capitalist countries. This belief ill-prepared him and the Soviet Union for the German invasion in June 1941.

In June 1939 Stalin dispatched General Georgi Zhukov to organize more-effective warfare against Japan in Manchuria. In August, Zhukov launched history's first campaign combining tanks, artillery, and aircraft at the battle of Nomonhan (as it is known in Japan) or Khalkhin-gol (in Russia). Although the Red Army decisively defeated the Japanese, that did not happen until the end of August. The lateness of that success in the war against Japan may have reinforced Stalin's motive for seeking an accommodation with Hitler. The Soviet-German Non-Aggression Pact signed on

August 23, 1939, shocked public opinion worldwide, but especially among communists. Stalin had portrayed himself as the primary defense against fascism and Nazism. Now national self-interest dictated another course. The pact included a secret clause calling for the division of Poland between Berlin and Moscow. It was followed up by trade agreements and Soviet annexations of the Baltic states and other territories in eastern Europe.

Stalin further secured his position by arranging a cease-fire in Manchuria, which became a Soviet-Japanese Neutrality Pact in April 1941. Repression in the Soviet Union was relaxed, but in the newly annexed lands, social groups representing national leaders were killed or sent to concentration camps. In November 1939, Stalin ordered the Red Army into Finland when the Finnish government rejected his demands for territorial concessions. The Finnish-Soviet war, the Winter War, revealed significant weaknesses in the Soviet army, though the greatly outnumbered Finns had no chance to win, especially as they lacked effective support from the Western powers. Stalin decided to negotiate, though by March 1940 the Red Army had recovered and the defeat of Finland was within reach.

Why Stalin was surprised by Operation Barbarossa is unclear. He received warnings, some from his own agents. Yet he seems to have believed that keeping Germany supplied with raw materials and food would forestall an attack, even after the Reich slowed down its promised deliveries. He did, however, order increased production of tanks. But the year that lapsed from the fall of France to the invasion was insufficient. The extension of the country's western borders did not help in defense; the new military lines were not completed by 1941, while the previous ones were weakened.

The organization of the state—which kept military and diplomatic decision making separate—the extensive terroristic use of secret police and censorship, and the recent purges inhibited effective government. Stalin compensated somewhat by his remarkable ability to remember details, a skill he used in asserting his power, but he never developed a coherent overall administration or strategy. Although he did travel abroad in his early years, he had limited foreign experience. He did not have the intellectual power of either Lenin or Trotsky.

At first, Stalin refused to believe that the German attack was in force. He did not appear to the public for two weeks, leaving it to others to bring the bad news to an unprepared public. The scale of the losses was staggering. German leaders boasted in mid-July that victory was theirs; half of the country's industry lay in German hands as well as much of its best agricultural land. Such claims were premature as the Red Army stopped the

Wehrmacht outside the gates of Moscow in late autumn. In spite of his limited military experience, Stalin appointed himself Supreme Commander and organized a state committee of defense with himself as its chair.

Stalin ordered a counteroffensive for December 1941, an act his generals thought highly ill-advised. In Zhukov he found a commander able to use limited reserves to turn the Germans back. A minor victory, it showed that the Germans were not invincible and strengthened public morale. At the same time, Stalin dropped communist rhetoric of the class struggle in favor of appeals to patriotism and Mother Russia. The campaign against the Russian Orthodox Church was also abandoned, and the Church rallied support to Russia's defense.

A Soviet campaign in spring 1942 was a disaster, and helped open the Ukraine for a renewed German offensive. In the process, Stalin became a learner, though he kept away from the front lines, directing the war by telephone. In 1942 he ordered no further retreats and forbade soldiers to surrender, holding their relatives responsible. Nazi racial atrocities and the killing of prisoners-of-war reinforced the will of Soviet citizens. Stalin refused General Andrei Vlasov's request for permission to withdraw to avoid encirclement in July 1942. The Germans captured Vlasov and permitted him to form a collaborationist army of anticommunists in 1944. Stalin even disowned his own son when he was captured and would not consider exchanging his release for that of some German officers.

Stalin conducted foreign policy with the assistance of Vyacheslav Molotov, who replaced Maxim Litvinov in the summer of 1939 as a signal to Hitler that led to the Non-Aggression Pact. An old-time, hard-line Bolshevik, Molotov worked closely with Stalin. But Stalin kept decision making in his own hands.

Stalin was the only wartime leader to be present at all three Allied summit conferences. He avoided negotiations from 1941 until the Tehran conference at the end of 1943 when he could act from strength, the German army having suffered a decisive defeat at Stalingrad early that year and now in steady retreat after the battle of Kursk in July. He continually reminded the western Allies of the cost in blood for the defeat of the Germans (four fifths of all casualties in Europe were on the eastern front), extracting as much diplomatic advantage as possible. The Americans extended massive aid in order to keep the Soviets in the war, but with none of the stipulations imposed on other recipients.

At Tehran, Stalin agreed to enter the war against Japan as the Americans wanted, but in return for concessions from China. He also demanded recognition of the Soviet annexations of 1939. Poland was to be compensated at

German expense for land the U.S.S.R. annexed. Stalin also expected reparations from the Germans. There are many examples of his ruthlessness against political opponents, national minorities, and Soviet officers. He had several thousand Polish officers murdered in 1940. At Tehran, he suggested to Churchill and Roosevelt that 50,000 German officers be summarily executed after the war, an indication of what would be in store as the Red Army swept into eastern Germany.

As the war ended, Stalin claimed all the accolades for himself. He took the title of generalissimo, after having named himself marshal of the Soviet Union in 1943. The relaxation of repression was reversed. He was more feared than ever, and was in a position to impose Stalinist regimes throughout eastern Europe. Those who would not submit to his leadership, such as the Chinese communists and Tito, became pariahs. Until his death on March 5, 1953, Stalin was the symbol of Soviet power. His leadership had propelled a weak, isolated state to the center of European politics for the next generation.

Tito, aka Josip Brozovitch or Broz (1892–1981)

Marshal Tito was born into a peasant family near Klanjec, Croatia, on May 25, 1892, and with the name Josip Brozovitch joined the Communist party in the 1920s. He was active in the Comintern (Communist International) from then until its disbandment during World War II. He used many pseudonyms before adopting that of Tito in 1934. Tito lived in Moscow for a time and was in Spain during the Spanish Civil War. He returned to Yugoslavia to head the Yugoslav Communist party and recruited Milovan Djilas, who became a close associate.

In June 1941 Tito became commander in chief of the partisans, a term that became current in the 1930s. During the war it referred to guerrilla activities in eastern Europe, but it was especially associated with Tito's movement.

Yugoslavia was occupied by German and Italian troops in April 1941. The government fled to Cairo, leaving the army under the control of Draza Mihailovic, who organized the Chetniks. The name derived from armed bands who had fought the Turks in earlier times. Tito's partisans and the Chetniks clashed in a civil war until the Germans drove each underground.

Tito moved his forces into Bosnia, where his main supporters were Croatians. Mihailovic kept his base in Serbia, with Serbs forming the core of the Chetniks, and maintained his loyalty to the monarchy and its exiled government. Rather than pursue the Germans, he chose to prepare for the liberation of the kingdom when the Germans were near defeat.

Tito initially advocated a revolutionary program, a policy he changed when Soviet victory failed to appear in 1942. In order to increase backing from the Western Allies, Moscow disbanded the Comintern and ordered the formation of broad political national fronts of communists and noncommunists. Tito complied, bringing a wide variety of ethnic and political groups into the partisan movement.

The wartime role of the partisans is shrouded in uncertainties and controversy. Tito emerged the victor in 1945, and his communist regime wrote the history of those years, portraying the partisans as unrelenting resisters and revolutionaries opposed to the Nazi occupation. The Chetniks were depicted as reactionaries. The story is more complex.

The partisans did fight the Germans, who mounted several campaigns against them. At times, though, Tito cooperated with them in order to defeat the Chetniks before an anticipated Anglo-American invasion. Like Mihailovic, Tito had his eye not only on the expulsion of the Wehrmacht but also on the postwar organization of the country.

Nonetheless, Tito turned a guerrilla force into a political movement with support from various nationalities in Yugoslavia. His charismatic leadership transformed local leaders with parochial interests into members of a pan-Yugoslav movement. More importantly, he managed to persuade Churchill and Roosevelt that the partisans more effectively fought the Germans than the Chetniks. The Tehran Conference of November 1943 recognized his movement as the main resistance force, and the Allies supplied him with much military aid. The Allied invasion of Italy also opened up new opportunities as the Italian occupation of Croatia collapsed.

In June 1944 Tito, driven almost to defeat by a final German offensive, agreed reluctantly to British demands that he enter a coalition government with Ivan Subasic, the prime minister of the government-in-exile. Tito now turned his attention to defeating the Chetniks, the main rival to the partisan conquest of Yugoslavia. Rapidly gaining political and military stature, Tito joined with the Red Army in liberating Belgrade in October. He now became the only serious future leader of the country. In March he formed a predominantly communist government, grounded in patriotism and reform, and was elected prime minister. His strength was great enough to enable him to reject British-Soviet proposals for the partition of Yugoslavia, and in 1948 he broke with Stalin to wield his own form of "national Communism." From then until his death on May 4, 1981, Tito held unchallenged power, undoubtedly the most successful resistance leader of the war.

Sir Henry Tizard (1885–1959)

One of World War II's leading scientists and science administrators, Henry Tizard was born into a navy family in Kent, England, on August 23, 1885. He studied mathematics and science at Oxford, graduating from Magdalen College in 1908. He also studied in Berlin, where he met his later nemesis, the physicist Frederick Lindemann. In World War II, science and technology played a greater role than in previous conflicts. Tizard was also a trained pilot, having served in World War I. Although his science specialty was physical chemistry, his background as a pilot and his wide interests in science, experience in management, and communication skills made it possible for him to bring together different professional communities.

Tizard headed the British Air Ministry's Scientific Survey of Air Defence from 1934 until 1940, usually known as the Tizard Committee. He also served in other science administrative positions, for example, as rector of the Imperial College. The great concern of the mid-1930s was to develop a means to defend Britain from the air. At the time, most believed that no defense was possible. The Scots physicist Robert Watson-Watt in 1934 demonstrated the possibility of radar (an acronym for *ra*dio *d*etection *a*nd *r*anging), though inventors in several countries made the same discovery in the mid-1930s.

Watson-Watt's work was known to Tizard, who supported his research and realized its possibilities. What was needed was a comprehensive radar scheme to link individual sets to a central command network that could then direct aircraft in the air from the ground. Tizard expertly joined his scientific understanding, administrative skills, and experience as a pilot in creating the Chain Home, so vital to defeating the Luftwaffe in the Battle of Britain in 1940, and in air defense after that.

Tizard also took up the problem of developing a variety of radar systems, including airborne radar, and the use of radio for navigation by aircraft. His involvement in a variety of war-related scientific projects led to his heading a mission to Canada and the United States in September 1940 to inform the North Americans of a variety of British scientific advances including the cavity magnetron in radar, but also ASDIC and the proximity fuse, among others. The cavity magnetron, invented early in 1940, was an electronic vacuum tube generating microwaves suitable for airborne radar. Impressed, the Americans established their own radar laboratory at the Massachusetts Institute of Technology two months later. ASDIC (acronym for *A*llied *S*ubmarine *D*etection *I*nvestigation *C*ommittee) was designed for submarine detection, though it was limited to distance and direction, and could not determine depth. Subsequently, the U.S. Navy developed a similar weapon, sonar. The proximity fuse was a radio emitting transceiver small enough to fit into an explosive projectile. It did not have to come into direct contact with its target in order to explode. It proved so effective in the air war that it was not fired over German occupied territory for fear an unexploded one would reveal its secret.

Tizard also was involved with the British investigation of an atomic bomb, assisting in establishing cooperation between Britain and the United States in the Manhattan Engineering project. His scientific work on aircraft fuels was also important to the war effort. It led to the system of octane rating now used globally.

Unfortunately, Tizard's talents were largely lost to the war effort by the personal antipathy between him and Frederick Lindemann (ennobled as Lord Cherwell in 1941), Churchill's close friend and science advisor.

After the war, Tizard worked on defense issues with the British dominions and helped to establish close connections between science and military defense. He retired in 1952 and died on October 9, 1959.

Harry S Truman (1884–1972)

Harris S Truman, the 33rd President of the United States, was born on May 8, 1884, and grew up on the family farm near Independence, Missouri. He failed to get into West Point because of poor eyesight. This prevented his getting a college education, as his family was too poor to pay the tuition anywhere else. He served in World War I. After the war, Truman soon turned to politics, becoming active in the state Democratic party machine. He served as a judge and was elected in 1934 to the United States Senate.

Truman rose to national prominence by chairing a Special Committee to Investigate the National Defense Program from early 1941. A strong supporter of Roosevelt's New Deal, he acquired a reputation for loyalty, honesty, and hard work.

Roosevelt picked him as his running mate to overcome a split in the Democratic party between progressive, pro-labor forces and southern conservatives. As a border state senator with a war record, Truman made a good candidate, though his relations with Roosevelt were never close. Even after the election, Truman, who held the president in high regard, had limited access to him. Particularly unfortunate was his unawareness of the administration's policies and decisions in foreign affairs.

Roosevelt's death on April 12, 1945, catapulted Harry Truman into prominence. At first, Truman lacked confidence in his ability adequately to follow Roosevelt's footsteps; wide segments of the population shared this view. But he soon surprised his critics. Feisty, diligent, and straight-talking, Truman's traits are celebrated in aphorisms such as "If you can't stand the heat, get out of the kitchen" or "The buck stops here."

Truman knew nothing of the atomic bomb project until becoming president. Roosevelt also had not confided in him the results of the Yalta conference; its substance had been kept secret. Undaunted, Truman publicly declared his intention to maintain Roosevelt's course.

The successful San Francisco conference, which established the United Nations, pleased him. But as the defeat of Germany neared and the Red Army occupied eastern Europe, conflicts grew. Truman believed that Moscow was reverting to prewar "power politics" to replace collective security. In a meeting with Molotov ten days after Roosevelt's death, Truman attacked the Soviets for violating the Yalta agreements, though he also expressed a desire to cooperate and to have the Soviets enter the war against Japan.

Although the war was coming to a conclusion, Truman continued the atomic bomb project. The Japanese showed no signs of surrendering; the battle for Okinawa indicated that the costs of an invasion would be high. An Interim Committee, chaired by Secretary of War Henry L. Stimson, was charged with deciding how to use the bomb. At its May 31 meeting, it recommended that the bomb be dropped without warning. Neither the committee nor Truman decided to use the bomb; rather, they never decided not to use it. Their discussions were on how to use it.

Truman met with Churchill (later Attlee) and Stalin for two weeks beginning on July 17 at Potsdam, a suburb of Berlin and symbol of German militarism. The day before, the first atomic bomb test showed that the United States had an awesome, unprecedented military weapon. Truman told Stalin that the United States had an unusually powerful new weapon, to which Stalin, who knew from spies of the project, replied that he hoped Truman would use it.

Possession of the bomb changed Truman's mood and has given rise to the notion that he turned to "atomic diplomacy" to reverse previous agreements with Stalin. Whatever the truth, Potsdam was contentious, with arguments erupting over Soviet policies in eastern Europe, Poland's borders, and German reparations. The Big Three did agree, however, to establish a council of foreign ministers that was to meet frequently to resolve differences.

At Potsdam, the United Kingdom, the United States, and China (China signed the Potsdam Declaration although it did not sit in on the Potsdam deliberations) issued an ultimatum to Japan to surrender unconditionally or face utter destruction. Truman knew that one of the sticking points for the Japanese was the future of the emperor. For this reason, the declaration made no reference to the emperor. Tokyo's response was "to treat [the ultimatum] with silent contempt." Truman then gave the go ahead to drop the available bombs; there were two on Tinian, location of the B-29 air bases in the Mariana Islands. The first fell on Hiroshima, August 6, the second on Nagasaki, August 9. The American public overwhelmingly approved and supported even more bombing.

Most of Truman's presidential years were after the war. He presided over the growing tensions of the Cold War. In 1947 he offered aid to Greece and Turkey to resist communist pressures, and authorized the Marshall Plan. The next year he ordered the desegregation of the armed forces, and responded to Soviet threats against Allied occupation rights in Berlin with the Berlin airlift.

In one of the great upsets of American electoral history, he defeated Thomas E. Dewey for the presidency in 1948. After that, he helped develop NATO and took the United States into the Korean War at the head of a UN coalition. The fall of the Chinese Nationalists to the communists in 1949, the "red scares," and the stalemate in the Korean war contributed to his great unpopularity by 1952. He chose not to run for reelection, and retired to develop his presidential library in Independence, Missouri. He died on December 26, 1972.

Isoruku Yamamoto (1884–1943)

Born on April 4, 1884, the son of a schoolteacher in Nagaoka, Japan, Isoruku Takano was one of Japan's most brilliant, cosmopolitan strategic thinkers and naval commanders. Yet he was enigmatic and willing to take great risks, sometimes against what he considered unlikely odds. He graduated from the Japanese Naval Academy before the battle of Tsushima, where the Japanese Navy trounced the Russian fleet. When his parents died, the 20-year-old Isoruku was adopted by the Yamamoto family, and he took Yamamoto as his family name.

He studied at Harvard from 1916 to 1918, with special interests in petroleum and air power. He became a master poker, bridge, and chess player. Back in Japan he briefly headed a new air training base before being assigned to Washington as a naval attaché (1925–1927).

In the 1930s Yamamoto ardently advocated building a strong navy based on aircraft carriers rather than battleships. In 1933 he was made commander of the 1st Carrier Division and reached the rank of vice admiral two years later. He opposed the limitations placed on Japanese naval tonnage, which he helped get altered. He also opposed those who advocated an extension of the war in China, and he did not want Japan to join the Axis. For these reasons there was danger that extremist militarists might assassinate him.

Yamamoto was made commander in chief of the Combined Fleet in 1939 and went to sea. Though he had little regard for the quality of the U.S. Navy, which he knew well, he also thought Japan had no chance of winning a war with the United States because of American industrial prowess. He came to believe, however, that the only chance for victory was a preemptive strike at the major U.S. Navy base at Pearl Harbor. If Pearl Harbor was destroyed, the Americans might accept Japan's demands against China. The attack on Pearl Harbor on December 7, 1941, appeared successful, and brought him enormous prestige and popularity. But it failed to cripple American naval power—in part because American carriers were at sea, in part because the enormous fuel supplies were not attacked, and in part because Pearl Harbor riveted Americans to the defeat of Japan as no previous action had.

The extension of Japanese power throughout Southeast Asia led Yamamoto to advocate another strike against the United States, this time at Midway. His idea was to draw the American fleet into a decisive action and further extend Japanese defenses in the western Pacific. Midway, however, was a Japanese disaster. In its planning, the campaign for Midway became increasingly complex and lost its focus. In addition, American intelligence uncovered the plan and Admiral Chester Nimitz devised a counterstroke that proved successful, though Japanese defeat was not inevitable.

Yamamoto continued as commander in chief, with some successes in the Solomon Islands. In April 1943, American naval intelligence learned the flight plan for one of Yamamoto's inspection tours. He would be within range of P-38s. Washington gave Nimitz permission to shoot him down, which was done on April 18. He died in the crash. The Japanese government did not reveal Yamamoto's death for some time, and never suspected the reason for it.

Georgi Zhukov (1896–1974)

Considered by some the greatest general of World War II, Georgi Zhukov was the son of peasants, born near Moscow on December 1, 1896. From his youth, he took an interest in self-cultivation; he lacked formal education. He was conscripted during World War I into the cavalry. After the war, he joined the Red Army, remaining in the cavalry, then entering the armored branch. His rise to military leadership began with his assignment to the

Outer Mongolia-Manchukuo border to organize resistance against the Japanese. In August 1939, he led history's first combined air, tank, and artillery operation at Khalkhin-gol (known as Nomonhan in Japanese) to trounce units of the Kwantung Army. In 1940 he was promoted to the newly established rank of General of the Army. That year he also led the takeover of Bessarabia.

In January 1941 Stalin promoted Zhukov to Chief of the General Staff, though he had no previous staff experience. He carried out various tasks during the summer of 1941 and then was removed from the General Staff and assigned to the Leningrad Army Group, though he remained on Stavka (the General Headquarters of the Armed Forces). In October Stalin reassigned him to the defense of Moscow, the rescue of which made Zhukov a national hero. When the Germans halted, he dispatched a counteroffensive on December 6 that continued into late winter of 1942.

When the renewed German campaign of 1942 poured into southern Ukraine and the Caucasus, Stalin advanced Zhukov to Deputy Supreme Commander, the position he retained until the end of the war. He spent most of the war in Moscow with Stalin planning strategy. As Deputy Supreme Commander, he organized operation Uranus, the titanic struggle against the Germans that ended with the destruction of their Sixth Army at Stalingrad in early 1943. For that victory, he became a marshal, the war's first on the Soviet side.

With his deputy Alexander Vasilevsky, Zhukov coordinated the major Soviet operations of the war, breaking the siege of Leningrad, planning the operations around the Kursk, and others. They coordinated the war's largest campaign, Bagration, against the German Army Group Center, which opened on June 23, 1944. It included 2,400,000 men, 5,200 tanks, and 5,300 airplanes.

Given the honor of taking Berlin as commander of the First Belorussian Army Group, Zhukov, flanked by Ivan Konev's First Ukrainian Army Group on his left and Konstantin Rokossovky's Second Belorussian on the right, opened the campaign to take Berlin on January 12, 1945. His Army Group came within 40 miles of Berlin before the end of the month. Stalin, however, ordered him to stop, and the rush to take Berlin did not begin again until mid-April. The final assault was slow, lasting over two weeks.

In the Soviet occupation of Germany, Zhukov was military governor and member of the Allied Control Council. He was second only to Stalin in popularity, a position that soon brought him obscurity. He was recalled from Germany in 1946 and assigned to a remote command. Only after Stalin's death, was he rehabilitated, becoming Defense Minister in 1955 under Khrushchev. In 1957, however, he was relieved of all posts and retired. Leonid Brezhnev rehabilitated him once again in 1965, and he received full honors at his death, which was on June 18, 1974.

Primary Documents of the War

Document 1
ROOSEVELT'S FIRESIDE CHAT OF
SEPTEMBER 3, 1939

Franklin Roosevelt brought the office of the presidency closer to the American people than any previous leader. One of the ways he did this was through periodic "fireside chats" in which he talked directly to the American public.

Radio, the new communications medium, made that possible. In many ways, radio was characteristic of World War II. Newspapers were typical of late-nineteenth-century mass communications and were especially important during World War I. Television, though in its infancy, did not become an important means of communication until the 1950s. Radio, however, meant that people who could not read could listen. It also meant that they could listen while they worked, cleaned up the kitchen, or sat around the table.

The following fireside chat came immediately after the outbreak of war in Europe. The United States was officially neutral. Congressional legislation forbade American citizens and companies to sell, trade, finance, or transport anything to nations at war. These "Neutrality Acts" were thought to be the nation's best guarantee that the United States would not get involved in another war. Though Roosevelt's view of this policy is not completely clear, this fireside chat clearly expresses his sympathy for the Polish people suffering from German aggression as well as that declaration of war by France and Great Britain. In November 1939 Congress amended the "Neutrality Acts" to permit Americans to sell arms to countries at war on condition that they paid for them in cash and transported them in non-American ships. This was known as the "Cash and Carry" policy.

My fellow Americans and my friends:

Tonight my single duty is to speak to the whole of America.

Until four-thirty this morning I had hoped against hope that some miracle would prevent a devastating war in Europe and bring to an end the invasion of Poland by Germany.

For four long years a succession of actual wars and constant crises have shaken the entire world and have threatened in each case to bring on the gigantic conflict which is today unhappily a fact.

It is right that I should recall to your minds the consistent and at times successful efforts of your Government in these crises to throw the full weight of the United States into the cause of peace. In spite of spreading wars I think that we have every right and every reason to maintain as a national policy the fundamental moralities, the teachings of religion and the continuation of efforts to restore peace—for some day, though the time may be distant, we can be of even greater help to a crippled humanity.

It is right, too, to point out that the unfortunate events of these recent years have, without question, been based on the use of force and the threat of force. And it seems to me clear, even at the outbreak of this great war, that the influence of America should be consistent in seeking for humanity a final peace which will eliminate, as far as it is possible to do so, the continued use of force between nations.

It is, of course, impossible to predict the future. I have my constant stream of information from American representatives and other sources throughout the world. You, the people of this country, are receiving news through your radios and your newspapers at every hour of the day.

You are, I believe, the most enlightened and the best informed people in all the world at this moment. You are subjected to no censorship of news, and I want to add that your Government has no information which it withholds or which it has any thought of withholding from you.

At the same time, as I told my press conference on Friday, it is of the highest importance that the press and the radio use the utmost caution to discriminate between actual verified fact on the one hand, and mere rumor on the other.

I can add to that by saying that I hope the people of this country will also discriminate most carefully between news and rumor. Do not believe of necessity everything you hear or read. Check up on it first.

You must master at the outset a simple but unalterable fact in modern foreign relations between nations. When peace has been broken anywhere, the peace of all countries everywhere is in danger.

It is easy for you and for me to shrug our shoulders and to say that conflicts taking place thousands of miles from the continental United States, and, indeed, thousands of miles from the whole American Hemisphere, do not seriously affect the Americas—and that all the United States has to do is to ignore them and go about its own business. Passionately though we may desire detachment, we are forced to realize that every word that comes through the air, every ship that sails the sea, every battle that is fought, does affect the American future.

Let no man or woman thoughtlessly or falsely talk of America sending its armies to European fields. At this moment there is being prepared a proclamation of American neutrality. This would have been done even if there had been no neutrality statute on the books, for this proclamation is in accordance with international law and in accordance with American policy.

This will be followed by a Proclamation required by the existing Neutrality Act. And I trust that in the days to come our neutrality can be made a true neutrality. It is of the utmost importance that the people of this country, with the best information in the world, think things through. The most dangerous enemies of American peace are those who, without well-rounded information on the whole broad subject of the past, the present and the future, undertake to speak with assumed authority, to talk in terms of glittering generalities, to give to the nation assurances or prophesies which are of little present or future value.

I myself cannot and do not prophesy the course of events abroad—and the reason is that, because I have of necessity such a complete picture of what is going on in every part of the world, I do not dare to do so. And the other reason is that I think it is honest for me to be honest with the people of the United States.

I cannot prophesy the immediate economic effect of this new war on our nation, but I do say that no American has the moral right to profiteer at the expense either of his fellow citizens or of the men, the women and the children who are living and dying in the midst of war in Europe.

Some things we do know. Most of us in the United States believe in spiritual values. Most of us, regardless of what church we belong to, believe in the spirit of the New Testament—a great teaching which opposes itself to the use of force, of armed force, of marching armies and falling bombs. The overwhelming masses of our people seek peace—peace at home, and the kind of peace in other lands which will not jeopardize our peace at home.

We have certain ideas and certain ideals of national safety, and we must act to preserve that safety today, and to preserve the safety of our children in future years.

That safety is and will be bound up with the safety of the Western Hemisphere and of the seas adjacent thereto. We seek to keep war from our own firesides by keeping war from coming to the Americas. For that we have historic precedent that goes back to the days of the Administration of President George Washington. It is serious enough and tragic enough to every American family in every State in the Union to live in a world that is torn by wars on other continents. Those wars today affect every American home. It is our national duty to use every effort to keep them out of the Americas.

And at this time let me make the simple plea that partisanship and selfishness be adjourned; and that national unity be the thought that underlies all others.

This nation will remain a neutral nation, but I cannot ask that every American remain neutral in thought as well. Even a neutral has a right to take account of facts. Even a neutral cannot be asked to close his mind or his conscience.

I have said not once, but many times, that I have seen war and that I hate war. I say that again and again. I hope the United States will keep out of this war. I believe that it will. And I give you assurance and reassurance that every effort of your Government will be directed toward that end.

As long as it remains within my power to prevent, there will be no blackout of peace in the United States.

Source: Franklin D. Roosevelt. *The Public Papers and Addresses of Franklin D. Roosevelt*, vol. 8, pp. 460–464. New York: Macmillan, 1941.

Document 2
THE ATLANTIC CHARTER

Although Prime Minister Winston Churchill and President Franklin Roosevelt engaged in a famous and revealing correspondence with one another beginning in September 1939, they did not meet until August 1941. Both wartime leaders secretly left their capitals accompanied by military staff officers to meet at Placentia Bay, off the coast of Newfoundland, from August 9 to August 12, 1941. The discussions aboard the American cruiser *Augusta* and the British battle cruiser *Prince of*

Wales covered a wide range of issues, especially the threat from Japan in East Asia. The conference concluded with the issuance of a statement of eight principles now known as the "Atlantic Charter." The military aspects of the conference were not made public, nor was the fact that Japan was a major topic of discussion.

Even though the United States was not at war when the Atlantic Charter was published, the Charter is the most important statement of Allied war aims. It was not a treaty and was never ratified by any legislative body. A close reading of its main points indicates that it was largely a document designed to elicit the support of American internationalists, anticolonialists, and advocates of free trade.

Historians as well as contemporaries have had very divided opinions about the importance of the Atlantic Charter. Nationalists in British colonies, for example, immediately appealed to London for the implementation of the provision of the third article. Many Americans also raised the same question, causing Churchill to declare that those provisions of the Charter only applied to Axis-occupied countries. The principles stated in the Charter were never enshrined in a treaty. Later agreements, such as the territorial changes in eastern Europe, did not accord with the will of the peoples concerned. On the other hand, the establishment of the International Monetary Fund and the World Bank realized some of the promises of points four and five. Finally, the vague principles of numbers six and eight led to the establishment of the United Nations.

What follows is taken from the report of the President to the United States Congress after his return.

The President of the United States and the Prime Minister, Mr. Churchill, representing His Majesty's Government in the United Kingdom, have met at sea.

They have been accompanied by officials of their two Governments, including high-ranking officers of their Military, Naval, and Air Services. The whole problem of the supply of munitions of war, as provided by the Lease-Lend Act, for the armed forces of the United States and for those countries actively engaged in resisting aggression has been further examined.

Lord Beaverbrook, the Minister of Supply of the British Government, has joined in these conferences. He is going to proceed to Washington to discuss further details with appropriate officials of the United States Government.

These conferences will also cover the supply problems of the Soviet Union. The President and the Prime Minister have had several conferences. They have considered the dangers to world civilization arising from the policies of military domination by conquest upon which the Hitlerite government of Germany and other governments associated therewith have embarked, and have made clear the stress which their countries are respectively taking for their safety in the face of these dangers. They have agreed upon the following joint declaration:

A joint declaration of the President of the United States of America and the Prime Minister, Mr. Churchill, representing His Majesty's Government in the United Kingdom, being met together, deem it right to make known certain common principles in the national policies of their respective countries on which they base their hopes for a better future for the world.

First, their countries seek no aggrandizement, territorial or other;

Second, they desire to see no territorial changes that do not accord with the freely expressed wishes of the peoples concerned;

Third, they respect the right of all peoples to choose the form of government under which they will live; and they wish to see sovereign rights and self-government restored to those who have been forcibly deprived of them;

Fourth, they will endeavor, with due respect for their existing obligations, to further the enjoyment by all States, great or small, victor or vanquished, of access, on equal terms, to the trade and to the raw materials of the world which are needed for their economic prosperity;

Fifth, they desire to bring about the fullest collaboration between all nations in the economic field with the object of securing, for all, improved labor standards, economic advancement, and social security;

Sixth, after the final destruction of the Nazi tyranny, they hope to see established a peace which will afford to all nations the means of dwelling in safety within their own boundaries, and which will afford assurance that all the men in all the lands may live out their lives in freedom from fear and want;

Seventh, such a peace should enable all men to traverse the high seas and oceans without hindrance;

Eighth, they believe that all of the nations of the world, for realistic as well as spiritual reasons, must come to the abandonment of the use of force. Since no future peace can be maintained if land, sea, or air armaments continue to be employed by nations which threaten, or may threaten, aggression outside of their frontiers, they believe, pending the establishment of a wider and permanent system of general security, that the disarmament of such nations is essential. They will likewise aid and encourage all other practicable measures which will lighten for peace-loving peoples the crushing burden of armaments.

Franklin D. Roosevelt
Winston S. Churchill

Source: United States, 77th Congress, lst Session, House Document No. 358. "Message of President Roosevelt to the Congress, August 21, 1941." Washington, D.C.: GPO, 1941.

Document 3
CHURCHILL'S TELEGRAM TO ROOSEVELT OF DECEMBER 7, 1940

As a result of "Cash and Carry," the British government and British manufacturers (as well as other belligerents such as France and Japan) could make purchases in the United States, thus helping to stimulate the production of war-related equipment. It also meant, however, that Britain had to finance those purchases through the transfer of gold to the United States and through the sale of assets outside of the United Kingdom. The result was that the United States became the world's largest holder of gold reserves. More importantly, the United Kingdom came to the verge of bankruptcy by the autumn of 1940.

President Roosevelt ran for reelection for an unprecedented third term in 1940. His opponent was a liberal, internationalist Wendell Willkie, a successful businessman who agreed with Roosevelt's overall foreign policy. Churchill did not wish to interfere in the American political process. On the other hand, British propaganda was very active during the 1940 American debate between the isolationists and the internationalists. The Battle of Britain, for example, became a primary vehicle for persuading Americans of the Nazi danger.

A month after the results of the November election returned Roosevelt to the White House, Churchill sent a lengthy telegram to the president. It is a remarkable single document. In it, Churchill surveyed the world scene and Britain's role in Europe and Asia. The United Kingdom and its Commonwealth allies were the sole countries fighting the Germans—in North Africa, in the air, and at sea. In East Asia, the British were nearly completely bereft of military forces.

At the close of his memorandum to the president, Churchill pointed out that Britain could no longer purchase weapons in the United States on a cash and carry basis.

London
December 7th, 1940

My Dear Mr. President:

As we reach the end of this year I feel that you expect me to lay before you the prospects for 1941. I do so strongly and confidently because it seems to me that the vast majority of American citizens have recorded their conviction that the safety of the United States as well as the future of our two democracies and the kind of civilisation for which they stand are bound up with the survival and independence of the British Commonwealth of Nations. Only thus can those bastions of sea-power, upon which the control of the Atlantic and the Indian Oceans depends, be preserved in faithful and friendly hands. The control of the Pacific by the United States Navy and of the Atlantic by the British Navy is indispensable to the security of the trade routes of both our countries and the surest means to preventing the war from reaching the shores of the United States.

2. There is another aspect. It takes between three and four years to convert the industries of a modern state to war purposes. Saturation point is reached when the maximum industrial effort that can be spared from civilian needs has been applied to war production. Germany certainly reached this point by the end of 1939. We in the British Empire are now only about half-way through the second year. The United States, I should suppose, was by no means so far advanced as we. Moreover, I understand that immense programmes of naval, military, and air defence are now on foot in the United States, to complete which certainly two years are needed. It is our British duty in the common interest as also for our own survival to hold the front and grapple with Nazi power until the preparations of the United States are complete. Victory may come before the two years are out; but we have no right to count upon it to the extent of relaxing any effort that is humanly possible. Therefore I submit with very great respect for your good and friendly consideration that there is a solid identity of interests between the British Empire and the United States while these conditions last. It is upon this footing that I venture to address you.

3. The form which this war has taken and seems likely to hold does not enable us to match the immense armies of Germany in any theatre where their main power can be brought to bear. We can however by the use of sea power and air power meet the German armies in the regions where only comparatively small forces can be brought into action. We must do our best to prevent German domination of Europe spreading into Africa and into Southern Asia. We have also to maintain in constant readiness in this Island armies strong enough to make the problem of an overseas invasion insoluble.

4. The first half of 1940 was a period of disaster for the Allies and for the Empire. The last five months have witnessed a strong and perhaps unexpected recovery by Great Britain; fighting alone but with invaluable aid in munitions and in destroyers placed at our disposal by the great Republic of which you are for the third time chosen chief.

5. The danger of Great Britain being destroyed by a swift overwhelming blow has for the time being very greatly receded. In its place there is a long, gradually maturing danger, less sudden and less spectacular but equally deadly. This mortal danger is the steady and increasing diminution of sea tonnage. We can endure the shattering of our dwellings and the slaughter of our civilian population by indiscriminate air attacks and we hope to parry these increasingly as our science develops and to repay them upon military objectives in Germany as our Air Force more nearly approaches the strength of the enemy. The decision for 1941 lies upon the seas; unless we can establish our ability to feed this Island, to import munitions of all kinds which we need, unless we can move our armies to the various theatres where Hitler and his confederate Mussolini must be met, and maintain them there and do all this with the assurance of being able to carry it on till the spirit of the continental dictators is broken, we may fall by the way and the time needed by the United States to complete her defensive preparations may not be forthcoming. . . .

10. A third sphere of danger [the second being the possibility of Vichy France joining the Axis] is in the Far East. Here it seems clear that the Japanese are thrusting Southward through Indo China to Saigon and other naval and air bases, thus bringing them within a comparatively short distance of Singapore and the Dutch East Indies. . . .

11. In the face of these dangers, we must try to use the year 1941 to build up such a supply of weapons, particularly aircraft, both by increased output at home in spite of bombardment, and through oceanborne supplies, as will lay the foundation of victory. . . .

12. The prime need is to check or limit the loss of tonnage on the Atlantic approaches to our Islands. This may be achieved both by increasing the naval forces which cope with attacks, and by adding to the number of merchant ships on which we depend. For the first purpose there would seem to be the following alternatives:

(1) [T]he reassertion by the United States of the doctrine of the freedom of the seas. . . .

(2) It would, I suggest, follow that protection should be given to this lawful trading by United States forces i.e. escorting battleships, cruisers, destroyers and air flotillas. . . .

(3) Failing the above, the gift, loan or supply of a large number of American vessels of war, above all destroyers already in the Atlantic, is indispensable to the maintenance of the Atlantic route. Further, could not United States naval forces extend their sea control over the American side of the Atlantic. . . .

(4) [Asking U.S. assistance to procure facilities in Ireland for British ships.][1]

13. The object of the foregoing measures is to reduce to manageable proportions the present destructive losses at sea. . . .

16. I am arranging to present you with a complete programme of munitions of all kinds which we seek to obtain from you, the greater part of which is of course already agreed. . . .

17. Last of all I come to the question of finance. The more rapid and abundant the flow of munitions and ships which you are able to send us, the sooner will our dollar credits be exhausted. They are already as you know very heavily drawn upon by payments we have made to date. Indeed as you know orders already placed or under negotiation, including expenditures settled or pending for creating munitions factories in the United States, many times exceed the total exchange resources remaining at the disposal of Great Britain. The moment approaches when we shall no longer be able to pay cash for shipping and other supplies. . . .

18. Moreover I do not believe the Government and people of the United States would find it in accordance with the principles which guide them, to confine the help which they have so generously promised only to such munitions of war and commodities as could be immediately paid for. You may be assured that we shall prove ourselves ready to suffer and sacrifice to the utmost for the Cause, and that we glory in being its champion. The rest we leave with confidence to you and to your people, being sure that ways and means will be found which future generations on both sides of the Atlantic will approve and admire.

19. If, as I believe, you are convinced, Mr. President, that the defeat of the Nazi and Fascist tyranny is a matter of high consequence to the people of the United States and to the Western Hemisphere, you will regard this letter not as an appeal for aid, but as a statement of the minimum action necessary to the achievement of our common purpose.

I remain,

Yours very sincerely, Winston S. Churchill

NOTE

1. Item 12(4) is paraphrased from the original wording.

Source: *Foreign Relations of the United States, 1940*, vol. 3, pp. 18–26. Washington, D.C.: GPO, 1957.

Document 4
PRESIDENT FRANKLIN D. ROOSEVELT'S ANNUAL
MESSAGE TO THE CONGRESS, JANUARY 6, 1941
(FOUR FREEDOMS SPEECH)

President Roosevelt's response to Churchill's appeal for arms in the face of the exhaustion of Britain's financial reserves is found in the following speech. The election campaign of 1940 stirred one of the greatest debates in the republic's history between advocates of intervention in the war on the side of the British or at least extending aid to them, and the isolationists, some of whom believed the president secretly wanted to take the country to war. The debate continued as American rearmament accelerated and the war in Europe and North Africa dragged on.

In this speech Roosevelt set his proposal for the United States to become the "arsenal of democracy" within the context of American defense policy and his general foreign policy goals. Roosevelt and many of his advisors were skeptical that Britain had run out of cash. This led Churchill to order British officials to show their books to the Americans in order to persuade them. Convinced of the need to act, Roosevelt at a press conference in December 1940 used the analogy of loaning a neighbor a garden hose in order to help him put out a fire. When the fire was out, the hose would be returned.

There were hurdles. American legislation prohibited loans to countries that had not repaid their World War I debts: Only Finland had done that. Roosevelt needed an approach that did not look like credit or subsidies. He also wanted a policy that would avoid the commitment of American men to military action. Lend-Lease was the answer.

Two months later, on March 11, Congress passed H. R. 1776 authorizing appropriations for what became known as Lend-Lease. The legislation authorized the president to extend aid to any nation whose defense he saw as vital to the defense of the United States. During the course of the next four years some 38 countries received some $42 billion in equipment and services from the United States.

Mr. President, Mr. Speaker, Members of the Seventy-seventh Congress:

I ADDRESS you, the Members of the Seventy-seventh Congress, at a moment unprecedented in the history of the Union. I use the word "unprecedented," because at no previous time has American security been as seriously threatened from without as it is today. . . .

Every realist knows that the democratic way of life is at this moment being directly assailed in every part of the world—assailed either by arms, or by secret spreading of poisonous propaganda by those who seek to destroy unity and promote discord in nations that are still at peace.

During sixteen long months this assault has blotted out the whole pattern of democratic life in an appalling number of independent nations, great and small. The assailants are still on the march, threatening other nations, great and small.

Therefore, as your President, performing my constitutional duty to "give to the Congress information of the state of the Union," I find it, unhappily, necessary to report that the future and the safety of our country and of our democracy are overwhelmingly involved in events far beyond our borders.

Armed defense of democratic existence is now being gallantly waged in four continents. If that defense fails, all the population and all the resources of Europe, Asia, Africa and Australia will be dominated by the conquerors. Let us remember that the total of those populations and their resources in those four continents greatly exceeds the sum total of the population and the resources of the whole of the Western Hemisphere—many times over. . . .

As long as the aggressor nations maintain the offensive, they—not we—will choose the time and the place and the method of their attack.

That is why the future of all the American Republics is today in serious danger. That is why this Annual Message to the Congress is unique in our history.

That is why every member of the Executive Branch of the Government and every member of the Congress faces great responsibility and great accountability.

The need of the moment is that our actions and our policy should be devoted primarily—almost exclusively—to meeting this foreign peril. For all our domestic problems are now a part of the great emergency.

Just as our national policy in internal affairs has been based upon a decent respect for the rights and the dignity of all our fellow men within our gates, so our national policy in foreign affairs has been based on a decent respect for the rights and dignity of all nations, large and small. And the justice of morality must and will win in the end.

Our national policy is this:

First, by an impressive expression of the public will and without regard to partisanship, we are committed to all-inclusive national defense.

Second, by an impressive expression of the public will and without regard to partisanship, we are committed to full support of all those resolute peoples, everywhere, who are resisting aggression and are thereby keeping war away from our Hemisphere. By this support, we express our determination that the democratic cause shall prevail; and we strengthen the defense and the security of our own nation.

Third, by an impressive expression of the public will and without regard to partisanship, we are committed to the proposition that principles of morality and considerations for our own security will never permit us to acquiesce in a peace dictated by aggressors and sponsored by appeasers. We know that enduring peace cannot be bought at the cost of other people's freedom. . . .

New circumstances are constantly begetting new needs for our safety. I shall ask this Congress for greatly increased new appropriations and authorizations to carry on what we have begun.

I also ask this Congress for authority and for funds sufficient to manufacture additional munitions and war supplies of many kinds, to be turned over to those nations which are now in actual war with aggressor nations.

Our most useful and immediate role is to act as an arsenal for them as well as for ourselves. They do not need man power, but they do need billions of dollars worth of the weapons of defense.

The time is near when they will not be able to pay for them all in ready cash. We cannot, and we will not, tell them that they must surrender, merely because of present inability to pay for the weapons which we know they must have.

I do not recommend that we make them a loan of dollars with which to pay for these weapons—a loan to be repaid in dollars.

I recommend that we make it possible for those nations to continue to obtain war materials in the United States, fitting their orders into our own program. Nearly all their material would, if the time ever came, be useful for our own defense. . . .

Let us say to the democracies: "We Americans are vitally concerned in your defense of freedom. We are putting forth our energies, our resources and our organizing powers to give you the strength to regain and maintain a free world. We shall send you, in ever-increasing numbers, ships, planes, tanks, guns. This is our purpose and our pledge." . . .

In the future days, which we seek to make secure, we look forward to a world founded upon four essential human freedoms.

The first is freedom of speech and expression—everywhere in the world.

The second is freedom of every person to worship God in his own way—everywhere in the world.

The third is freedom from want—which, translated into world terms, means economic understandings which will secure to every nation a healthy peacetime life for its inhabitants—everywhere in the world.

The fourth is freedom from fear—which, translated into world terms, means a world-wide reduction of armaments to such a point and in such a thorough fashion that no nation will be in a position to commit an act of physical aggression against any neighbor—anywhere in the world.

That is no vision of a distant millennium. It is a definite basis for a kind of world attainable in our own time and generation. That kind of world is the very antithesis of the so-called new order of tyranny which the dictators seek to create with the crash of a bomb.

To that new order we oppose the greater conception—the moral order. A good society is able to face schemes of world domination and foreign revolutions alike without fear.

Since the beginning of our American history, we have been engaged in change—in a perpetual peaceful revolution—a revolution which goes on steadily, quietly adjusting itself to changing conditions—without the concentration camp or the quick-lime in the ditch. The world order which we seek is the cooperation of free countries, working together in a friendly, civilized society.

This nation has placed its destiny in the hands and heads and hearts of its millions of free men and women; and its faith in freedom under the guidance of God. Freedom means the supremacy of human rights everywhere. Our support goes to those who struggle to gain those rights or keep them. Our strength is our unity of purpose.

To that high concept there can be no end save victory.

Source: Congressional Record: Proceedings and Debates of the 77th Congress. First Session. Vol. 87, Pt. 1, 44–47. Washington, D.C.: GPO, 1941.

Document 5
UNITED NATIONS DECLARATION, JANUARY 1, 1942

Churchill welcomed the Japanese attack on the United States. Combined with the German war against the Soviet Union, it meant that Germany would lose the war.

Although there had been many contacts between British and American officials, there was as yet no clear coordination of policies between the United States and the United Kingdom before December 1941. Churchill proceeded as quickly as possible to Washington, D.C., where he and his staff met with President Roosevelt and American military officials from December 22, 1941, through January 14, 1942.

Among their discussions was a statement of the war aims of the "united nations." The declaration was issued on January 1, 1941, signed by the United States, China, the Soviet Union, and the United

Kingdom. Twenty-two other governments later signed it. During the course of the war a further 19 nations joined.

The declaration repeated in part the principles of the Atlantic Charter. It did not expressly look forward to the establishment of a new international body to replace the defunct League of Nations; Roosevelt, however, supported the establishment of such an organization and during the war the United States became the primary nation fostering its creation.

From April 25 to June 26, 1945, a conference was held in San Francisco, California, to approve a charter for the United Nations. Delegates from 50 nations attended. The following document was the one proclaimed on January 1, 1942.

A joint Declaration by the United States, the United Kingdom, the Union of Soviet Socialist Republics, China, Australia, Belgium, Canada, Costa Rica, Cuba, Czechoslovakia, Dominican Republic, El Salvador, Greece, Guatemala, Haiti, Honduras, India, Luxembourg, Netherlands, New Zealand, Nicaragua, Norway, Panama, Poland, South Africa, Yugoslavia

The Governments signatory hereto,

Having subscribed to a common program of purposes and principles embodied in the joint Declaration of the President of the United States of America and the Prime Minister of the United Kingdom of Great Britain and Northern Ireland dated August 14, 1941, known as the Atlantic Charter.

Being convinced that complete victory over their enemies is essential to defend life, liberty, independence and religious freedom, and to preserve human rights and justice in their own lands as well as in other lands, and that they are now engaged in a common struggle against savage and brutal forces seeking to subjugate the world,

DECLARE:

(1) Each Government pledges itself to employ its full resources, military—or economic, against those members of the Tripartite Pact and its adherents with which such government is at war.

(2) Each Government pledges itself to cooperate with the Governments signatory hereto and not to make a separate armistice or peace with the enemies.

The foregoing declaration may be adhered to by other nations which are, or which may be, rendering material assistance and contributions in the struggle for victory over Hitlerism.

Done at Washington
January First, 1942

Source: United States. Department of State. *A Decade of American Foreign Policy,* *1941–1949*, pp. 2–3. Washington, D.C.: GPO, 1950.

Document 6
THE CASABLANCA CONFERENCE AND THE POLICY OF UNCONDITIONAL SURRENDER

President Roosevelt and Prime Minister Churchill met in a suburb of Casablanca, French Morocco, from January 14 to January 24, 1943. Most of the conference was devoted to discussing military strategies and plans, especially the continuing operations in the Mediterranean Sea and the strategic bombing campaign in Europe. At a press conference following the meetings, Roosevelt made the following comments, which include the phrase "unconditional surrender." Those words did not appear in the official communiqué of the conference, leading to speculation that "unconditional surrender" had not been discussed or agreed upon.

In fact, the idea had been frequently discussed before the conference, especially by the Americans. Similar phrases such as "total victory" and "absolute defeat" had also been used. Roosevelt probably announced "unconditional surrender" to reassure American public opinion and those who saw the war as a struggle against fascism that there would be no compromises made with fascists. Eisenhower's "deal" with Vichy French leaders in Algeria to end French resistance had led to vociferous criticism.

It has been charged that the policy of "unconditional surrender," though it may have encouraged resistance movements within occupied Europe, stiffened the Nazis' will to fight and made the war against Japan in the Pacific more difficult to end.

"UNCONDITIONAL SURRENDER" STATEMENT, JANUARY 24, 1943

Transcript of Press Conference

THE PRESIDENT: This meeting goes back to the successful landing operations last November, which as you all know were initiated as far back as a year ago, and put into definite shape shortly after the Prime Minister's visit to Washington in June.

After the operations of last November, it became perfectly clear, with the successes, that the time had come for another review of the situation, and a planning for the next steps, especially steps to be taken in 1943. That is why we came here, and our respective staffs came with us, to discuss the practical steps to be taken by the United Nations for prosecution of the war. We have been here about a week. . . .

I think it can be said that the studies during the past week or ten days are unprecedented in history. Both the Prime Minister and I think back to the days of World War I when conferences between the French and British and ourselves very rarely lasted more than a few hours or a couple of days. The Chiefs of Staffs have been in intimate touch; they have lived in the same hotel. Each man has become a definite personal friend of his opposite number on the other side.

Furthermore, these conferences have discussed, I think for the first time in history, the whole global picture. It isn't just one front, just one ocean, or one continent—it is literally the whole world; and that is why the Prime Minister and I feel that the conference is unique in the fact that it has this global aspect. . . .

Another point. I think we have all had it in our hearts and heads before, but I don't think that it has ever been put down on paper by the Prime Minister and myself, and that is the determination that peace can come to the world only by the total elimination of German and Japanese war power.

Some of you Britishers know the old story—we had a General called U. S. Grant. His name was Ulysses Simpson Grant, but in my, and the Prime Minister's, early days he was called "Unconditional Surrender" Grant. The elimination of German, Japanese and Italian war power means the unconditional surrender by Germany, Italy and Japan. That means a reasonable assurance of future world peace. It does not mean the destruction of the population of Germany, Italy, or Japan, but it does mean the destruction of the philosophies in those countries which are based on conquest and the subjugation of other people.

([T]his meeting is called the "unconditional surrender" meeting.)[1]

While we have not had a meeting of all of the United Nations, I think that there is no question—in fact we both have great confidence that the same purposes and objectives are in the minds of all of the other United Nations—Russia, China, and all the others.

And so the actual meeting—the main work of the Committee—has been ended, except for a certain amount of resultant paper work—has come to a successful conclusion. I call it a meeting of the minds in regard to all military operations, and, thereafter, that the war is going to proceed against the Axis Powers according to schedule, with every indication that 1943 is going to be an even better year for the United Nations than 1942.

THE PRIME MINISTER: I agree with everything that the President has said, and I think it was a very happy decision to bring you gentlemen here to

Casablanca to this agreeable spot, Anfa Camp, which has been the center—the scene—of much [of] the most important and successful war conference which I have ever attended or witnessed. Nothing like it has occurred in my experience, which is a long while—the continuous work, hours and hours every day from morning until often after midnight, carried on by the Staffs of both sides, by all the principal officers of the two nations who are engaged in the direction of the war.

NOTE

1. The parenthetical statement is in the printed text, with no indication as to its source.

Source: United States. Department of State. *Foreign Relations of the United States, Conference at Casablanca, 1943*, pp. 726–728. Washington, D.C.: GPO, 1968.

Document 7
THE TEHRAN CONFERENCE, NOVEMBER 28–DECEMBER 1, 1943

The first conference among the Big Three—that is, the leaders of the United States, the Soviet Union, and the United Kingdom—was held at Tehran from November 28 through December 1, 1943. Although the Tehran Conference was overshadowed by the Yalta Conference 14 months later, it can be considered more important. Almost all the issues later dealt with by Roosevelt, Stalin, and Churchill were discussed and basically agreed to at Tehran. The Soviet Union agreed to enter the war against Japan within three months of the defeat of Germany. The Western Allies announced their intention to invade the continent in May of 1944 (delayed until June 6). Stalin announced that the Red Army would open a simultaneous offensive.

During the conference Roosevelt and his immediate staff stayed at the Russian embassy, as it was considered too dangerous for the president to travel back and forth to the more distant American embassy. Roosevelt attempted to play a mediating role between the Russian dictator and the British prime minister, to the annoyance of Churchill. In addition, Churchill was ill, and the United States by the end of 1943 was beginning to replace the British Empire and Commonwealth as the most important military opponent of Germany in the West.

The most important decision, was the future of Germany. The policy of unconditional surrender meant that the Allies would be responsible for the future of the country, how it would be treated, and its form of government. The details were worked out at the Yalta and Potsdam conferences, but the initial proposals were laid down in Tehran.

The following document is from the notes taken by Charles Bohlen, who was present at the state dinner on November 29, 1943. A career diplomat, he had served in Russia after 1933. In 1940 he was sent to Tokyo where he was interned for six months after the attack on Pearl Harbor. After his release he returned to Moscow and served as interpreter for Roosevelt at the Tehran conference.

SECRET

The most notable feature of the dinner was the attitude of Marshal Stalin toward the Prime Minister. Marshal Stalin lost no opportunity to get in a dig at Mr. Churchill. Almost every remark that he addressed to the Prime Minister contained some sharp edge, although the Marshal's manner was entirely friendly. He apparently desired to put and keep the Prime Minister on the defensive. At one occasion he told the Prime Minister that just because Russians are simple people, it was a mistake to believe that they were blind and could not see what was before their eyes.

In the discussion in regard to future treatment of Germans, Marshal Stalin strongly implied on several occasions that Mr. Churchill nursed a secret affection for Germany and desired to see a soft peace.

Marshal Stalin was obviously teasing the Prime Minister for the latter's attitude at the afternoon session of the Conference, he was also making known in a friendly fashion his displeasure at the British attitude on the question of OVERLORD.

Following Mr. Hopkins' toast to the Red Army, MARSHAL STALIN spoke with great frankness in regard to the past and present capacity of the Red Army. He said that in the winter war against Finland, the Soviet Army had shown itself to be very poorly organized and had done very badly; that as a result of the Finnish War, the entire Soviet Army had been reorganized; but even so, when the Germans attacked in 1941, it could not be said that the Red Army was a first class fighting force. That during the war with Germany, the Red Army had become steadily better from [the] point of view of operations, tactics, etc., and now he felt that it was genuinely a good army. He added that the general opinion in regard to the Red Army had been wrong, because it was not believed that the Soviet Army could reorganize and improve itself during time of war.

In regard to the future treatment of Germany, MARSHAL STALIN developed the thesis that he had previously expressed, namely, that really effective measures to control Germany must be evolved, otherwise Germany would rise again within 15 or 20 years to plunge the world into another war. He said that two conditions must be met:

(1) At least 50,000 and perhaps 100,000 of the German Commanding Staff must be physically liquidated.

(2) The victorious Allies must retain possession of the important strategic points in the world so that if Germany moved a muscle she could be rapidly stopped.

MARSHAL STALIN added that similar strong points now in the hands of Japan should remain in the hands of the Allies.

THE PRESIDENT jokingly said that he would put the figure of the German Commanding Staff which should be executed at 49,000 or more.

THE PRIME MINISTER took strong exception to what he termed the cold blooded execution of soldiers who had fought for their country. He said that war criminals must pay for their crimes and individuals who had committed barbarous acts, and in accordance with the Moscow Document, which he himself had written, they must stand trial at the places where the crimes were committed. He objected vigorously, however, to executions for political purposes.

MARSHAL STALIN, during this part of the conversation, continuously referred to Mr. Churchill's secret liking for the Germans.

With reference to the occupation of bases and strong points in the vicinity of Germany and Japan, THE PRESIDENT said those bases must be held under trusteeship.

MARSHAL STALIN agreed with the President.

THE PRIME MINISTER stated that as far as Britain was concerned, they do not desire to acquire any new territory or bases, but intended to hold on to what they had. He said that nothing would be taken away from England without a war. He mentioned specifically, Singapore and Hong Kong. He said a portion of the British Empire might eventually be released but that this would be done entirely by Great Britain herself, in accordance with her own moral precepts. He said that Great Britain, if asked to do so, might occupy certain bases under trusteeship, provided others would help pay the cost of such occupation.

MARSHAL STALIN replied that England had fought well in the war and he, personally, favored an increase in the British Empire, particularly the area around Gibraltar. He also suggested that Great Britain and the United States install more suitable government[s] in Spain and Portugal, since he was convinced that Franco was no friend of Great Britain or the United States. In reply to the Prime Minister's inquiry as to what territorial interests the Soviet Union had, MARSHAL STALIN replied, "[T]here is no need to speak at the present time about any Soviet desires, but when the time comes, we will speak." Although the discussion between Marshal Stalin and the Prime Minister remained friendly, the arguments were lively and Stalin did not let up on the Prime Minister throughout the entire evening.

Source: United States. Department of State. *Foreign Relations of the United States, Conferences at Cairo and Tehran, 1943*, pp. 552–555. Washington, D.C.: GPO, 1961.

Document 8
THE YALTA CONFERENCE: THE DECLARATION ON
LIBERATED EUROPE

Among the most controversial agreements of World War II diplomacy is the Yalta declaration on "Liberated Europe."

The Yalta conference was held in the Crimea, a resort area of the Soviet Union, from February 4 until February 11. The Third Reich was clearly approaching collapse, though there were still military decisions to be made. The main discussions, however, centered around the occupation of Germany and the territorial and political changes in eastern Europe. Without Churchill's or Chiang Kai-shek's knowledge, the United States agreed to recognize Soviet rights in Mongolia, the southern part of Sakhalin Island, and the Kurile Islands in return for Soviet entrance into the war against Japan.

The most contentious issue of the conference was the formation of the Polish government and Poland's postwar borders. As the Red Army had moved into Poland during the summer and fall of 1944, a provisional government of Polish communists organized as the "Polish Committee of National Liberation" began to form a government. Both Churchill and Roosevelt wished to have the Polish government-in-exile in London participate in the restructuring of the new Polish government. Stalin procrastinated, and the so-called Lublin government, named at the city where it was resident, essentially became the government of Poland.

The Declaration on Liberated Europe also applied to other countries throughout Europe. In the course of the next two years, all the eastern Europe countries, from Poland in the north through Bulgaria in the south became communist dictatorships. The Declaration on Liberated Europe proved a sham.

Roosevelt's role in this is not settled. Did he agree to this declaration as a part of an overall policy to keep the Soviet Union in the alliance and to bring it into the war against Japan? Did he realize that it was essentially "window dressing" designed to satisfy American public opinion? Was it necessary in order to bring the Soviet Union into the United Nations? Was it the best he could achieve in February 1945?

Whatever the answers to these questions, the Declaration on Liberated Europe remains one of the primary statements of the Allies regarding their vision of postwar Europe.

The Declaration was Part II of the Protocols of the Conference.

DECLARATION ON LIBERATED EUROPE

The following declaration has been approved:

The Premier of the Union of Soviet Socialist Republics, the Prime Minister of the United Kingdom, and the President of the United States of America have consulted with each other in the common interests of the peoples of their countries and those of liberated Europe. They jointly declare their mutual agreement to concert during the temporary period of instability in liberated Europe the policies of their three governments in assisting the peoples of the former Axis satellite states of Europe to solve by democratic means their pressing political and economic problems.

The establishment of order in Europe and the rebuilding of national economic life must be achieved by processes which will enable the liberated peoples to destroy the last vestiges of Nazism and Fascism and to create democratic institutions of their own choice. This is a principle of the Atlantic Charter—the right of all peoples to choose the form of government under which they will live and the restoration of sovereign rights and self-government to those peoples who have been forcibly deprived of them by the aggressor nations.

To foster the conditions in which the liberated peoples may exercise these rights, the three governments will jointly assist the people in any European liberated state or former Axis satellite state in Europe where in their judgment conditions require (a) to establish conditions of internal peace; (b) to carry out emergency measures for the relief of distressed peoples; (c) to form interim governmental authorities broadly representative of all democratic elements in the population and pledged to the earliest possible establishment through free elections of governments responsive to the will of the people; and (d) to facilitate where necessary the holding of such elections.

The three governments will consult the other United Nations and provisional authorities or other governments in Europe when matters of direct interest to them are under consideration.

When, in the opinion of the three governments, conditions in any European liberated state or any former Axis satellite state in Europe make such action necessary, they will immediately consult together on the measures necessary to discharge the joint responsibilities set forth in this declaration.

By this declaration we reaffirm our faith in the principles of the Atlantic Charter, our pledge in the Declaration by the United Nations, and our determination to build in cooperation with other peace-loving nations world order under law, dedicated to peace, security, freedom and general well-being of all mankind.

In issuing this declaration the Three Powers express the hope that the Provisional Government of the French Republic may be associated with them in the procedure suggested.

Source: United States. Department of State. *Foreign Relations of the United States. Diplomatic Papers. The Conferences at Malta and Yalta, 1945,* pp. 971–973. Washington, D.C.: GPO, 1955.

Document 9
THE POTSDAM ULTIMATUM

The Manhattan Engineer District project to design and build an atomic bomb reached its fruition on July 16 when the world's first nuclear detonation lighted the New Mexico desert. The final wartime conference opened the next day in Potsdam, a suburb of Berlin and center of Prussian/German monarchical and military authority.

President Roosevelt had died in April, so the new president Harry Truman headed the United States delegation to Potsdam. He was at Potsdam when word of the successful explosion of the first atomic bomb reached him. The war against Japan continued, with the prospect of an invasion of Japan with thousands of casualties on both sides. On July 26 the United States, joined by Britain and China, issued an ultimatum that called for Japan's unconditional surrender.

The ultimatum and the dropping of atomic bombs on Hiroshima on August 6 and on Nagasaki on August 9 are among the most traumatic events of the war. Contrary to popular opinion, there was never a decision by American authorities to drop the bombs. Their only question was how to use the bombs most effectively to end the war. Militarists within Japan were determined to fight to the very end, making the invasion so costly that the United States and its allies would not persevere to an unconditional surrender. Only the emperor Hirohito's intervention brought the war to an end.

POTSDAM PROCLAMATION, JULY 26, 1945

Proclamation by the heads of Governments, United States,
China and the United Kingdom

(1) We, the President of the United States, the President of the National Government of the Republic of China and the Prime Minister of Great Britain, representing the hundreds of millions of our countrymen, have conferred and agree that Japan shall be given an opportunity to end this war.

(2) The prodigious land, sea and air forces of the United States, the British Empire and of China, many times reinforced by their armies and air fleets from the west are poised to strike the final blows upon Japan. This military power is sustained and inspired by the determination of all the Allied nations to prosecute the war against Japan until she ceases to resist.

(3) The result of the futile and senseless German resistance to the might of the aroused free peoples of the world stands forth in awful clarity as an example to the people of Japan. The might that now converges on Japan is immeasurably greater than that which, when applied to the resisting Nazis, necessarily laid waste to the lands, the industry and the method of life of the whole German people. The full application of our military power, backed by our resolve, will mean the inevitable and complete destruction of the Japanese armed forces and just as inevitably the utter devastation of the Japanese homeland.

(4) The time has come for Japan to decide whether she will continue to be controlled by those self-willed milita(r)istic advisers whose unintelligent calculations have brought the Empire of Japan to the threshold of annihilation, or whether she will follow the path of reason.

(5) Following are our terms. We will not deviate from them. There are no alternatives. We shall brook no delay.

(6) There must be eliminated for all time the authority and influence of those who have deceived and misled the people of Japan into embarking on world conquest, for we insist that a new order of peace, security and justice will be impossible until irresponsible militarism is driven from the world.

(7) Until such a new order is established and until there is convincing proof that Japan's war-making power is destroyed, points in Japanese territory to be designated by the Allies shall be occupied to secure the achievement of the basic objectives we are here setting forth.

(8) The terms of the Cairo Declaration shall be carried out and Japanese sovereignty shall be limited to the islands of Honshu, Hokkaido, Kyushu, Shikoku and such minor islands as we determine.

(9) The Japanese military forces, after being completely disarmed, shall be permitted to return to their homes with the opportunity to lead peaceful and productive lives.

(10) We do not intend that the Japanese shall be enslaved as a race or destroyed as (a) nation, but stern justice shall be meted out to all war criminals, including those who have visited cruelties upon our prisoners. The Japanese government shall remove all obstacles to the revival and strengthening of democratic tendencies among the Japanese people. Freedom of speech, of religion, and of thought, as well as respect for the fundamental human rights shall be established.

(11) Japan shall be permitted to maintain such industries as will sustain her economy and permit the exaction of just reparations in kind, but not those industries which would enable her to re-arm for war. To this end, access to, as distinguished from control of raw materials shall be permitted. Eventual Japanese participation in world trade relations shall be permitted.

(12) The occupying forces of the Allies shall be withdrawn from Japan as soon as these objectives have been accomplished and there has been established in accordance with the freely expressed will of the Japanese people a peacefully inclined and responsible government.

(13) We call upon the Government of Japan to proclaim now the unconditional surrender of all the Japanese armed forces, and to provide proper and adequate assurances of their good faith in such action. The alternative for Japan is prompt and utter destruction.

Potsdam July 26, 1945

Harry S Truman
Winston Churchill
by H.S.T.
President of China
by wire

Source: United States. Department of State. *The Conferences of Berlin*, II, pp. 1474–1476. Washington, D.C.: GPO, 1960.

Document 10
MEMORANDUM BY THE JOINT CHIEFS OF STAFF TO THE SECRETARY OF STATE, AUGUST 3, 1944

The small size of the United States Army, indeed that of its entire military establishment in the 1930s, placed it among the world's minor powers. World War II changed that. By 1944 the United States was the world's premier military power. Its two-ocean navy dwarfed that of other countries. Its air force possessed fighter planes, bombers, and transport planes in numbers and technical quality far beyond any other power. Its army exceeded 8,000,000 men and women, fewer than that of the Soviet Union, but much better armed and organized. The Pentagon, built as a temporary structure across the Potomac River in Washington, was the symbol as well as the center of a new American global military presence.

The Joint Chiefs of Staff, the planning agency of the American military, along with the Combined Chiefs of Staff of both the United States and the United Kingdom, organized the plans for victory in Europe and Asia. It also prepared for the postwar world. During the war, new international conditions and rapidly changing technologies suggested that the role of the United States in maintaining world peace would be significantly changed.

The document which follows illustrates the Joint Chiefs' view of the U.S. defense position and how it best might be secured into the future as of August 1944. The major missing factor is, of course, the successful development of the atomic bomb.

MEMORANDUM BY THE JOINT CHIEFS OF STAFF TO THE SECRETARY OF STATE

Subject: Fundamental Military Factors in Relation to Discussions Concerning Territorial Trusteeships and Settlements

1. Discussions are to be held in the near future with representatives of the three other principal United Nations concerning the proposed future international organization. While these discussions are intended to be exploratory only, it is possible that directly or indirectly, questions concerning territorial settlements may arise. Should this be the case, it appears certain that on some questions of this nature, Russian aspirations will be found in conflict with those of the British on the one hand, and with those of China on the other. The interests of the United States would undoubtedly be involved, particularly as to the future status of the Japanese Mandated Islands, and British and Chinese interests could be expected to come in conflict, especially as to Hong Kong.

2. The question of whether the subject of territorial settlements should be discussed during these conversations—either specifically as to certain areas, or in general terms as to the trusteeship or other status of such areas under the General International Organization—is an important matter of policy which should be determined only after thorough examination of all factors involved. Among the basic factors which must be given full weight

in determining the United States policy in this regard is the over-all military situation as it can be foreseen both before and after the defeat of Japan.

3. While the war with Germany is well advanced toward a final conclusion, the defeat of Japan is not yet in sight. The defeat of Germany will leave Russia in a position of assured military dominance in eastern Europe and in the Middle East. While it is true that on the fall of Germany the United States and Britain will occupy and control western Europe, their strength in that area will thereafter progressively decline with the withdrawal of all but their occupational and enforcement forces, for employment against Japan, or for demobilization.

4. At present, the war against Japan is being carried on almost entirely by the United States. . . . Whether or not Russia enters the war, the fall of Japan will leave Russia in a dominant position on continental Northeast Asia in so far as military power is concerned.

5. The land forces of Russia can provide a major contribution by being brought to bear directly against the most powerful element of Japanese military strength—her Army. The air forces of Russia or of the United States, operating from Siberian or Korean bases, would provide the most effective short range land-based air attack against the heart of Japan. Should Russia promptly and effectively enter the war after the fall of Germany, she would bring her great land and air forces into action directly against Japan, thereby materially shortening the war and effecting vast savings in American lives and treasure. Should Russia abstain from such action, due to our untimely pressing the subject of territorial settlement—or any other avoidable cause—we must be prepared to accept responsibility for a longer war. . . .

7. The successful termination of the war against our present enemies will find a world profoundly changed in respect of relative national military strengths, a change more comparable indeed with that occasioned by the fall of Rome than with any other change occurring during the succeeding fifteen hundred years. . . . There are technical and material factors which have contributed greatly to this change. Among these are the development of aviation, the general mechanization of warfare and the marked shift in the munitioning potentials of the great powers.

8. After the defeat of Japan, the United States and Russia will be the strongest military powers in the world. This is due in each case primarily to a combination of geographical position and extent, manpower, and vast munitioning potential. While the United States can protect its military power into many areas overseas, it is nevertheless true that the relative strength and geographic positions of these two powers are such as to preclude the mili-

tary defeat of one of these powers by the other, even if that power were allied with the British Empire.

9. As a military power, the British Empire in the post-war era will be in a lower category than the United States and Russia. . . . Nearly all the essential factors of national power in the post-war era will have altered, to the disadvantage of the British Empire.

10. Notwithstanding her vast population and area, China possesses at present but little military strength. This condition will not be improved prior to her extensive industrialization, which in turn is dependent on the firm establishment of political unity and a stable government. . . .

11. As a military power, France will be found in a category below the British Empire. Nevertheless, France after her recovery will be in a position to exert a greater effort than Britain in land operations on the European continent, because of her high degree of economic self-sufficiency and the very considerable munitioning capacity she will eventually possess after the reacquisition of the Lorraine ore fields and the reconstruction of her industry.

12. In spite of her resources in manpower, Italy, because of her very notable deficiencies in essential mineral reserves, must remain a relatively minor military power, largely dependent upon others for her munitioning needs.

Source: United States. Department of State. *Foreign Relations of the United States*, 1944, vol. I, pp. 700–703. Washington, D.C.: GPO, 1966.

Document 11
GIULIO DOUHET ON AIR POWER

The airplane became a reality in 1903. Its military significance was immediately recognized, though exactly what its importance would be was not clear. During World War I, airplanes were largely used for reconnaissance, though they also were used to bomb enemy targets.

Between 1918 and 1939 the airplane made great strides in size and speed, making it a serious instrument of war. Views on air power varied between those who saw it primarily as an auxiliary of ground forces and those who advocated air forces as an independent strategic force. The former thought that aircraft should be used to locate the enemy and to add to the firepower of ground-based artillery. Advocates of an independent strategic air force often argued that the threat of strategic bombing from the air would be the decisive factor in any future war.

Giulio Douhet was one of the first writers on the topic of strategic air power. A military officer in Italy, he became minister of aviation in Mussolini's Fascist government. His *Command of the Air* appeared in

Italy in 1921. It circulated among like-minded military officers in the United States in an unpublished translation until its publication in English during the war.

The importance of strategic bombing during World War II remains controversial. Even the importance of Douhet to the thinking of its supporters remains unclear. In Britain, the Royal Air Force, commanded by Hugh Trenchard, was an independent branch of the armed forces. Germany also had an air force, the Luftwaffe, separate from the army, but it had no independent strategic role, having been created as a means of bypassing the influence of the already established army. The United States air force was a part of the army until after World War II.

The following selection from *Command of the Air* outlines Douhet's theory of the role of air power in future conflict. He believed, as did many advocates of air power, that the airplane alone could be the decisive factor in future conflicts.

Since war had to be fought on the surface of the earth, it could be waged only in movements and clashes, of forces along lines drawn on its surface. Hence, to win, to gain control of the coveted area, one side had to break through the fortified defensive lines of the other and occupy the area. As making war increasingly required the entire resources of nations, in order to protect themselves from enemy invasion warring nations have been forced to spread out their forces along battle lines constantly extended as the fighting went on, to a point where, as in the last war, the lines extended over practically the whole battlefield, thus barring all troop passage either way.

Behind those lines, or beyond certain distances determined by the maximum range of surface weapons, the civilian populations of the warring nations did not directly feel the war. No enemy offensive could menace them beyond that predetermined distance, so civilian life could be carried on in safety and comparative tranquillity. The battlefield was strictly defined; the armed forces were in a category distinct from civilians, who in their turn were more or less organized to fill the needs of a nation at war. There was even a legal distinction made between combatants and noncombatants. And so, though the World War sharply affected whole nations, it is nonetheless true that only a minority of the peoples involved actually fought and died. The majority went on working in safety and comparative peace to furnish the minority with the sinews of war. This state of affairs arose from the fact that *it was impossible* to invade the enemy's territory without first breaking through his defensive lines.

But that situation is a thing of the past; for now *it is possible* to go far behind the fortified lines of defense without first breaking through them. It is air power which makes this possible.

The airplane has complete freedom of action and direction; it can fly to and from any point of the compass in the shortest time—in a straight line—by any route deemed expedient. Nothing man can do on the surface of the earth can interfere with a plane in flight, moving freely in the third dimension. All the influences which have conditioned and characterized warfare from the beginning are powerless to affect aerial action. . . .

The airplane, in contrast [to movements on land], can fly in any direction with equal facility and faster than any other means of conveyance. A plane based at point A, for example, is a potential threat to all surface points within a circle having A for its center and a radius of hundreds of miles for its field of action. Planes based anywhere on the surface of this same circle can simultaneously converge in mass on point A. Therefore, an aerial force is a threat to all points within its radius of action, its units operating from their separate bases and converging in mass for the attack on the designated target faster than with any other means so far known. For this reason air power is a weapon superlatively adapted to offensive operations, because it strikes suddenly and gives the enemy no time to parry the blow by calling up reinforcements. . . .

In fact, we have no difficulty in imagining what would happen when areas of 500 to 2,000 meters in diameter in the center of large cities such as London, Paris, or Rome were being unmercifully bombed. With 1,000 bombers of the type described—an actual type in use today, not a hypothetical type in some blueprint of the future—with their necessary maintenance and replacements for daily losses, 100 such operating squadrons can be constituted. Operating 50 of these daily, such an aerial force in the hands of those who know how to use it could destroy 50 such centers every day. This is an offensive power so far superior to any other offensive means known that the power of the latter is negligible in comparison.

As a matter of fact, this same offensive power, the possibility of which was not even dreamed of fifteen years ago, is increasing daily, precisely because the building and development of large, heavy planes goes on all the time. The same thing is true of new explosives, incendiaries, and especially poison gases. What could an army do faced with an offensive power like that, its lines of communication cut, its supply depots burned or blown up, its arsenals and auxiliaries destroyed? What could a navy do when it could no longer take refuge in its own ports, when its bases were burned or blown up, its arsenals and auxiliaries destroyed? How could a country go on living and working under this constant threat, oppressed by the nightmare of imminent destruction and death? How indeed! We should always keep in mind that aerial offensives can be directed not only against objectives of least physical resistance, but against those of least moral resistance as well. For instance, an infantry regiment in a shattered trench may still be capable of some resistance even after losing two-thirds of its effectives; but when the working personnel of a factory sees one of its machine shops destroyed, even with a minimum loss of life, it quickly breaks up and the plant ceases to function.

All this should be kept in mind when we wish to estimate the potential power of aerial offensives possible even today. To have command of the air means to be in a position to wield offensive power so great it defies human imagination. It means to be able to cut an enemy's army and navy off from their bases of operation and nullify their chances of winning the war. It means complete protection of one's own country, the efficient operation of one's army and navy, and peace of mind to live and work in safety. In short, it means to be in a position to win. To be defeated in the air, on the other hand, is finally to be defeated and to be at the mercy of the enemy, with no chance at all of defending oneself, compelled to accept whatever terms he sees fit to dictate.

This is the meaning of the "command of the air."

Source: Giulio Douhet. *The Command of the Air.* Trans. Dino Ferrari, pp. 8–9, 16, and 22–23. New York: Coward-McCann, 1943; New York: Arno Press, 1972 repr.

Document 12
GENERAL OF THE ARMY HENRY "HAP" ARNOLD ON STRATEGIC BOMBING

Henry "Hap" Arnold headed the United States Army Air Forces from its creation as an independent organization within the United States Army in June 1941. Arnold was a lifelong advocate of air power. He learned to fly at the hands of the Wright brothers before World War I, but joined the service too late to participate in the war in Europe. He was a disciple of William "Billy" Mitchell, an early American advocate of air power and maverick who was court-martialed in 1925 for his criticism of military leaders.

In the 1920s and 1930s Arnold pressed for the creation of an effective independent bombing force. During the 1930s he was more responsible than any other man for the B-29, the Boeing Superfortress, the most advanced bomber of the war. Coming into production too late for the European theater, the B-29 was deployed in China in June 1944, and in large numbers in the western Pacific. Altogether the B-29 flew nearly 35,000 sorties, dropping 170,000 tons of bombs, including the two atomic bombs on Hiroshima and Nagasaki.

Under Arnold's leadership the USAAF grew from 20,000 men and antiquated planes into a force of 2,400,000 men with some 80,000 aircraft. In addition to overseeing the administration of this great expansion, Arnold also sat on the U.S. Joint Chiefs of Staff and the Combined Chiefs of Staff.

In the following passages from his memoirs, we can gain a sense of Arnold's drive to prove the value of bombing. His belief that the war could be won from the air if the Air Force was given full support is not shared by all historians. But his enthusiasm for the impact of and need for unrestrained bombing was widely shared by his fellow airmen.

The Doolittle raid Arnold refers to took place in April 1942 when 16 B-25s from the aircraft carrier *Hornet* attacked Japan with minimal damage. Its purpose was to reassure the American public that the war was being carried to Japan and to show that the Japanese homeland was vulnerable to air attacks.

The four-engine bomber was the first positive answer to the need arising from the United States' modification of the Douhet theories, which we had been teaching as an abstract science at the Air Corps Tactical School for several years. Ever since Versailles, Germany had been considered the next enemy by most strategists, including Billy Mitchell, whose notion, however, that Japan would come flying to attack us "some fine Sunday morning" was less heeded.

The large bomber was the center of the "bomber controversy." If one thinks of the state of the world in 1936, the year the Spanish Civil War began, the year after Mussolini invaded Ethiopia, the year immediately before Japan went into China proper, the year in which Hitler's remilitarization of the Rhineland took place, it would seem that the time was overdue for some kind of clear-cut thinking about American air power to have started in the War Department. It hadn't. And in that connection, this is a good place to note one or two facts that are sometimes oversimplified.

Despite popular legend, we could not have had any real air power much sooner than we got it. By that, I mean the genuine nucleus of air power, able to expand quickly, enough to meet whatever demands were made upon it, that was foreshadowed technically by the appearance of the four-engine bomber, and which was to obtain its real Magna Carta in the office of President Roosevelt on September 28, 1938.

Unbelieving men in high places, battleship admirals, generals, and others who seized on Billy Mitchell's sins to eliminate him, didn't eliminate air power at all, nor retard it half so much as has been said. Actually they didn't even eliminate Billy. They broke his heart, but from the day of his trial public opinion was mostly on his side. The point is, that kind of public opinion couldn't help air power then in any, conclusive degree, and no other kind of public opinion was ready.

So far on my trip across the Pacific [in June 1944] no one had hazarded the time for the defeat of Japan, except LeMay. Neither Admiral Nimitz nor General Richardson nor their staffs talked about when the war would be over. But while I was on Guam, I received the preliminary report of Francis d'Olier upon the strategic bombing in Germany, in which he said that bombing had not only hastened the end of the war there, but had had a most disastrous effect upon Germany's production. The attacks on oil and transportation, and the prevention of the movement of coal from the Ruhr had been in the words of Speer himself "tragic" and "a nightmare." I didn't see the whole report then, naturally, but reading that much of it caused me to do some serious thinking about Japan. . . .

While I was at Saipan, I watched 520 B-29s take off for Osaka, carrying 3000 tons of bombs. It was quite a contrast to Doolittle's 18 planes, with their 15 tons, and the first B-29 mission a year ago with 68 planes and 181 tons.

That same day I received a cablegram from General Marshall in which he stated there would be a meeting of the Joint Chiefs of Staff, with the President, to discuss the subject, "Can we win the war by bombing?" . . .

The strategic bombing must be unhampered in its organization, administration, logistics, and operations. It must have a free hand to drop the greatest number of bombs in the shortest possible time. That meant the administrative delay in getting bombs, gasoline, and such things must be stopped. The Army and Navy must keep their hands off the actual bombing operations.

Meanwhile, I prepared and later sent off a cablegram to General Marshall, outlining my ideas.

1. Continue with our present plans and occupy Kyushu to get additional bases for forty groups of heavy bombers.

2. Give priority to B-29 attacks and the Kyushu operation so as to step up bombing attacks.

3. Make plans for complete destruction of Japan proper, using B-29's from the Marianas and Okinawa, heavy bombers and attacking planes from Kyushu, and carrier planes to cover areas not completely covered by other planes.

4. Give priority to, and take off all administrative restrictions to bombing efforts, and put all postwar activities into much lower priorities.

5. Continue plans for the main effort by group troops for landing on Honshu, but keep it on a "live," but postponed, basis.

Source: H. H. Arnold, *Global Mission,* pp. 157, 566–567. New York: Harper and Row, 1949; New York: Arno, 1972 repr.

Document 13
CHARLES DE GAULLE ON THE NEED FOR A PROFESSIONAL ARMY

The dramatic increase in the firepower of automatic weapons, especially the machine gun, combined with mass, conscript armies to bring about the stalemated, immobile front lines of World War I. The bloodletting and high casualties appalled all observers, but few could imagine what sort of military forces, what tactics, or what equipment might break the logjam. Among the critics of the conduct of the war was Charles de Gaulle, an infantry officer wounded several times and taken prisoner in 1916. De Gaulle's postwar career was lackluster, though as a protégé of Henri Pétain, Marshall of France and victor of Verdun, he was well-known among military circles.

Like J.F.C. Fuller and Basil Liddell Hart in Britain, Erich von Manstein and Heinz Guderian in Germany, de Gaulle argued that tanks offered a solution. In *Le Fil de l'epée* (*The Edge of the Sword,* 1932), and *Vers l'armée de métier* (translated as *The Army of the Future,* but more accurately means *Towards a Professional Army,* 1934), he advocated the formation of a professional, career army, smaller in size than the huge, mass armies favored by French republicans and the French military establishment. Linked to a strong, armored force, a lean, elite army could provide the defensive and offensive force at less cost and more effectiveness. De Gaulle's civilian critics feared that the type of army he wanted for France would run the risk of becoming isolated from the general French population. The political consequences could be an army less subject to civilian control.

De Gaulle's writings were controversial and made no headway against the orthodoxy of the French General Staff. He managed to gain the support of Paul Reynaud, a centrist politician who became prime minister in March 1940. De Gaulle commanded a tank regiment from 1937, but a full tank division was only being formed in 1940 when Reynaud named him its commander. Two months later, German Panzers swept through northwestern France, leading to a French collapse.

It is true that at all times France has tried to obscure the breaches in her frontiers by fortifications. She is still doing the same. . . . But these fortifications, quite apart from the fact that they must be given adequate garrisons, are very limited in depth. Besides, they leave the whole of the northern region exposed. And how can one foresee the effects that would be produced on the defenders by modern methods of attack, aircraft, super-heavy tanks and poisonous gases? Moreover, one must take into consideration the possibilities of surrender. For, of all the trials of war, the hardest, on the whole, is reserved for beleaguered troops. The impression of finding oneself surrounded by assailants, the horrible feeling of isolation, the fact of having to live with one's wounded, the continual drain on one's strength which cannot be renewed, very soon undermine the morale of troops. And when to such shocks, suffered at the beginning of a campaign, are added those of one's baptism of fire, one needs extraordinary cohesion to resist them. Hence, of course, the supreme glory with which popular instinct surrounds the valiant defenders of strongholds. But hence also, of course, the complete surrenders which are the constant fate of indifferent garrisons. . . .

How, then, are we to compensate for all that is usually unsound and awkward in the initial actions of the French, except by building up a special body of men firmly welded together? . . .

The moment has come when, to our mass of reserves and of recruits . . . we must add a maneuvering instrument which is capable of acting without delay, that is to say, one which is permanent in its force, coherent, broken to battle. Without a professional army there can be no French defence.

Source: Charles de Gaulle. *The Army of the Future.* Translation of *Vers l'armée de métier.* Philadelphia: Lippincott, 1941. Repr. Westport, CT: Greenwood Press, 1976, pp. 40–42.

Document 14
HENRY DEWOLF SMYTH'S REPORT ON THE DEVELOPMENT OF THE ATOMIC BOMB

The research, development, and engineering of the atomic bomb during World War II were undoubtedly the greatest technological and scientific achievement of those years. Although only a handful of scientists and physicists understood the potential of the new weapon in 1939, by August 1945 any informed person who read the newspaper had some idea that the history of the world, the history of warfare, had been forever changed.

The Manhattan Project, as the effort by the United States was called, brought together an international team of scientists and engineers. Under the direction of General Leslie Groves, the project cost over $2 billion with a work force of more than 600,000.

Much of the technical details about the development of the bomb remained secret, but General Groves commissioned Professor Henry Smyth, chair of the Department of Physics at Princeton University and consultant to the project, to write a report for release to the general public.

The report was written before the first successful explosion in New Mexico on July 16, 1945, with further thoughts added after that date.

What follows is Prof. Smyth's general summary and call for a public discussion on the future use of this new knowledge.

GENERAL SUMMARY

Present Overall Status

13.1. As the result of the labors of the Manhattan District organization in Washington and in Tennessee, of the scientific groups at Berkeley, Chicago, Columbia, Los Alamos, and elsewhere, of the industrial groups at Clinton, Hanford, and many other places, the end of June 1945 finds us expecting from day to day to hear of the explosion of the first atomic bomb devised by man. All the problems are believed to have been solved at least well enough to make a bomb practicable. A sustained neutron chain reaction resulting from nuclear fission has been demonstrated; the conditions necessary to cause such a reaction to occur explosively have been established and can be achieved; production plants of several different types are in operation, building up a stock pile of the explosive material. Although we do not know when the first explosion will occur nor how effective it will be, announcement of its occurrence will precede the publication of this report. Even if the first attempt is relatively ineffective, there is little doubt that later efforts will be highly effective; the devastation from a single bomb is expected to be comparable to that of a major air raid by usual methods.

13.2. A weapon has been developed that is potentially destructive beyond the wildest nightmares of the imagination; a weapon so ideally suited to sudden unannounced attack that a country's major cities might be destroyed overnight by an ostensibly friendly power. This weapon has been created not by the devilish inspiration of some warped genius but by the arduous labor of thousands of normal men and women working for the safety of their country. Many of the principles that have been used were well known to the international scientific world in 1940. . . .

The Questions before the People

13.7. We find ourselves with an explosive which is far from completely perfected. Yet the future possibilities of such explosives are appalling, and their effects on future wars and international affairs are of fundamental importance. Here is a new tool for mankind, a tool of unimaginable destructive power. Its development raises many questions that must be answered in the near future.

13.8. Because of the restrictions of military security there has been no chance for the Congress or the people to debate such questions. They have been seriously considered by all concerned and vigorously debated among the scientists, and the conclusions reached have been passed along to the highest authorities. These questions are not technical questions; they are political and social questions, and the answers given to them may affect all mankind for generations. In thinking about them the men on the project have been thinking as citizens of the United States vitally interested in the welfare of the human race. It has been their duty and that of the responsible high government officials who were informed to look beyond the limits of the present war and its weapons to the ultimate implications of these discoveries. This was a heavy responsibility. In a free country like ours, such questions should be debated by the people and decisions must be made by the people through their representatives. This is one reason for the release of this report. It is a semi-technical report which it is hoped men of science in this country can use to help their fellow citizens in reaching wise decisions. The people of the country must be informed if they are to discharge their responsibilities wisely.

Source: Henry DeWolf Smyth. *Atomic Energy for Military Purposes. The Official Report on the Development of the Atomic Bomb under the Auspices of the United States Government, 1940–1945*, pp. 223 and 226. Princeton: Princeton University Press, 1948.

Document 15
THE POLITICAL PROGRAM OF THE CONSEIL NATIONAL DE LA RÉSISTANCE

Resistance to occupation by the enemy has been an aspect of war from the beginning of human history. World War II differs from previous conflicts, however, in the extent of resistance and the political importance of resistance (and collaboration as well) in the domestic development of occupied countries.

Among the most important resistance movements of the war was the resistance in France. Various social and ideological elements of French society came together by 1943 to form a united front with a common program. They not only wanted to expel the Germans from France, they also wanted to create a new France, one in which the political and social divisions typical of prewar France would no longer cripple the will of the nation.

In 1943 various factions resisting the Germans came together to form a national association of resistance. They recognized Charles de Gaulle as their representative and leader abroad. Domestically, they proposed a platform of social and economic reform.

The following is a statement of the National Council of the Resistance [C.F.L.N.] program for postwar France. It was adopted unanimously on March 15, 1944. The first part of the two-part document deals with plans for underground resistance activities. This is the second part.

II. MEASURES TO BE ADOPTED AFTER THE LIBERATION

United concerning our goals, united on the means to attain them—the swift Liberation of our land—the delegates from the movements, groups, parties and political currents represented in the C.N.R. proclaim their determination to remain united after the Liberation:

1. In order to establish the Provisional Government of the Republic formed by General de Gaulle to defend the political and economic independence of the nation and to reestablish French power, grandeur, and the universal mission of France.

2. In order to assure the punishment of traitors and the eviction from the administration and professional life of all those who have dealt with the enemy or have actively associated themselves with the policy of the governments of collaboration.

3. In order to see to the confiscation of the property of traitors and black marketeers, the establishment of a progressive tax on war profits and in general on all profits realized at the expense of the people and the nation during the occupation, as well as the confiscation of all enemy property, including the shares in French and colonial businesses that the Axis Governments and their nationals have acquired since the Armistice—these shares to become inalienable national property.

4. In order to assure:

> the establishment of the broadest possible democracy by allowing the people to voice their desires through the reestablishment of universal suffrage;
>
> full liberty of thought, conscience and expression;
>
> freedom of the press—an honest press, independent of the State, powerful economic interests and foreign influences;
>
> freedom of association, freedom to meet and demonstrate;
>
> the inviolability of the home and of private correspondence;
>
> respect for the individual;
>
> absolute equality of all citizens before the law;

5. In order to effect the necessary reforms:
(a) Economic:

the establishment of a true economic and social democracy, with the requisite eviction of the great economic and financial feudatories from the direction of the economy;

rational organization of the economy, assuring the subordination of special interests to the general interest, and freed from the professional dictatorship installed in the image of the fascist states;

the development of national production following a state plan, established after consultation with the representatives of all interested groups;

the return to the nation of the great monopolies, fruits of the labor of all, of energy resources, of the underground riches of the country, of the insurance companies and the major banks;

the development and support of producers', buyers', and sellers' cooperatives in both agriculture and manufacturing;

the right of qualified workers to rise to administrative and management positions in businesses, and workers' participation in the running of the economy.

(b) Social:

the right to work and the right to leisure, in particular by the reestablishment and the improvement of labor contracts;

a major readjustment of wages and the guarantee of a level of wages and working conditions which will assure every worker and his family security, dignity, and the chance of a decent life;

guaranteed purchasing power through a policy of monetary stabilization;

the reestablishment of the traditional liberties of an independent trade-union movement with broad powers in the organization and management of the economic and social life of the country;

a complete social security system, providing all citizens with the means of existence when they are unable to secure it themselves, a system whose management is shared by those concerned and by the State;

security of employment, regulation of hiring and firing, the reestablishment of shop delegates;

raising and guaranteeing the standard of living of agricultural workers by a policy of farm price supports, improving and extending the experience of the Office du Blé [Office of Wheat], by social legislation giving agricultural workers the same treatment as industrial workers, by a system of insurance against crop failures, by the establishment of fair rates for share-croppers and tenant-farmers, by facilitating access to farm-ownership by young farm families, and by the institution of a program of making farm equipment available;

a pension system permitting aged workers to end their days in dignity;

indemnification for war damages, payments and pensions for victims of fascist terror;

an extension of political, social and economic rights to native and colonial populations;

a meaningful opportunity for all French children to have the benefits of education and access to the best of French culture, whatever their family's financial status, so that the highest positions in society are truly open to all those with the capacity to fill them, thus bringing into being a real elite, of merit rather than of birth, constantly renewed from the people.

Thus a new Republic will be founded, which will sweep away the reactionary regime installed by Vichy and return to our democratic and popular institutions the effectiveness which they lost through the corrupting and treasonous activity that preceded the surrender. Thus we will make possible a democracy which brings together effective control by the representatives of the people and stable government.

The unity of the representatives of the Resistance, for present and future action, in the highest interests of the nation, should be a symbol of confidence and a stimulus to all Frenchmen. It should inspire them to banish all particularist sentiment, that divisiveness which can restrict their action and serve only the enemy.

Forward, then, in the union of all Frenchmen around the C.F.L.N. and its president, General de Gaulle. Forward to battle. Forward to victory, so that France may live.

[The organizational membership of the C.F.L.N. follows.]

Source: Peter Novick. *The Resistance vs Vichy: The Purge of Collaborators in Liberated France*, pp. 198–201. London: Chatto and Windus, 1968.

Document 16
THE YUGOSLAV RESISTANCE UNDER TITO

The most successful resistance movement was that in Yugoslavia. The Germans and the Italians occupied Yugoslavia in April 1941 on the eve of the invasion of the Soviet Union. The Yugoslav government went into exile, leaving behind a Serbian-led underground army, known as the Chetniks, under the leadership of Draza Mihailovic. Josip Broz, generally known by his underground name of Tito, organized the

Yugoslav communists into a guerrilla force opposing the German and Italian occupation. They were known as the Partisans.

The relations between the Chetniks and the Partisans remain controversial. The Partisans emerged victorious at the end of the war. Tito's postwar government executed Mihailovic as a collaborator and labeled the Chetniks as reactionary supporters of a defunct regime. Whatever the historic reality, the Partisans emerged in 1945 in control of the country, and in a position making them strong enough to restructure the multiethnic society of Yugoslavia and to resist the influence of the Soviet Union.

The following document includes excerpts from one of Tito's wartime speeches, given on November 29, 1943. It illustrates his ideas and the promises of the Partisans for the future of their country.

Our People's Liberation struggle can be divided into four stages. These are as follows. . . .

The first stage. The causes of such a quick capitulation of Yugoslavia and the enslavement of our country by German, Italian, Hungarian, and Bulgarian invaders are today quite clear to the majority of our people. The twenty-year-old oppression of the various nationalities of Yugoslavia (such as the Croats, the Macedonians, the Slovenes and others) by a handful of great-Serb hegemonists; further, the unprecedented corruption of the ruling circles inside the country and their affiliations with the most reactionary circles abroad, especially in Germany and Italy, for the purpose of keeping themselves in power; then the unprecedented treachery and espionage inside the Yugoslav Army, especially in the General Staff,—all these things were causes of the catastrophic and disgraceful defeat of the Yugoslav armies in the war. This defeat had catastrophic consequences for the people of Yugoslavia. The king and government fled abroad with the group of people responsible for such a fate having overtaken the country. Yugoslavia was carved up and became the booty of aggressors such as history has rarely seen. In the country there broke out unprecedented terror, and exterminations were carried out not only of the most progressive elements but of the entire Serbian population of Croatia, Bosnia and Herzegovina, and Vojvodina, and of the Slovene population of Slovenia, and so on. The German and Italian aggressors brought to power in Croatia the bloody ustashi monsters, and in Serbia the loathsome traitor Nedic; and with the help of these men they began to execute their diabolical plan for the extermination of Slavs in the Balkans. In this grievous situation, I can say with certitude the most grievous situation in the history of our peoples, there was one single organisation in the country, one which for twenty years had, so to speak, been outside the law and had been persecuted by all who came to power in Yugoslavia,—and now it has placed in the service of its enslaved country all its experience and organisational skill, and all its tried and trusted fighters. It was only the Communist Party which led the people into armed revolt, which never lost heart but raised high the standard of the Liberation Struggle, and which, together with its people, has remained steadfast. (*Loud shouts of approval. Cries of "Long live the Communist Party."*). . . .

The second stage of the People's Liberation Struggle began. Brigades, divisions, and army corps were formed, and whole areas were liberated from the enemy and their ustashi and chetnik henchmen. Our young People's Liberation Army showed at its very outset that it was capable of discharging even the most onerous tasks. Numerous towns were liberated, for example: Livno, Glamoc, Mrkonjicgrad, Jajce, Kljuc, Bihac, Krupa, Slunj, etc. The creation of the People's Liberation Army gave a new impetus to the uprising in areas which had been relatively quiet until then.

In this period the People's Liberation Struggle assumed an increasingly stable character and because of that gained the confidence of an ever increasing number of people in all parts of Yugoslavia.

The people's liberation committees, which until that time had been set up in liberated territory, now began to be set up in semi-liberated territory as well, and even in occupied territory, for this new nucleus of people's authority was becoming increasingly popular among the people and in increasing measure gained their confidence. . . .

The historic assembly of the Anti-Fascist Council of People's Liberation of Yugoslavia was convoked in Bihac. . . .

The setting up of the Anti-Fascist Council of People's Liberation of Yugoslavia was one of the greatest achievements of the People's Liberation Struggle up to that time. The foundations were laid on which could be built a new, more just social order in the territories of Yugoslavia. The foundations were laid on which could be built true brotherhood and the equality of all the nationalities of Yugoslavia, the foundations of a just, truly democratic people's government. (*"Loud shouts of approval. Applause."*) . . .

As a result of events outside our country, i.e., as a result of the victories of the glorious Red Army on the Eastern Front and the annihilation of Hitler's elite armies (*Cries of "Long live the unconquerable Red Army"*), conditions were created for the victories of the other Allies, the British and Americans in Africa, conditions were created for the Allied landings in Sicily, and finally in Italy, and for the capitulation of Hitler's chief partner, Fascist Italy. Here I must emphasise that a great part was played in the elimination of Italy from the conflict by our People's Liberation Army which throughout the whole war pinned down sixteen to twenty Italian divisions. Just before the capitulation of Italy, units of our People's Liberation Army, going over again to the offensive after the Fifth enemy offensive, liberated almost the whole of Eastern Bosnia, the greater part of central Bosnia and the Bosnian Krajina. (*"Loud shouts of approval. Applause."*) . . .

As has been shown earlier, the situation in Yugoslavia and in the world has completely changed in the past year. Thanks to the victories of the Red Army, Hitler's war machine is on the brink of catastrophe; a victory over this, the greatest enemy of mankind is not far off. In the course of this year the fascist bloc has disintegrated. Italy has been eliminated from the conflict. Even greater confusion and disintegration reign among Hitler's satellites. The relations between the Allies, the Soviet Union, Britain, and America, are becoming increasingly close (*Applause*); and this was very much in evidence at the Moscow Conference of representatives of the three great Allied powers. All these factors also have an enormous significance for our People's Liberation Struggle. Faith in imminent victory and in final liberation for our people from the yoke of the occupier is gaining ground among increasingly widespread sections of the population; and this can be seen in the large numbers of new recruits who are flocking wholesale to the ranks of the People's Liberation Army and in the fact that many outstanding political, cultural, and other public figures from all parts of Yugoslavia are joining our People's Liberation Struggle. From another point of view, all these things bring influence to bear upon the increasingly swift disintegration of the puppet state machines of Pavelic and Nedic and, consequently, upon the weakening of the occupier's position in our country. (*Applause.*)

Source: Josip Broz Tito, *Selected Speeches and Articles, 1941–1961.* Zagreb, Yugoslavia: Naprijed, 1963, pp. 40–46; also reprinted in Henry M. Christman, editor, *The Essential Tito*, pp. 40–46. New York: St. Martin's Press, 1970.

Document 17
BRITISH STRATEGIC OPERATIONS EXECUTIVE AND RESISTANCE TO AXIS OCCUPATION

Prime Minister Winston Churchill authorized the creation of the Special Operations Executive (SOE) in July 1940 as the British Empire and Commonwealth continued to pursue the war against Germany without allies. It was a secret organization carrying out several forms of subversive actions against the Germans of occupied Europe, and later in other parts of the world. Churchill once described the SOE as a fourth branch of the services, charged with conducting "ungentlemanly warfare."

The government in London was still working out an overall strategy for the defeat of Germany in 1940. Gaining allies in the United
States and the Soviet Union was important, but meanwhile the
United Kingdom had to use whatever tactics were at hand. A naval
blockade would reduce German imports, but that would be a measure slow to take effect with the Soviet Union providing Germany
with much needed raw materials. Strategic bombing was as yet un-
tried, and Bomber Command was still being built up. A land army
preparing for a future invasion was another option, but with limited
manpower and the need to manufacture arms, that would also be a
long-term goal.

The following excerpts from an SOE memorandum of November
1940 lay out both the SOE's estimation of the situation in Europe as well
as the prospects for encouraging resistance to the Axis occupiers.

'Subversive Activities in Relation to Strategy.' SOE's first general direc-
tive from the Chiefs of Staff, 25 November 1940, COS (40)27(0) in CA B
80156.

MEMORANDUM

This paper has been prepared with a view to guiding the Special Operations Executive as to the direction in which subversive activities can best assist our strategy.

STRATEGICAL PLANNING OF SUBVERSIVE ACTIVITIES

It is essential that subversive activities should be planned with due regard
to our strategical policy. Similarly our strategy and current plans should
take account of the contribution which subversive activities should make towards the military and economic offensive. . . .

FUTURE OFFENSIVE STRATEGY

As our forces expand, our policy will be directed towards exploiting our
amphibious power to the full, with the object of striking with land forces at
outlying enemy positions. By such operations we shall aim at stretching our
enemies, using up their resources, straining their communications, and
gaining positions from which we can tighten the blockade, strike deeper at
our enemies and generally support revolt against them.

In particular, the elimination of Italy comes first among our strategical
aims, and would be a strategical success of the first order towards the defeat
of Germany, which is our main object.

Apart from the aim of eliminating Italy, our major strategy in 1941 is
likely to be a strategy of attrition. We shall maintain and wherever possible

intensify blockade and the air offensive, and generally endeavour to wear down the resistance of our enemies by amphibious and other offensive operations within the limits of our resources.

It is not our intention to build up an army comparable in size with the German army. Our aim, while building up very powerful air and naval forces and maintaining our merchant shipping tonnage, is to create an army which, in addition to providing for our needs at home and overseas, will be capable of providing a striking force on the Continent when the morale of the enemy forces has been considerably weakened. The process of undermining the strength and spirit of the enemy armed forces, especially those in the occupied territories, should be the constant aim of our subversive organisation.

On a long view, it should be the particular aim of our subversive organisation to prepare the way for the final stage of the war when, by coordinated and organised revolts in the occupied countries and by a popular rising against the Nazi party inside Germany, direct and decisive military operations against Germany herself may be possible.

LOCALITIES IN WHICH SUBVERSIVE ACTIVITIES
SHOULD BE ORGANISED

In the present stage of the war it is quite impracticable to state with any certainty or precision the localities where military operations will take place in the future. The most we can do is to define those areas where we think that subversive activities will be most likely to assist our strategy or interfere with that of the enemy. . . .

ENEMY COUNTRIES

In Germany and Italy our constant aim should be to create political disunity, discontent, economic disorganisation and dislocation of communications. . . .

ENEMY-OCCUPIED COUNTRIES IN EUROPE

In the enemy-occupied countries we should also create economic disorganisation and dislocation of communications. While maintaining the national spirit and passive resistance to our enemies, our aim should be to undermine the morale of the enemy, to eliminate the influence of any pro-enemy elements and generally to keep alive pro-Ally feeling. . . .

FRENCH NORTH AND WEST AFRICA

In view of the uncertain political future of the French Colonial Empire it is not possible at present to lay down a definite strategical policy. We are of opinion that present activities should be confined to work of an exploratory nature, and to the fostering of pro-British feelings among the local population. Particular care should be taken not to precipitate native risings in Morocco. . . .

NEUTRAL COUNTRIES IN EUROPE

In any neutral countries from which the enemy draws supplies, our activities should be directed towards causing the maximum interference with such supplies. In particular, immediate destruction of communications by rail and road, especially of oil to Germany, in Roumania, would be of great assistance.

Preparations for destruction of communications between Germany and Italy and the south and east through Yugoslavia, Hungary and Bulgaria should also be made in case of further Axis moves to the southeast and arrangements subsequently to create economic disorganisation so as to hinder the enemy from exploiting the resources of the occupied areas.

In Spain and Portugal preparations should be made to delay an enemy advance from the Pyrenees towards Portugal and Gibraltar by destruction of communications, guerrilla warfare, and economic disorganisation. At the same time, preparations should be made for co-operation with our own offensive action in South-Western Spain, Tangier, Spanish Morocco, the Azores, Canary Islands, Madeira, the Cape Verdes and the Balearics.

In Switzerland we would lay special stress on the immediate interruption of trade—particularly coal trade between Germany and Italy, so long as Swiss neutrality is not endangered by our action.

MIDDLE EAST

Subversive operations in the Middle East—including Italian East Africa, Turkey, Syria, Iraq, Iran, Libya and the Dodecanese—are under a Special Operations Executive representative who works in close touch with the Commander-in-Chief, Middle East.

In Italian East Africa and Libya efforts should be directed to the harrying of enemy communications and destruction of his supplies, particularly in the ports: and to raising the tribes to revolt when we are in a position to take advantage strategically of such a situation.

In the Dodecanese in particular the way should be paved for our own offensive operations.

FAR EAST

We feel that any subversive operations in the Far East designed to meet the situation of war with Japan should be carried out in close cooperation with the Commander-in-Chief, Far East, at Singapore, and we are not at present in a position to offer guidance.

Source: David Stafford. *Britain and European Resistance, 1940–1945: A Survey of the Strategic Operations Executive with Documents*, pp. 219–223. Toronto and Buffalo: University of Toronto Press, 1980. The original document is in the Public Record Office, Kew Gardens, U.K.

Appendix

Military and Civilian Deaths during World War II

	Military Deaths (in 1,000s)	Civilian Deaths (in 1,000s)	Total Deaths
Australia	23	12	35
Austria	230	145	375
Belgium	10	78	88
Britain	270	50	320
Bulgaria	32	3	35
Canada	37	0	37
China	1,350–2,200	8–18,000?	21,000?
Czechoslovakia	250	90	340
Finland	84	16	100
France	210	360	570
Germany	4,500	2,000	6,500
Greece	73	390	463
Hungary	180	290	470
India	30	1,500[1]	1,530
Italy	400	100	500
Japan	2,000	350–1,000	3,000
Jews	0	5,900[2]	5,900

Netherland	6	200	206
New Zealand	10	2	12
Norway	2	8	10
Poland	320	5,480	5,800
Romania	350	200	550
South Africa	7	0	7
U.S.S.R.	10,000	15–17,000	27,000
U.S.A.	300	0	300
Yugoslavia	410	1,200	1,610
TOTAL	21,934	54,024	76–77,000

1. Died in 1943 famine caused by dislocations in world food supplies
2. 80 percent of Jews living in Europe before the war; 35 percent of Jews worldwide

Most figures, especially of civilian deaths, are estimates and have been rounded off. The true cost in the number of human lives will never be known, though it seems clear that old figures of 35–40,000 are too small.

Authorities differ significantly in their estimates, especially for eastern Europe, the Soviet Union, and China. See I.C.B. Dear and M.R.D. Foot, *The Oxford Companion to World War II* (Oxford and New York: Oxford University Press, 1995), p. 290; Louis L. Snyder, *Guide to World War II,* Westport, Conn.: Greenwood, 1982, p. 126.

Glossary of Selected Terms

Axis: Mussolini's term for the Italian-German alliance, the Pact of Steel, signed in May 1939. Japan joined in September 1940 when it signed the Tripartite Pact with Italy and Germany.

Bretton Woods Conference: Held in Bretton Woods, New Hampshire, in July 1944 to plan the postwar international financial and trade system.

Casablanca Conference: Attended by Roosevelt and Churchill in Morocco in January 1943. Future strategy in North Africa and Europe, the war against U-boats in the Atlantic, and strategic bombing were primary topics. The conference is best known for the announcement of the policy of unconditional surrender.

Combined Bomber Offensive (CBO): The cooperation of the British Bomber Command and the United States Army Air Force in the strategic air war against Germany, especially after January 1943.

Combined Chiefs of Staff (CCS): The military command committee established in December 1941 linking the American and the British chiefs in a common, global strategy planning organization. It met on a continuing basis in Washington and participated in major Allied conferences.

Dumbarton Oaks Conference: Representatives from the United States, United Kingdom, and the Soviet Union convened at the Dumbarton Oaks Estate in Washington, D.C., to plan the organization of the United Nations.

Grand Alliance: Term coined by Churchill, alluding to the Grand Alliance against Louis XIV of France in which his ancestor, the First Duke of Marlborough, played a leading role. Generally used to refer to the cooperation among the United Kingdom, the Soviet Union, and the United States. The United Kingdom and the Soviet Union signed a treaty of alliance, but the United States did not.

International Monetary Fund (IMF): Agency of the United Nations, planned at Bretton Woods and implemented in 1945. Its role is to facilitate international trade and reduce exchange rate fluctuations.

Joint Chiefs of Staff (JCS): The American chiefs of the Navy, Army, and Army Air Force after 1942. They also represented the United States in the Combined Chiefs of Staff (CCS).

Lend-Lease: Legislation passed by the U.S. Congress in March 1941 authorizing the president to lend or lease equipment and services to any nation whose defense he considered vital to American national defense.

Operation Bagration: The Red Army's offensive, the war's largest in numbers of men, against Germany, which opened on June 23, 1944.

Operation Overlord: The Anglo-American invasion of western Europe which began on D-Day, June 6, 1944.

Operation Torch: The Anglo-American invasion of North Africa, which began on November 8, 1942.

Potsdam Conference: The last conference among the leaders of the Allied nations, it opened in July 1945 with Truman, Churchill, and Stalin present. British elections during the conference led to Churchill's replacement by Attlee.

Royal Air Force of Great Britain (RAF): An independent branch of the British armed forces, beginning in April 1918. It included Fighter Command for defense and Bomber Command for strategic bombing as well as other branches.

Schutzstafel (SS): Literally protection squad, an elite Nazi organization responsible for party security as well as the operation of concentration and death camps.

Special Operations Executive (SOE): A separate branch of the British war effort against Germany engaged in undercover activities.

Tehran Conference: Held in the capital of Iran at the end of November 1943 and the first day of December, it was the first meeting in which Stalin, Churchill, and Roosevelt were all present. Broad issues of military strategy in Europe and Asia were discussed, and plans were initiated for the postwar treatment of Germany, reparations, border realignments, war crimes trials, and the organization of the United Nations.

Vichy: Collaborationist government in France named after its capital, a resort in central France. Created by the French National Assembly after the signing of an armistice with Germany in June 1940, its "head of state" was Marshal Henri Pétain.

Wehrmacht: Literally "defense power," the name of the combined German armed forces under Hitler from 1938.

Yalta Conference: Second meeting of the "Big Three," the leaders of the Soviet Union, the United Kingdom, and the United States. Held in February 1945 in the Crimea, Ukraine, and attended by Churchill, Roosevelt, and Stalin. The conference discussed major issues in the postwar settlement. Most troublesome was the Soviet imposition of procommunist governments in eastern Europe, though on other issues Allied cooperation continued.

Annotated Bibliography

BOOKS

Adams, Michael C. C. *The Best War Ever: America and World War II*. Baltimore: Johns Hopkins University Press, 1994. Critical of the view that the war was a good war.

Addington, Larry. *The Blitzkrieg Era and the German General Staff, 1941–1965*. New Brunswick, N.J.: Rutgers University Press, 1971. The history of the German Army's strategy of blitzkrieg from the nineteenth century to the beginning of World War II.

Addison, Paul. *The Road to 1945*: *British Politics and the Second World War*. London: Cape, 1975; Pimlico, 1994. An account of the changes in British politics during the war that led to the victory of the Labour party in the July 1945 elections.

Ambrose, Stephen E. *Citizen Soldiers: The U.S. Army from the Normandy Beaches to the Bulge to the Surrender of Germany, June 7, 1944–May 7, 1945*. New York: Simon and Schuster, 1997. A compelling narrative of the American campaign in the defeat of Germany, emphasizing the common soldiers' experiences.

———. *Eisenhower*. Vol. 1, *Soldier, General of the Army, President-Elect, 1890–1952*. New York: Simon and Schuster, 1983. The most authoritative biography of the Supreme Commander.

Balfour, Michael. *Propaganda in War: Organisations, Policies, and Publics, in Britain and Germany 1939–1945*. London and Boston: Routledge and Kegan Paul, 1979. A thorough, comparative study of German and British wartime propaganda.

Bartov, Omer. *Hitler's Army: Soldiers, Nazis and War in the Third Reich.* New York: Oxford University Press, 1991. Challenges the view that the German army's behavior in the war against Russia was different than that of racist Nazi formations.

Baudot, Marcel, Alvin D. Coox, and Thomas R. H. Havens., eds. *The Historical Encyclopedia of World War II.* New York: Facts-on-File, 1977, 1989. A reference work by an international team of historians; it includes a chronology, bibliographies, and list of films.

Bauer, Yehuda. *A History of the Holocaust.* New York: Franklin Watts, 1982. A balanced view by a leading Holocaust scholar.

Beck, Earl R. *The European Home Fronts, 1939–1945.* Arlington Heights, Ill.: Harlan Davidson, 1993. A comparative history of major European societies at war.

Bell, Philip M. *Origins of the Second World War in Europe.* London: Longmans, 1986. A standard survey with an excellent bibliography.

Bennett, Ralph. *ULTRA and the Mediterranean Strategy, 1941–1945.* London: Hamish Hamilton, 1989. A thorough treatment of the use of ULTRA (the British intelligence messages created by the decryption of German radio signals enciphered by the ENIGMA machine) on the conduct of Allied operations in the Mediterranean theater.

Bischof, Günter, and Stephen Ambrose, eds. *Eisenhower and the German POWs: Facts against Falsehood.* Baton Rouge, La.: Louisiana State University Press, 1992. A collection of essays refuting the charge that Eisenhower deliberately caused the deaths of thousands of German prisoners of war after the surrender of Germany.

Blum, John M. *V Was for Victory: Politics and American Culture during World War II.* New York: Harcourt Brace Jovanovich, 1976. A standard account of various aspects of American culture during the war.

Bosworth, R. J. B. *Explaining Auschwitz and Hiroshima: History Writing and the Second World War 1945–1990.* London and New York: Routledge, 1994. A study of the way historians and their publics have dealt with their nation's role during World War II.

Browning, Christopher. *Ordinary Men: Reserve Police Battalion 101 and the Final Solution in Poland.* New York: Harper Collins, 1992. Using postwar court records and interviews, Browning showed how regular Germans participated in genocidal acts.

Bullock, Alan. *Hitler and Stalin: Parallel Lives.* London: Harper Collins, 1991. Author of an early biography of Hitler compared the thoughts and actions of the century's most important dictators.

Burns, James M. *Roosevelt: The Soldier of Freedom, 1940–45.* New York: Harcourt Brace Jovanovich, 1970. The second volume of a classic study of Roosevelt's wartime administration.

Buruma, Ian. *The Wages of Guilt: Memoirs of War in Germany and Japan*. New York: Farrar, Straus, and Giroux, 1994. A comparison of the ways in which the Germans and Japanese have and have not come to terms with their countries' wartime pasts.

Calder, Angus. *The People's War: Britain, 1939–1945*. London: Pimlico, 1969, 1992; New York: Pantheon, 1969. An extensive, partly anecdotal, history of British society at war; filled with numerous examples of ordinary people and the impact of war on their lives.

Calvocoressi, Peter, Guy Wint, and John Pritchard. *Total War: Causes and Course of the Second World War*. 2nd ed. 2 Vols. New York: Pantheon; London: Viking, 1989. A thorough account of the war in Europe and the Asian-Pacific theater with a focus on diplomacy and military campaigns.

Campbell, D'Ann. *Women at War with America: Private Lives in a Patriotic Era*. Cambridge, Mass.: Harvard University Press, 1984. A survey of various groups of women, attempting to interpret their role in the war in terms of their own understanding.

Carver, Michael, ed. *The War Lords: Military Commanders of the Twentieth Century*. Boston and Toronto: Little, Brown and Company, 1976. A collection of 43 essays by leading military historians; 30 are on important World War II commanders from all sides of the conflict.

Churchill, Winston S. *The Second World War*. 6 Vols. London: Chartwell and Boston: Houghton Mifflin, 1948–1953 and various editions. Only memoirs of a "Big Three" statesman. He included extensive materials from memoranda and other official papers he wrote or had access to during the war.

Clemens, Diane. *Yalta*. London and New York: Oxford University Press, 1970. A sober, balanced appraisal of the conference and Roosevelt's role in it.

Cook, Haruko Taya, and Theodore F. Cook. *Japan at War: An Oral History*. New York: New Press, 1992. A comprehensive collection of recollections of the war by Japanese civilians and military persons within the country and in areas occupied by Japan.

Crane, Conrad C. *Bombs, Cities, and Civilians: American Airpower Strategy in World War II*. Lawrence, Kans.: University Press of Kansas, 1993. A study of the United States Army Air Force strategic bombing of Japan in the context of wartime technology, geographic conditions, and the leadership of Curtis LeMay.

Curley, Stephen. "The War and Film in the United States and Britain." In Loyd E. Lee, ed. *World War II in Asia and the Pacific and the War's Aftermath, with General Themes*. Westport, Conn.: Greenwood Press, 1998. Surveys the historiography of the extensive secondary literature on war-related films, especially those produced during the war in the United

States and Great Britain, but also includes books about films produced in other Western countries.

Dallek, Robert. *Franklin D. Roosevelt and American Foreign Policy, 1932–1945.* New York: Oxford University Press, 1979. Exhaustive, authoritative account of American foreign policy under Roosevelt.

Dawidowicz, Lucy S. *The War against the Jews, 1933–1945.* New York: Holt, Rinehart and Winston, 1976. Part I outlines the development of anti-Semitism and genocide in Nazi Germany; Part II recounts Jewish reaction and resistance to genocide.

Deakin, F. W. *The Brutal Friendship: Mussolini, Hitler, and the Fall of Italian Fascism.* London: Weidenfeld and Nicolson; New York: Harper and Row, 1962; Garden City, N.Y.: Anchor Books, 1966. An account of Hitler and Mussolini's alliance.

Dear, I.C.B., and M.R.D. Foot. *The Oxford Companion to World War II.* Oxford and New York: Oxford University Press, 1995. Essays by more than 140 World War II experts on all aspects of the conflict; unfortunately it lacks an index.

Divine, Robert A. *Roosevelt and World War II.* Baltimore: Johns Hopkins University Press, 1969; Penguin Books, 1975. A brief study of Roosevelt's wartime diplomacy.

Dower, John. *War without Mercy: Race and Power in the Pacific War.* New York: Pantheon Books; London: Faber, 1986. Examines the racist aspects of the conflict on both the Japanese and American sides.

Drea, Edward J. *MacArthur's ULTRA: Codebreaking and the War against Japan, 1942–1945.* Lawrence, Kans.: University Press of Kansas, 1992. Expert examination of the operational use of intelligence in MacArthur's Southwest Pacific Area.

Eisenhower, Dwight D. *Crusade in Europe.* Garden City, N.Y.: Doubleday, 1948. A ghost-written account that avoids the controversial aspects of the Allied invasion of western Europe.

Ellis, John. *World War II: A Statistical Survey.* New York: Facts-on-File, 1993. Also published as *The World War II Databook: The Essential Facts and Figures for All Combatants.* London: Aurum, 1993. Compact and fact-filled, but presented in a readable and easily understandable way.

Foot, M.R.D., and J. M. Langley. *Resistance: An Analysis of European Resistance to Nazism.* London: Eyre Methuen, 1976. Coauthored by a member (Foot) of the British Strategic Operations Executive, which assisted European resistance movements. Breaks the resistance movements down into intelligence, escape, and sabotage, with an emphasis on the military significance of resistance movements.

Frank, Anne. *The Diary of a Young Girl: The Definitive Edition.* New York: Doubleday, 1995. Diary of a precocious 14-year-old German-Jewish girl in hiding in Amsterdam during the war. Died in Bergen-Belsen concentration camp. This edition restored the sections of this remarkable diary not previously published.

Freidel, Frank B. *Franklin D. Roosevelt.* 4 vols. Boston: Little, Brown, 1952–1973. A comprehensive, standard account of the president's public life.

Fritz, Stephen G. *Frontsoldaten: The German Soldier in World War II.* Lexington, Ky.: University Press of Kentucky, 1995. Examines the experiences of the ordinary German soldier, using diaries, letters, and memoirs.

Fussell, Paul. *Wartime: Understanding and Behavior in the Second World War.* New York: Oxford University Press, 1989. Acerbic personal reflections of the war and the idiocy of military life utilizing selective memoirs from other participants.

Glantz, David M., and Jonathan House. *When Titans Clashed: The Red Army and the Wehrmacht, 1941–1945.* Lawrence, Kans.: University Press of Kansas, 1995. Best one-volume account and analysis of the war's most extensive military front.

Greenfield, Kent R. *American Strategy in World War II.* Baltimore: Johns Hopkins University Press, 1963. A key outline by the U.S. Army's chief historian of the official histories of the war.

Hersey, John. *Hiroshima.* New York: A. A. Knopf, 1946. A brief classic account based on the experiences of survivors; a key document in forming American public opinion on the dropping of the bomb.

Hilberg, Raul. *The Destruction of the European Jews.* 3 Vols. New York: Holmes & Meier, 1984. Thorough, detailed, pathbreaking analysis of the Holocaust.

Hinsley, F. H. *British Intelligence in the Second World War.* Abridged edition. New York: Cambridge University Press, 1993. Summary of the official history of British intelligence by a historian and participant in ULTRA.

Horne, Alistair. *To Lose a Battle: France, 1940.* New York: Penguin; London: Papermac, 1990. Readable, informative portrait of the German attack and defeat of France.

Howard, Michael E. *The Mediterranean Strategy in the Second World War.* London: HMSO; New York: Praeger, 1968. Authoritative statement of British strategy and the dispute between the British and Americans over the importance of the Mediterranean in the defeat of the Axis.

Ienaga, Saburo. *The Pacific War, 1931–1945.* New York: Random House, 1978. Unique narrative commentary on the war from a Japanese historian who dissented from the nationalists' view of the conflict.

Iriye, Akira. *The Origins of the Second World War in Asia and the Pacific.* London and New York: Longman, 1987. Excellent introduction to the historiography and story of the conflict in Asia and the Pacific.

———. *Power and Culture: The Japanese-American War.* Cambridge, Mass.: Harvard University Press, 1981. A comparison of Japanese and American diplomacy in their cultural contexts by a leading American practitioner of international history.

Jaeckel, Eberhard. *Hitler's Weltanschauung: A Blueprint for Power.* Middletown, Conn.: Wesleyan University Press, 1972. In-depth analysis of Hitler's ideas, their origins, and their consequences.

James, D. Clayton, and Anne Sharp Wells. *From Pearl Harbor to V-J Day: The American Armed Forces in World War II.* Chicago: Ivan R. Dee, 1995. Brief survey of American military planning, technology, and doctrine followed by overviews of the major operations in Europe and the Pacific. Includes consideration of generals at the top as well as the GIs.

Jeffries, John W. *Wartime America: The World War II Home Front.* Chicago: Ivan R. Dee, 1996. Surveys the American homefront, concluding that these were ambiguous years, with some positive achievements, but with many of the experiences not good, even lamentable.

Kahn, David. *The Codebreakers: The Story of Secret Writing.* New York: MacMillan, 1967. Narrates the development of sending, receiving, and breaking secret messages with special focus on the twentieth century and World War II.

Keegan, John. *Six Armies in Normandy: From D-Day to the Liberation of Paris, June 6th-August 25th, 1944.* New York: Viking, 1982. Brilliant narrative of the Normandy invasion by a leading military historian.

Keegan, John, ed. *Encyclopedia of World War II.* New York: Gallery, 1977, 1990. Includes essays on battles, weapons of the war, and important wartime leaders.

———, ed. *Routledge Who's Who in World War II.* London: Routledge, 1995. Includes brief biographies of key personalities from all aspects of the war.

———, ed. *The Times Atlas of the Second World War.* New York: Harper, 1989. Indispensable for tracking the course of military campaigns.

Kennett, Lee. *G.I.: The American Soldier in World War II.* New York: Scribner's, 1987; Norman, Okla.: University of Oklahoma Press, 1997. A group portrait of the Americans at war, based on official records and personal accounts.

Kimball, Warren F. *Forged in War: Roosevelt, Churchill, and the Second World War.* New York: William Morrow, 1997. Argues that the leaders' personalities did not significantly shape policy and defends Roosevelt at Yalta.

———. *The Juggler: Franklin Roosevelt as Wartime Statesman.* Princeton: Princeton University Press, 1991. A sympathetic retelling of Roosevelt's wartime administration by the editor of the Roosevelt-Churchill wartime correspondence.

Koppes, Clayton R., and Gregory D. Black. *Hollywood Goes to War: How Politics, Profits and Propaganda Shaped World War II Movies.* New York:

Free Press, 1987. Details the ways the American Office of War Information influenced Hollywood producers to make films following official propaganda guidelines. A good introduction to wartime American feature filmmaking.

Lee, Loyd E., ed. *World War II in Asia and the Pacific and the War's Aftermath, with General Themes. A Handbook of Literature and Research.* Westport, Conn.: Greenwood Press, 1998. Historiographic essays on the war in Asia and the Pacific, including essays on film, literature, music, culture, religion, and the postwar world.

————, ed. *World War II in Europe, Africa, and the Americas, with General Sources. A Handbook of Literature and Research.* Westport, Conn.: Greenwood Press, 1997. Comprehensive collection of historiographic essays on military and other themes relating to the war in Europe and its participants, with the "state of the question" on each topic; includes bibliographies.

Lewin, Ronald. *The American Magic: Codes, Ciphers and the Defeat of Japan.* New York: Farrar, Straus, Giroux; Harmondsworth, U.K.: Penguin, 1982. Details the breaking of the Japanese diplomatic code as well as other codes by American cryptographers.

————. *ULTRA Goes to War.* New York: McGraw-Hill, 1978. Early assessment of the use of ULTRA by a popular British historian.

Liddell Hart, Basil H. *History of the Second World War.* London: Cassell, 1970; New York: Putnam, 1971; Perigree, 1982. Classic history, published posthumously, by a British military theorist and journalist with contacts among high-ranking officers within the British and German armies.

Linderman, Gerald F. *The World within War: America's Combat Experience in World War II.* New York: Free Press, 1997. A sympathetic portrait of American soldiers, emphasizing the Pacific war and the suffering, isolation, and psychological stresses the soldiers experienced.

Lingeman, Richard R. *Don't You Know There's a War On? The American Home Front, 1941–1945.* New York: Putnam, 1970. Popular, anecdotal account of American society during the war.

Lukacs, John. *The Last European War: September 1939/December 1941.* Garden City, N.Y.: Anchor/Doubleday, 1976; London: Routledge and Kegan Paul, 1977. Relates the early phases of the war in Europe from the attack on Poland to the expansion of that war into a worldwide conflict.

Marrus, Michael R. *The Holocaust in History.* Hanover, N.H.: University Press of New England, 1987. Short, comprehensive survey of the research and issues relating to all aspects of the Holocaust.

Marwick, Arthur. *The Home Front: The British and the Second World War.* London: Thames and Hudson, 1976. An early study of the impact of the war on British society.

Masterman, J. C. *The Double-Cross System in the War of 1939 to 1945*. London: Yale University Press, 1972. A secret history of one of Britain's most successful spy operations written immediately after the war. "Double-cross" turned all German spies sent to Britain. Published in 1972 to restore confidence in the country's secret intelligence service.

Michel, Henri. *The Shadow War: Resistance in Europe 1939–1945*. London: André Deutsch, 1972. A classic account of the various resistance movements throughout Europe.

Milward, Alan S. *War, Economy and Society, 1939–1945*. London: Lane; Berkeley: University of California Press, 1977. A standard account of how major societies mobilized for the war and its impact on their economies.

Morison, Samuel Eliot. *History of the United States Naval Operations in World War II*. 15 Vols. Boston: Little, Brown, 1947–1962. The well-written, semiofficial history of the United States Navy by a lifelong student of naval and maritime affairs.

———. *The Two-Ocean War: A Short History of the United States Navy in the Second World War*. Boston, Toronto, and London: Little, Brown and Company, 1963. An abridged edition of his fifteen-volume history.

Murray, Williamson. *The Change in the European Balance of Power, 1938–1939*. Princeton: Princeton University Press, 1984. Shows the rapid changes in military strength among the European powers in the two years preceding the German attack on Poland.

Overy, Richard J. *The Air War 1939–1945*. New York: Stein and Day Publishers, 1980. The best single-volume survey of the equipment and strategies of the major belligerents, and their successes and failures.

———. *Why the Allies Won*. London: Jonathan Cape; New York: W. W. Norton, 1995. A thorough exploration of the economic, material, strategic, moral, and political factors in the defeat of the Axis powers.

Paxton, Robert O. *Vichy France: Old Guard and New Order, 1940–1944*. New York: Columbia University Press, 1972. Argues that the collaboration of the French Vichy government was more than just opportunistic.

Perrett, Bryan, and Ian Hogg. *Encyclopedia of the Second World War*. Novato, Calif.: Presidio, 1989. Includes major battles, wartime personalities, weapons, and code names.

Polenberg, Richard. *War and Society: The United States, 1941–1945*. Philadelphia: J. B. Lippincott Company, 1972. A breakthrough examination of the impact of the war on American society.

Polmar, Norman, and Thomas B. Allen. *World War II: America at War: 1941–1945*. New York: Random House, 1991. Features an extensive chronology and entries on individual topics and leaders in the war.

Prange, Gordon W., Donald M. Goldstein, and Katherine V. Dillon. *At Dawn We Slept: The Untold Story of Pearl Harbor*. New York: Penguin, 1981,

1988, 1991. Based on an exhaustive investigation of Japanese and American sources regarding the surprise attack at Pearl Harbor.

Reynolds, David. *The Creation of the Anglo-American Alliance, 1937–1941: A Study in Competitive Co-Operation.* London: Europa, 1981; Chapel Hill, N.C.: University of North Carolina Press, 1982. Important study on the differing goals of the United States and the British Empire leading up to the war.

Reynolds, David, et al., eds. *Allies at War: The Soviet, American and British Experience, 1939–1945.* New York: St. Martin's Press, 1994. Post–Cold War essays by scholars from the former Soviet Union, the United Kingdom, and the United States, based on newly released documents and new perspectives of the war years.

Rhodes, Richard. *The Making of the Atomic Bomb.* New York: Simon & Schuster, 1986. Most comprehensive study of the American Manhattan Engineering District project to develop the bomb, including scientific, administrative, and political history.

Robbins, Keith. *Munich 1938.* London: Cassell, 1968. An account sympathetic to Chamberlain's predicament in opposing Hitler's aggressive goals against Czechoslovakia.

Rock, William. *Chamberlain and Roosevelt: British Foreign Policy and the United States, 1937–1940.* Columbus: Ohio State University Press, 1988. On the less-than-positive relations between the two world leaders during the crises leading up to the war.

Royal Institute of International Affairs Staff, comp. *Chronology and Index of the Second World War, 1938–1945.* London and Westport: Meckler, 1990. Reprint of 1947 edition. A detailed day-by-day chronology of the war, fully indexed.

Sainsbury, Keith. *The Turning Point: Roosevelt, Stalin, Churchill, and Chiang Kai-Shek, 1943: The Moscow, Cairo, and Tehran Conferences.* New York: Oxford University Press, 1985. Examines the 1943 conferences as the formative meetings among the Allied diplomats and leaders.

Schaffer, Ronald. *Wings of Judgment—American Bombing in World War II.* New York and Oxford: Oxford University Press, 1985. A revisionist approach to strategic bombing, finding it inefficient and immoral.

Sherry, Michael S. *The Rise of American Air Power: The Creation of Armageddon.* New Haven, Conn., and London: Yale University Press, 1987. A critique of American use of air power before, during, and after the war.

Sherwin, Martin J. *A World Destroyed: The Atomic Bomb and the Grand Alliance.* New York: Knopf, 1973; Vintage, 1977. The development of the bomb and the politics of its use.

Smurthwaite, David. *The Pacific War Atlas, 1941–1945.* New York: Facts-on-File; London: HMSO, 1995. A commemorative atlas of the Pacific theater.

Spector, Ronald H. *Eagle against the Sun: The American War with Japan*. New York: Free Press/Macmillan, 1985. The war in the western Pacific told from an American viewpoint.

Speer, Albert. *Inside the Third Reich: Memoirs*. New York: Macmillan, 1970. Memoirs of an administrator and confidant of Hitler, written during his imprisonment for war crimes.

Stokesbury, James L. *A Short History of World War II*. New York: Morrow, 1980. An excellent brief introduction to the background and course of the war.

Taylor, Telford. *The Anatomy of the Nuremberg Trials: A Personal Memoir*. New York: Knopf, 1992. Best account of the trials, their legal foundation, the personalities involved, the proceedings, the defeats, and the results.

Terkel, Studs. *"The Good War": An Oral History of World War II*. New York: Pantheon, 1984. A celebrated collection of interviews and recollections about the war from persons both famous and obscure.

Thorne, Christopher. *The Issue of War: States, Societies, and the Far Eastern Conflict of 1941–1945*. New York: Oxford University Press; London: Hamish Hamilton, 1985. Also published as *The Far Eastern War: States and Societies 1941–45*. London: Unwin Paperbacks, 1986. Pioneer investigation of the domestic political and international relationships brought on by the war in Asia.

Toland, John. *The Rising Sun: The Decline and Fall of the Japanese Empire*. New York: Random House, 1970. The East Asian-Pacific War emphasizing Japan.

Tuttle, William M., Jr. *"Daddy's Gone to War": The Second World War in the Lives of America's Children*. New York and Oxford: Oxford University Press, 1993. Pathbreaking look at the impact of the war on children.

Vining, Donald, ed. *American Diaries of World War II*. New York: Pepys, 1982. An introduction to an important genre of World War II writing.

Volkogonov, Dmitri. *Stalin: Triumph and Tragedy*. Rocklin, Calif.: Prima Publishing, 1992. Critical evaluation of the Soviet dictator using post–Cold War archival findings about Stalin and the war.

Weigley, Russell F. *Eisenhower's Lieutenants: The Campaigns of France and Germany, 1944–1945*. Bloomington, Ind: Indiana University Press, 1990. Excellent examination of the leaders, strategies, and Allied operations in the invasion of western Europe.

Weinberg, Gerhard L. *A World at Arms: A Global History of World War II*. New York and Cambridge: Cambridge University Press, 1994. Most complete one-volume history of the war, emphasizing military and diplomatic developments, and integrating all theaters.

Werrell, Kenneth P. *Blankets of Fire: U.S. Bombers over Japan during World War II*. Washington, D.C.: Smithsonian, 1996. The best introduction to the development and deployment of the B-29 during the war in the Pacific.

Wheal, Elizabeth-Anne, Stephen Pope, and James Taylor. *A Dictionary of the Second World War*. New York: Peter Bedrick Books, 1990. Also published as *Meridian Encyclopedia of the Second World War*. New York: Penguin, 1989, 1992, and as *The Macmillan Dictionary of the Second World War*. London: Macmillan, 1995. Contains substantial entries, maps, and a chronology.

Willmott, H. P. *Empires in the Balance. Japanese and Allied Strategies in the Pacific*. Annapolis: Naval Institute Press, 1982. Penetrating analyses into grand strategy in East Asia and the Pacific in its global context.

———. *The Great Crusade: A New Complete History of the Second World War*. New York: Free Press, 1989. A global approach to the strategies of the war without attempting a complete history (in spite of the subtitle).

Wilt, Alan F. *War from the Top: German and British Military Decision Making during World War II*. Bloomington, Ind.: Indiana University Press, 1990. Compares Hitler and Churchill as wartime leaders, taking advantage of contemporary research.

Winkler, Allan M. *Home Front U.S.A.: America during World War II*. Arlington Heights, Ill.: Harlan Davidson, 1986. Surveys recent research and insights into the social history of the war in the United States.

Winterbotham, Frederick W. *The ULTRA Secret*. New York: Harper and Row, 1974. The book that revealed the British breaking of the German Enigma machine's system of encryption.

Wohlstetter, Roberta. *Pearl Harbor: Warning and Decision*. Stanford, Calif.: Stanford University Press, 1962. Examines all aspects of the American intelligence failure leading up to the surprise attack on Pearl Harbor.

Woodward, Llewellyn. *British Foreign Policy in the Second World War*. 5 Vols. London: HMSO, 1970–1976. The official, authoritative history of British foreign policy; revised to take account of ULTRA documentation.

World War Two Studies Association. *Newsletter*. Previously American Committee for the History of World War II, *Newsletter*. Department of History, Kansas State University, Manhattan, KS 66506–1002. 1968– .

Wright, Gordon. *The Ordeal of Total War, 1939–1945*. New York: Harper and Row, 1968. Outstanding, one-volume history of Europe at war, covering all aspects of the war years.

Wyman, David S. *The Abandonment of the Jews: America and the Holocaust 1941–1945*. New York: Pantheon Books, 1984. Finds the Allies guilty of not having done enough to rescue European Jews before and during the war.

FILM AND ELECTRONIC SOURCES
World War II and Film

Aldgate, Anthony. *Britain Can Take It: The British Cinema in the Second World War*. Edinburgh: Edinburgh University Press, 1994. A comprehensive survey of the British film industry and its output during the war.

Bowker's Complete Video Directory. New Providence, N.J.: Reed, 1997. Published annually, this has a very extensive (over 800) listing of videotapes and films relating to World War II. Brief descriptions are included, as well as information about purchasing or renting of videotapes.

Butler, Ivan. *The War Film*. South Brunswick and New York; London: A.S. Barnes; Tantivy Press, 1974. Includes a chapter on World War II, with a list of important wartime and war-related films.

Dick, Bernard. *The Star Spangled Screen: The American World War II Film*. Lexington, Ky.: University Press of Kentucky, 1985. A history of Hollywood wartime productions based on studio archives and files.

Doherty, Thomas Patrick. *Projections of War: Hollywood, American Culture, and World War II*. New York: Columbia University Press, 1993. Hollywood war films within the larger context of American culture.

Doneson, Judith E. *The Holocaust in American Film*. Philadelphia, Pa., New York; and Jerusalem: The Jewish Publication Society, 1987. A history of anti-Semitism in film and television from the 1930s to the 1980s.

Hyams, Jay. *War Movies*. New York: Gallery Books, 1984. Covers all wars, but includes a discussion of World War II films.

Klisz, Anjanelle. *Video Source Book*. Detroit, Mich.: Gale Research, 1995. A catalog of videotapes available for rent or purchase. Some entries include a brief description of the video. Not as comprehensive as *Bowker's Complete Video Directory*, but cheaper and more readily available.

Langman, Larry, and Ed Borg, eds. *Encyclopedia of American War Films*. New York and London: Garland, 1989. A comprehensive listing of American films, including documentaries and propaganda films. Each film is briefly described.

Manvell, Roger. *Films and the Second World War*. South Brunswick, N.J.: A. S. Barnes, 1974. Popular, standard discussion of feature films and documentaries made in all major belligerent countries.

Parish, James Robert. *The Great Combat Pictures: Twentieth-Century Warfare on the Screen*. Metuchen, N.J. and London: Scarecrow, 1990. A comprehensive, but selective description of combat films with information about producers, directors, cast, screenwriters, and others.

Schatz, Thomas. *Boom and Bust: The American Cinema in the 1940s*. New York: Charles Scribner's Sons; London: Simon & Schuster and Prentice Hall International, 1997. An anthology of important essays about the American film industry and its productions during the 1940s, with special emphasis on the war.

Wetta, Frank J., and Stephen J. Curley. *Celluloid Wars: A Guide to Film and the American Experience of War.* New York; Westport, Conn.; and London: Greenwood, 1992. Two chapters list films produced during the war, and films produced about the war after 1945.

Select Filmography of World War II Documentaries

Air Force Story, Part I, 1906–1942, Part II, 1942–1944; Part III, 1943–1947, American. The origins of the U.S. Army Air Force, the development of new technologies and aircraft through the strategic bombing campaigns of World War II in Europe, North Africa, and the Pacific. More-detailed films of individual operations are also available. Length: each part, 120 minutes.

America at War (1935–1954), American. From the March of Time Collection; includes the Home Front, Friend and Foe (in three parts), and American Defense (in two parts). Also available as individual cassettes. Length: 678 minutes, six cassettes.

Battle of Midway (1942), American. Director, John Ford. An original color film of the key Pacific battle of June 3–6, 1942. Won an Academy Award as best documentary. Length: 18 minutes.

Genocide (1981), American. Director, Arnold Schwartzman. Produced by the Simon Wiesenthal Center in Los Angeles, this documentary traces the plight of Jews from the post–World War I era through the establishment of death camps and failure of the international community to aid Jewish emigration or to protest their treatment. Received an Academy Award.

The Liberators: Fighting on Two Fronts in WWII (1992), American. Directors, Nina Rosenblum and Bill Miles. Film about African American soldiers in the European theater; controversial because of its attempt to link African American civil rights issues with the liberation of Dachau concentration camp. Length: 90 minutes.

Memphis Belle (1944), American. Director, William Wyler. The Flying Fortress Memphis Belle led a squadron in a daytime attack on a submarine base in Wilhelmshaven, Germany. Filmed by the Photographic Section of the U.S. Eighth Air Force, this is a factual, realistic, action filled depiction of the mission. Length: 43 minutes, color.

The Negro Soldier (1944), American. Directors, Frank Capra and Stuart Heisler. Showed why African Americans should support the war and why they were good soldiers. Originally intended as a part of the *Why We Fight* series. Length: 40 minutes.

San Pietro (1944), American. (Often erroneously titled *The Battle of San Pietro.*) Director, John Huston. A bloody, one-half hour film of an American infantry division's fight in Italy. Includes civilians from the village of San Pietro, in southern Italy. Ranking military authorities did not want it shown to troops, but General George C. Marshall overruled their objections.

Shoah (1985), French. Director, Claude Lanzmann. Interviews of survivors, perpetrators, and bystanders of the death camps to give a fresh examination of their horrors and atrocities. No wartime footage is shown, relies on memories and recollections to narrate the Holocaust in this greatly acclaimed documentary. Length: 570 minutes.

Triumph of the Will (1935), German. Director, Leni Riefenstahl. Considered by many the finest propaganda film ever made, *Triumph of the Will*, though not a wartime film, alleged to document the 1934 Nazi Party rally at Nuremberg. It shows the vitality and expansionist goals of the Nazi party. The Nuremberg events were carefully staged in preparation for the filming. It includes marching Nazis, youth, SA members, troops, speeches by Nazi leaders, and ceremonies honoring martyred Nazis. Length: 110 minutes in its shortened version; it should be seen in its full, four-hour entirety.

Victory at Sea (1950–1954), American. Twenty-six-part series covering all aspects of the war at sea, in the Atlantic, the Mediterranean, and the Pacific. Richard Rodgers composed the award-winning music, which is performed by the National Broadcasting Company orchestra. Length: 30 minutes each. A condensed version issued in 1954 is 97 minutes.

Victory through Air Power (1943), American. Director, H. C. Potter. A feature length, Walt Disney animated history lesson on air power and how the bomber could win the war. Based on a book by Alexander de Seversky of the same name.

Why We Fight. Director and series supervisor, Frank Capra. There were seven films produced in this series during the war and used as training films in the United States military. Capra used captured enemy film, footage from feature films and newsreels, as well as scenes shot in studios. At first, they were only shown to servicemen and workers in war plants, but they were eventually projected on commercial theater screens as well. They are listed as follows:

The Battle of Britain (1943), American. Director, Frank Capra. The British people absorb German Luftwaffe attacks as the RAF Fighter Command defeats the Germans in the air. Length: 53 minutes. (*Why We Fight* series)

The Battle of China (1944), American. Director, Frank Capra. Depicts an unrealistic account of Chinese resistance by Chiang Kai-shek's Nationalists to Japanese invasion and occupation; includes original footage. Length: 65 minutes. (*Why We Fight* series)

The Battle of Russia (1943), American. Director, Anatole Litvak. Used Soviet newsreel film to depict the heroic struggle of the Soviet peoples against the German onslaught of 1941–1942. Length: 83 minutes. (*Why we Fight* series)

Divide and Conquer (1943), American. Director, Frank Capra. Extensive coverage of the years of military success for the Third Reich: the invasion of Scandinavia; Blitzkrieg against the Netherlands, Belgium, and France; and the Battle of Britain. Length: 60 minutes. (*Why We Fight* series)

The Nazis Strike (1942), American. Directors, Frank Capra and Anatole Litvak. Depicts the German takeover of Austria and Czechoslovakia, and the invasion and occupation of Poland. Length: 40 minutes. (*Why We Fight* series)

Prelude to War (1942), American. Director, Frank Capra. Details the Axis coalition of Germany, Italy, and Japan, comparing them to gangsters. Covers Japanese invasion of Manchuria, Italian fascism, German Nazism, and American military unpreparedness. Won an Academy Award for Best Documentary. Length: 52 minutes. (*Why We Fight* series)

War Comes to America (1945), American. Director, Frank Capra. An Edenic America, prosperous, and fun-loving, whose way of life and love of freedom are threatened by Axis aggression. Ends with the attack on Pearl Harbor and President Roosevelt's speech before Congress of December 8, 1941. Length: 67 minutes. (*Why We Fight* series)

The World at War (1971), British. Twenty-six-part series produced by the British Broadcasting Corporation covers the entire war with original archival footage, interviews of military and civilian leaders, and other wartime films. Each episode is 52 minutes.

Select Filmography of World War II Feature Films

Back to Bataan (1945), American. Director, Edward Dmytryk. Reenactment of American and Filipino defeat at Bataan in 1942 and the ensuing "Death March." Length: 97 minutes.

Casablanca (1942), American. Director, Michael Curtiz. Classic Hollywood movie starring some of the industry's best actors, set in French Morocco under the Vichy, collaborationist regime.

Destination Tokyo (1944), American. Director, Delmer Daves. Submarine crew puts meteorologist ashore to guide first air raids over Tokyo.

49th Parallel (also titled The Invaders, 1941), British. Director, Michael Powell. High adventure of six Germans set ashore; their submarine is sunk in the Gulf of St. Lawrence; they fight their way to neutral U.S. territory, meeting various representatives of Canadian pluralist, democratic society along the way.

The Great Dictator (1940), American. Director, Charles Chaplin. Chaplin satire in which he resembles Hitler in the character of Adenoid Hynkel; Jack Oakie mimics Mussolini as Benzino Napoloni. The film was later criticized for its handling of concentration camps, whose horrors were not well known in 1940.

Guadalcanal Diary (1943), American. Director, Lewis Seiler. Based on the best-selling book of the same name by Richard Tregaskis; a realistic representation of combat.

Gung Ho! (1943), American. Director, Ray Enright. Commando adventure story on Makin Island, 1942, based on the exploits of the Second Marine Raider Battalion, who took up the Chinese motto "Gung Ho!" (work together) and popularized it.

In Which We Serve (1942), British. Director, Noel Coward. The story of the building, career, and sinking of a destroyer and its crew, based on the real-life fate of HMS *Kelley* and its commander, Lord Louis Mountbatten.

Lifeboat (1944), American. Director, Alfred Hitchcock. Survival story raising wartime morale and psychological questions; occupants of a lifeboat take on the captain of the German submarine that sank their ship.

Nine Men (1943), British. Director, Harry Watt. A re-creation of the North African campaign, bringing together a mix of characters to depict their interactions under combat stress.

North Star (1943), American. Director, Lewis Milestone. Lillian Hellman script, pro-Soviet; features happy peasants despoiled by German invaders; the 1957 reedited version bowdlerized (distorted) the script, turning it into an anti-Soviet story.

Sahara (1943), American. Director, Zoltan Korda. An odd assortment of Allied soldiers (and one German POW) in their M-3 tank hold off 500 Germans of the Afrika Korps at an oasis, allowing reinforcements to arrive before the battle of El Alamein.

So Proudly We Hail (1943), American. Director, Mark Sandrich. Early portrayal of women nurses at the scene of combat in the Pacific, at Corregidor, and Bataan.

The Story of G. I. Joe (also titled *War Correspondent*) (1945), American. Director, William A. Wellman. General Eisenhower called it the best war film. The Italian campaign as seen by the renowned journalist Ernie Pyle.

They Were Expendable (1945), American. Director, John Ford. Men who ran PT boats in early stages of the war in the Philippines; an engrossing story.

Thirty Seconds over Tokyo (1944), American. Director, Mervyn LeRoy. Reenactment of Doolittle raid of April 1942, using real names of participants; based on a book by Ted Lawson, one of the pilots who lost a leg after crashing in China.

Wake Island (1942), American. Director, John Farrow. First World War II movie of an American unit in action. Marines hold out for two weeks against overwhelming odds in December 1941. The film became one of the most popular in training camps.

A Walk in the Sun (1945), American. Director, Lewis Milestone. The Salerno, Italy, beachhead; a platoon of ordinary soldiers take on Germans holed up in a farmhouse. The terror of combat is balanced by focusing on the personalities of each man.

The Way Ahead (1944), British. Director, Carol Reed. A socially diverse unit recruited after the disaster at Dunkirk serves in North Africa.

CD-ROMs on World War II

There are many CD-ROMs available. The following list is very selective, with war games left out. This is a rapidly changing area. For reviews of new CD-ROMs, see especially *Library Journal* and *Software and CD-ROM Reviews on File.*

The Day after Trinity: J. Robert Oppenheimer and the Atomic Bomb (1995), Voyager. Includes the documentary film of the same name plus interviews and documents.

The Electronic Encyclopedia of World War II (1993), Marshall Cavendish. Expensive and exhaustive, this is based on a 12-volume print encyclopedia. It incorporates over 3,000 pages of text, with more than 700 color and 1,100 black-and-white photographs.

FDR (1996), Corbis. An extensive collection of photographs, videos, voice recordings, archival material relating to President Roosevelt's career.

Lest We Forget: A History of the Holocaust (1996), Logos Research System. Videos, over 500 still photographs and texts narrate the history of the Third Reich, the experiences of the Holocaust, and the aftermath. Contains much graphic material.

Normandy: The Great Crusade (1994), Discovery Communications, Inc. The Anglo-American invasion of Europe in June 1944, complete with 40 minutes of video clips, photographs, letters, selections from diaries and maps.

The Simon and Schuster D-Day Encyclopedia (1994), Simon and Schuster. The text of the print encyclopedia plus videos, interviews, and photographs.

Wings: London Blitz to Pearl Harbor (1997), Discovery Channel Multimedia. Details of more than 700 World War II aircraft.

Wings over Europe (1995), Discovery Channel Multimedia. Two CD-ROM set with details on the war's planes, key battles, pilots, and video clips, and includes a flight simulator.

World War II (1993), Compton's NewMedia and Quanta Press. A comprehensive selection of documents with black-and-white photographs.

World War II. Encyclopedia: The European Theater (1994), Attica Cybernetics. An extensive collection of photographs, radio recordings and videos from the BBC and the British Imperial War Museum.

Internet Sources

There are tens of thousands of Web sites relating to World War II. Web sites range from individuals who post their own photographs and diaries, to archival and text sources. In this rapidly changing arena, users must be prepared to discover new sources and to learn that old ones have been discontinued. In using a Web browser, note that there are several ways to access sites relating to the war. "World War II" is most common, but "World War 2," "World War Two," the "Second World War," and "World War, 1939–1945" (the Library of Congress classification) are also used.

Good general links for access to history information include the following. Each has links to other sites.

History Index:

> http:/english-www.hss.cmu.edu/history/

Index of Resources for Historians:

> http://kuhttp.cc.ukans.edu/history/index.html

World War II on the Web:

> http://www.geocities.com/Athens/Oracle/2691/links.htm has a comprehensive set of links to nearly 300 sites relating to the war.

WW II Resources:

> http://sunsite.unc.edu/pha contains links to more than 1,000 sites with primary sources and original documents.

Access to the United States National Archives and Records Administration is on:

> http://www.nara.gov/nara.nai.html includes texts, photographs, sound recordings, and maps.

Film and Video Database:

> http/us.imdb.com/ is advanced database of hundreds of thousands of films, including those of World War II. It includes extensive information about each film, often indicating where it may be acquired.

Two sites for World War II discussions are:

> listserv@ubvm.cc.buffalo.edu. To subscribe, send the following: "subscribe wwii-l (plus your name)."

http://www.cis.ohio-state.edu/hypertext/faq/usenet/world-war-2/faq.html

Michigan State University is the site for several academic discussion pages sponsored by the National Endowment for the Humanities. H-War includes military topics from all periods and geographic areas. There is no site devoted solely to World War II. For a list of the available sites, contact http:h-net.msu.edu/about/lists.html.

Index

Page numbers for major belligerents and major leaders refer only to substantive entries.

About the Author

LOYD E. LEE is Professor of History and Chair of the Department at the State University of New York, College at New Paltz. He is the editor of *World War II in Europe, Africa, and the Americas, with General Sources*: *A Handbook of Literature and Research* (Greenwood, 1997), and the author of *The War Years*: *A Global History of the Second World War* (1989), *The Politics of Harmony*: *Civil Service, Liberalism, and Social Reform in Baden, 1800–1850* (1980), and other publications on German and global history.